Talking
with
Psychopaths
and Savages

GUILTY BUT INSANE

Born in 1948 in Winchester, Hampshire, **Christopher Berry-Dee** is descended from Dr John Dee, Court Astrologer to Queen Elizabeth I, and is the founder and former Director of the Criminology Research Institute (CRI), and former publisher and Editor-in-Chief of *The Criminologist*, a highly respected journal on matters concerning all aspects of criminology from law enforcement to forensic psychology.

Christopher has interviewed and interrogated over thirty of the world's most notorious killers – serial, mass and one-off – including Peter Sutcliffe, Ted Bundy, Aileen Wuornos, Dennis Nilsen and Joanna Dennehy. He was co-producer/interviewer for the acclaimed twelve-part TV documentary series *The Serial Killers*, and has appeared on television as a consultant on serial homicide, and, in the series *Born to Kill?*, on the cases of Fred and Rose West, the 'Moors Murderers' and Dr Harold Shipman. He has also assisted in criminal investigations as far afield as Russia and the United States.

Notable book successes include: *Monster* (the basis for the movie of the same title, about Aileen Wuornos); *Dad Help Me Please*, about the tragic Derek Bentley, hanged for a murder he did not commit (subsequently subject of the film *Let Him Have It*); and *Talking with Serial Killers*, Christopher's international bestseller, now, with its sequel, *Talking with Serial Killers: World's Most Evil*, required reading at the FBI Behavioral Analysis Unit Academy at Quantico, Virginia. His *Talking with Psychopaths and Savages: A Journey Into the Evil Mind*, was the UK's bestselling true-crime title of 2017; its successor volume, *Talking with Psychopaths and Savages: Beyond Evil,* was published in the autumn of 2019. In 2020 a new edition of his *Talking with Serial Killers: Dead Men Talking* appeared, and he has since published *Talking with Serial Killers: Stalkers, Talking with Psychopaths and Savages: Mass Murderers and Spree Killers, Talking with Serial Killers: Sleeping with Psychopaths* and, in 2023, *Talking with Psychopaths and Savages: Letters from Serial Killers*. He is the UK's bestselling true-crime writer.

https://www.christopherberrydee.com//

Christopher Berry-Dee

Talking
with
Psychopaths
and Savages

GUILTY BUT INSANE

A chilling study of serial killers' minds

First published in the UK by John Blake Publishing
an imprint of The Zaffre Publishing Group
A Bonnier Books UK company
4th Floor, Victoria House
Bloomsbury Square
London WC1B 4DA
England

Owned by Bonnier Books
Sveavägen 56, Stockholm, Sweden

www.facebook.com/johnblakebooks
twitter.com/jblakebooks

First published in paperback in 2024

Paperback ISBN: 978-1-78946-693-5
Trade paperback: 978-1-78946-690-4
Ebook ISBN: 978-1-78946-692-8
Audiobook ISBN: 978-1-78946-691-1

British Library Cataloguing-in-Publication Data:

A catalogue record for this book is available from the British Library.

Design by www.envydesign.co.uk

Printed and bound in Great Britain by Clays Ltd, Elcograf S.p.A

1 3 5 7 9 10 8 6 4 2

Every reasonable effort has been made to trace copyright-holders of material reproduced in this book, but if any have been inadvertently overlooked the publishers would be glad to hear from them.

John Blake Publishing is an imprint of Bonnier Books UK
www.bonnierbooks.co.uk

For
Sir Ludovic 'Ludo' Henry Coverley Kennedy, FRSL
(1919–2009)

Contents

Prologue

*'Insanity — a perfectly rational adjustment to
the insane world.'*

R.D. LAING: QUOTED IN *THE GUARDIAN,* 1972

Before I drag you screaming and protesting to the edge of the bottomless abyss that is homicidal insanity, let me offer you the traditional Filipino greeting '*Mabuhay*'. And why? Well, about halfway through the research and writing of this book I took a well-deserved holiday in my favourite county, the Philippines. Manila is now a filthy place, so after a few days I boarded a PAL flight to Mactan-Cebu airport in Lapu-Lapu City, after which I booked into my usual hotel, the Cebu Parklane International.

Much, much cleaner than Manila is Cebu City. It was almost flattened by Super Typhoon Odette in 2021, and it amazed me how resilient the people were in putting it back together again in such a short time. If some big city in the

UK suffered a similar disaster, I can imagine the council's rebuilding team still mumbling and stumbling around among piles of debris a year later, sucking their pencils, clueless as what to do next, perhaps considering whether it might be best to leave things as they were.

Now, it goes without saying that in many British cities the traffic is bad, but in the Philippines motoring madness reigns supreme. Crossing any street with millions of cars, trucks, jeepneys, trikes and motorbikes, all going in every direction known to humankind, at excessive speeds, can be a lethal exercise. I can confirm, however, that they all have exceedingly good brakes – and I believe there is an excellent reason for this: squashing a westerner results in a lot of paperwork with maybe a suspended licence if one can bribe the cops to get one off the hook. I soon got the hang of it: I simply stepped off a pavement, and with a quick glance nonchalantly strolled across the road, accompanied by the screech of rubber, clouds of exhaust smoke, polite and encouraging waves from the drivers and ever-so-soft toots from their horns.

But here's a thing. It seems that the fire engines, ambulances and police cars on their way to an emergency stick to the 30mph speed limit; and they *do* stop at red lights. You can hear their sirens from miles away; then with red and blues flashing, they creep past at a snail's pace, slowing down every few hundred yards to allow a banana seller to move his barrow of fruit out of the middle of the road or for an extended family of eighteen to alight a jeepney. It's quite remarkable, but have I not said in previous books that the Filipinos are the friendliest people on planet Earth?

That is, of course, if you are not the victim of a crazed rapist-cum-serial killer, because at the time of writing one young girl is going missing every twenty-four hours in Cebu City alone – at least twenty at the current tally as I type this, their bodies dumped like garbage. The city is gripped in fear; young women are terrified about going out at night.

Is this the work of a lone-wolf killer, or of a group of men bundling girls into a van? The cops are clueless. In fact, there is currently a serial killer epidemic ravaging the Philippines, with hundreds of young girls, some as young as twelve, being snatched from the streets and barangays every day. And this in a country that was once a stranger to homicide on such a scale.

It is murder madness. And if you, dear reader, think that this is a mad, mad way to start a book, be aware that there is madness aplenty to come. So let's crack on.

CHRISTOPHER BERRY–DEE
UK AND EL NIDO, PALAWAN, PHILIPPINES
christopherberrydee.com

Introduction

'In a mad world, only the mad are sane.'
AKIRA KUROSAWA: JAPANESE FILMMAKER AND PAINTER

Years ago, I adopted the term 'Murder Road', a metaphorical journey along which are many twists and turns, many crossroads too. And at some of these crossroads, two lives meet; one is extinguished while the other goes on as if nothing untoward has happened. Welcome to your road trip into homicidal insanity.

Mental illness is a serious subject. It can provoke heated debate during the adversarial shenanigans that, more often than not, play out in murder trials – especially in the US. This book contains examples of such behaviour in spades.

Yes, 'tis true that I am often accused of being devoid of tact or discretion; that I am meddlesome and exasperating. It is also true that when my mood demands it I am no stranger to alcohol or tobacco and furthermore have acquainted myself with a few of the so-called seven deadly sins. Here, I might quote Mary Danvers, Baroness Stocks: 'We don't call it sin today, we call it self-expression.' Mary was well cool, if you ask me. So next time you find yourself in a confessional box and asked to give penitence, tell Father Michael Goodmichael: 'Nah, I ain't sinned, I just self-expressed myself,' before being frogmarched down the nave and booted out of the front door.

But the thing is, why advertise these seven deadly sins in the first place – we humans are curious, are we not? So hands up anyone who has not tried out at least one of them – purely for experimental purposes, of course.

I have digressed.

We all love adventurous road trips because we learn so many exciting new things, do we not? This sense of exploring starts pretty much from the moment we first open our eyes and see things and sense physical touch. The root of 'to explore' is the Latin *explorare*, meaning 'investigate' or 'search out'. Later in our lives, when we want to explore a new place, we hope to see interesting things and get to know its people but, as often *is* the case, what we *hope* to find we *don't find*. Example: one books a glossy-looking holiday online, let's say one in Spain. But, oops-a-daisy, when one arrives on the costa de España with the now irascible wife and moaning kids traipsing behind, your hotel looks like it's half-built or half-demolished, with the khazi having been heaved over the balcony, now lying in fragments some two hundred feet below, with her explaining in modest terms: 'You *are* an asshole, Derek. We should have gone to Butlin's, as my mother told you. She and Dennis have been going there ever since their honeymoon forty years ago!'

Many of my readers will doubtless email me to insist that Spain is an amazing place to visit, so I must not, in fear of my life, disagree with them. But as my books are not available in Spanish, I just plucked the country out of my Sherlock Holmes deerstalker. Many adventures do have their ups and downs, though, don't they – as evidenced in the *Only Fools and Horses* episode 'The Unlucky Winner Is...' (Season 6, Episode 4). If you have not watched this belter of a sitcom, then you should.

Let's move breezily along our road towards Madnessville. Before the invention of the motor car, we truly appreciated and absorbed our surroundings. Whereas today we zip through towns and villages in our motors as if these places are of no consequence. We zoom along with maybe a sigh of, 'Ah, how sweet', upon passing through a village pretty enough for any chocolate box. We glance at these places, but in reality we don't see much at all; we are always in too much of a hurry, you see... rush, rush, rush, to go someplace, and more often than not we miss many interesting things along our way.

Case in point: the first chapter in this book is set in the civil parish of Loxton, in northern Somerset. The village itself has many of the rustic flavours of bygone times: quaint thatched cottages with tiny leaded windows; sitting rooms so small you couldn't swing a cat around in them, and apple trees and a vegetable patch out back. In this respect, not much has changed today. Then there are the big houses smelling of old money with shiny new Range-Rovers that never go off-road in their lives; leafy up-hill, down-dale narrow lanes, a Norman-built church with the obligatory 200-year-old yew parked among the graves – all easily unseen as one rockets, staring straight ahead, along the nearby M5. Yes, dear reader, Loxton could be described as an idyllic backwater. Yet it was once the site of a dreadful event, and the perpetrator's skeleton now lies deep in a damp grave here.

So: this book is all about enjoying (or *not*) trips along several not so-easy-to-drive 'murder roads'. To relish (or *not*) various allsorts of homicidal flavours on our travels.

'Hey Christopher, get with the programme, will you, please?' I hear you mutter under your breath. Fair enough! Let's get straight to the heart of the matter: murder and madness. And first of all, I have to introduce something that will crop up frequently in my narrative: the M'Naghten rule. For most true-crime-minded-readers, this is a fussy legal standard that seemed to have cemented itself into the law books back in the 1840s. But its roots go back way further. Let me now bring into *play* the Code of Hammurabi, a Babylonian legal text created by a king in around 1750 BCE. This ancient standard still exists in various modified forms today. And oh boy, isn't it well abused!

Why '*play*'? you may ask. Well past times will regularly act as the backdrop to the stage we are soon to view from our seats in the stalls – OK, OK, from the comfort of our warm homes. For my opening scene, I present the attempted murder of a king in his royal box at the King George Theatre (no prizes here for guessing the king's name) in Drury Lane, London. When he stood to attention as the national anthem started to play, a rotten scoundrel fired a red-hot ball at him – and missed. (C'mon guys and gals, I mean the royal box in any theatre is no bigger than an 8 x 10-foot creosoted garden shed. How could anyone miss a target in one of those – and at point-blank range, too?) After the clouds of white gunpowder smoke cleared away – along with those in the seats down below, and the thespians who vanished stage left into the wings – the would-be assassin roundly apologised to the king, which did him no good at all, as you can imagine.

Point-of-fact: criminal case courtrooms *are* stages, upon which legally, medically and forensically educated people become the principal cast. In some countries, including the UK of course, they are obliged to put on costumes, wear wigs and black gowns (just as actors might) to add solemnity to the occasion. In the US, however, only judges wear black gowns; many down-at-heel public defenders are often dressed as if their wardrobe has been pinched from a bin bag dumped outside a charity shop.

Just like an actor, the KC – with rakish aplomb and twinkling eyes – deliberately pauses as he or she measures out their case, for dramatic effect. They are the legal eagles who can turn from a quiet, softly spoken advocate into a pit bull terrier in a heartbeat; they keep the jurors leaning forward to catch every utterance, backsides superglued to their seats.

During the execution of the US serial killer Ted Bundy at Florida State Prison, crowds gathered outside wearing T-shirts bearing the slogan 'Burn Bundy Burn'. I liked that very much indeed, most especially the placard pictured leaning against a mobile burger van, which read 'Sizzling Bundy Burgers'. That's what I call enterprising. However, in the UK, with the likes of serial killer Peter Sutcliffe, we find headlines that are a tad less exhilarating, and distinctly more PC, such as: 'The Yorkshire Ripper sentenced to life in prison'... with the codicil 'But if the shrinks have their way and cure him of his bullshit paranoid schizophrenia mental illness, he could be *your* next-door neighbour within thirty years.'

Sutcliffe pulled the wool over the eyes of some of the best shrinks, some of whom had been practising their 'profession' for thirty years. 'He's insane, stark raving bonkers... he is a maniac,' they said. Was he heck. Far from it. If you ask me, he was saner than many of the psychiatrists who evaluated him.

Moving on, let me quote from the 1999 movie *The Green Mile*, inspired by a Stephen King novel. 'What happens on the Mile, stays on the Mile. Always has, always will.' For me, that resonates with the secretive treatments and other goings-on inside our secure metal-health facilities, and for good reason. But there can be no valid reasons these days for not revealing the unpalatable truths of how the parole system, so often easily manipulated by self-opinionated forensic psychiatrists, allows many of the most dangerous offenders their freedom – in some instances to kill, kill and kill again. This book serves as a demand that homicidal sexual psychopaths, especially serial killers (who cannot be 'cured' or 'rehabilitated') must *never* be allowed to walk among us ever again. Let them live out the remainder of their stultifyingly boring days, sweating in a tiny, cramped box within the 'Belly of the Beast'. At least – unlike their victims – they are still breathing.

Can I say 'Fuck them. Let them rot'? Yes, why not!

A hard, perhaps non-Christian stance to adopt, but as I see it life *should* mean life: they should only leave prison wearing a pine box. Yet, there are those on the extreme-leaning-so-far-left-as-if-about-to-topple-over who argue somewhat pitifully that to remove any hope of release leaves this murderous ilk without any hope at all. Do these do-gooders forget that these monsters – whether totally mad or sane – have removed *all* hope and any *future* from their deceased victims? That they have caused irreparable life-long emotional damage to next of kin, friends and colleagues? Of course they forget. I regard these people as disdainful asses.

As I now unsteadily climb down from my Speakers' Corner soapbox in Hyde Park, the reader will, I am sure, want to get into the nitty-gritty of homicidal madness most foul. If your author appears to go off-track along our road trip and into the minds of those who definitely have more than a few screws loose, you may begin to think that Christopher himself has a few screws loose too.

All that said, I would like you, the reader, to become interactive with this book; have some 'fun' – as in solving a Rubik's Cube in a mind-twisting judicial context. So at the end of some of the chapters, I will pose scenarios for you to consider, as if you were a member of a jury. And if it pleases you, it will be for *you* to decide: 'Is the offender sad, bad, mad, or truly evil?' There are five distinct differences there to consider. And after having read all the information that we know about a given case, you will – of course – be compassionate and – without fear or prejudice – forthright in your determinations.

Christopher, let's not fool ourselves that a murder trial is a search for the truth. It's anything but. It's a legal stage set with actors: a bewigged judge all wrapped up in ermine, the lawyers in gowns and horsehair wigs; psychiatrists who most often disagree with colleagues let alone their own thinking, with the better side winning, even at the cost of true justice... Oh, and I have settled the bill.

> Sir Ludovic 'Ludo' Kennedy: to the author while dining at Langan's Brasserie, London, 1994

So, step forward an attractive forty-seven-year-old woman named Noreen O'Connor. I will leave it for you, the reader, as a metaphorical member of her trial jury, to consider which of the five categories listed above applies to her.

Noreen O'Connor:
possessed by a demon?

'I plucked someone's eyeballs out and it is not Maria that is dead. It is the evil that was in her eyes.'

Noreen O'Connor (1907–83), upon her arrest in
Loxton, Somerset, England

Loxton

What follows is not a well-documented case. But I love my country; I mean I really *do* get an educational kick out of its venerable history. So let's travel to Loxton, a quaint Somerset English civil parish, with a population of some 214 as of 2021. That's right, a mere 214 residents. And for the benefit of any American readers, Loxton is a village and *not* to be confused with a city, which our cousins across the pond label almost any place with a population of six people or so.

In case you didn't know it, although I am sure that you do, Loxton derives its name from the Lox Yeo River, the name meaning 'settlement' (from the pre-seventeenth-century

English 'tun') on said watercourse. It was first mentioned in the Domesday Book of 1086, under the name 'Lochestone'. To confuse both myself and the reader, Loxton was also known as 'Lokestone' in the Red Book of the Exchequer (1212) and as the more familiar 'Loxton' in Somerset's Fine Court Rolls (1259). Lox' is maybe of Old Welsh origin, in which language it would indicate either 'winding stream' or 'bright one'

Well, I did say that this book was a road trip of sorts, did I not?

Murder afoot in Loxton

So, dear reader, it's time for you to join your fellow true-crime aficionados for the drive to Loxton. We climb aboard a preserved 1954-ish AEC Regal IV, which is an underfloor-engined, single-decker bus. In the pamphlet (page 2) on your seat you will note the reference to old workings among Loxton's surrounding hills. Somerset has more holes in it than Swiss cheese, you know. I highlight this because at one time mining was abundant in them thar hills: for calamine, lead, copper and more recently yellow ochre, which, as every sable-brush-sucking artist knows, is used by Daler-Rowney and Winsor & Newton in their paints. Back in the nineteenth century, the stark raving mad Richard Dadd used lots of yellow ochre in his beautiful paintings, while he was a patient in what was then known as 'Broadmoor Criminal Mental Asylum' – today known as the more PC-friendly 'Broadmoor Hospital'.

In 1954, sleepy Loxton came to national attention when a forty-seven-year-old state-registered nurse-cum-housekeeper, Miss Noreen O'Connor, murdered an elderly German-born *Jungfer* (spinster) Friederika Maria 'Marie' Buls, by plucking out her eyes. Hey, one doesn't hear about that sort of thing going on every day, does one? Let alone in out-of-the-way places such as picture-postcard Loxton.

A friend of mine, 'The Boris', and I once visited Noreen's grave in the cemetery of the village's Norman-built St Andrew Church. If you are of a mind to, you can visit her grave too without even leaving your chair. You can see it on Google Earth. You will need good eyesight, though. However, if you look carefully in the bottom-right-hand corner of the aerial photo – taken at an altitude of approximately 450 kilometres – the first grave you'll spot (although it's a wee bit fuzzy) is that of Noreen O'Connor. Her story is a Stephen-King-mess-your-pants-novel come true.

St Andrew Church

'Dying is a very dull, dreary affair. And my advice to you is to have nothing whatever to do with it.'

W. Somerset Maugham: attributed
last words, 1965

It was ever-so-nice churchwarden Jane and her husband who greeted me and The Boris, and led us along a downhill/uphill narrow footpath draped either side by bramble bushes, through a wooden gated arch and onto church grounds. To the left, set into lush green grass that looked as if it had been recently clipped with a hairdresser's precision, was Noreen's grave: a slab of weathered white limestone about two metres in length, a metre wide, and around fifteen centimetres deep. Just visible on it are the words: 'Noreen O'Connor (1907–83)'.

Tissues at the ready, please, because en route to Loxton I had bought a bouquet of flowers from a petrol station. These I lovingly placed as I knelt down to say a short prayer. I think that's a good thing to do, don't you? Jane silently stood back at a respectful distance, head bowed, hands clasped in front her, and obviously moved by my pious gesture. It's about respect, you see. It was a remarkable thing for me to do, because your author is penny-pinching-meaner than Scrooge; tighter than the rear end of a mallard duck on a village pond, some say, and I happily agree with them. Jane went on to give me and The Boris a tour of this delightful little church. You can see photos of it online. It's what I call a 'proper church'. It is quite unlike modern religious edifices. You know the types – usually abandoned 7/11 stores, with A-frames parked outside telling would-be cushion-kneelers: 'Pastor Peter Goodbody and Mrs Bernice Goodbody Welcome All to His Evangelical House of God: reopening one day when the roof is fixed. Children admitted if on a lead.'

Hey guys, I am not suggesting for one millisecond that these pastors are anything other than devout, even when they still wear bell-bottom trousers, black socks and white trainers. Gosh, I would never say anything like that. Speaking personally, unless I lived in America's Bible Belt, and had a fondness for the singer Travis Tritt, or some old Southern gospel music (which, in truth, I love), I stay well clear of vicars and the like. Especially at any Sunday service when the song 'Nearer, my God, to Thee' comes up. As you will know, it is rumoured to have been the last song most of the passengers on the RMS *Titanic* heard being played before the allegedly unsinkable ship sank – but at least the band was dead right on that score!

Jane then took us on a tour of the graveyard. Boneyards are not usually up my street because it kinda spoils my day. For the life or death of me, I still don't quite understand why visitors to even the nicest villages find themselves compelled to take a wander around lots of headstones; peering at the names and dates of the people buried below – deceased folk whom one has never met, nor ever wanted to meet, and could not give two hoots about. I am sure the reader knows what I am taking about. I once heard a parent scream out to a boisterous child: '*Tommy! Stop* jumping up and down on that concrete slab... somebody is underneath it, for f★★k's sake!' That's so British, isn't it?

Here's the interesting part: Jane explained that Noreen is buried facing east, in the same direction allocated to all God-fearing folk. I think that the general idea is that if the deceased suddenly spring back to life – which is somewhat unlikely – they will face the sun rising on each new day, and not due west as would be the case for murderers or non-Christians. To prove her point, Jane showed us the graves of the Tiarks family who are buried close by and include Noreen's former employer, German-born Frank Tiarks. All point resolutely east.

Indeed, so well loved by Loxton residents was Noreen that after she passed away, aged seventy-six, in a charity-run mental healthcare unit in Northampton, the village had a whip-round. It paid for her funeral and brought her to her final resting place at the church where she had once been a devote member of the congregation. That's a nice thing to do, isn't it just?

So, what about Noreen's narrative, as sketchy as it may be?

As a starter for ten, we know zilch about her early life. We do know that she took over the position of nursemaid/housekeeper to Mrs Emily 'Emmy' and Mr Frank Tiarks from German-born spinster Friederika Alwine Maria Buls – more familiarly 'Marie' – who, in 1939, was interned just as World War II broke out. Emmy Tiarks passed away in 1943, by which time Frank was confined to a wheelchair, being pretty much housebound due to a hunting accident and now reliant on Noreen to look after his needs.

Noreen took to the quiet life, so much so that she immersed herself in fundraising for a new school to be based in the village hall. She attended Sunday service at St Andrew Church, and helped the local vicar with fetes and car boot sales. A very, *very* nice lady, I say.

For his part, Frank Tiarks was a generous man. He was a former merchant banker in London, and his family name can be traced back decades in the village's history. Out of the blue, he bought a detached cottage with an upper bedroom, which he called 'Gardeen'. It is still situated on Christon Road, Loxton. This property he would later bequeath to Noreen O'Connor, along with a trust fund of £20,000, shares and his cars, upon his death in 1952 – the equivalent of over £700,000 in today's money. Way to go Noreen, you hit the jackpot!

Frank liked Noreen. And, if I can share a confidence

and be frank with you, if I had been mega-rich Frank in my wheelchair, being spoon-fed most of my meals wearing a bib, the impish streak in me would have enjoyed the attentions of this much younger carer. Occasionally, Frank holidayed with Noreen to South Africa aboard the Union-Castle Line's *Pendennis Castle*, and enjoyed Cape Town where he had many friends. Noreen also drove Frank around in a car specially adapted for him. He was often seen at local cricket matches with her by his side, and why not? Tall, slim, with light shoulder-length hair, smartly dressed and with finely turned ankles, she could turn any man's head – the green eyes of some women too. Noreen was middle class-ish and well spoken; she occasionally wore a brown Dior astrakhan coat and low heels. But then something allowed the rot to set in – or maybe it was the Devil incarnate suddenly emerging in Loxton.

After Frank's death in 1952, aged seventy-seven, Noreen invited frail *Haushälterin* Marie Buls now (since freed from internment) to live with her in Gardeen. There was no codicil in Frank's will that made this a legal stipulation. Noreen, to a fault a compassionate Christian, and knowing that previously Marie had suffered two strokes and by 1954 had also broken her leg – by all accounts an injury that kept her largely confined to her bedroom – freely welcomed her. 'Noreen nursed her devotedly,' note Nicola Sly and John Van der Kiste, in their excellent book *Somerset Murders* (2008).

What comes next is straight out of the 1973 horror movie *The Exorcist*. Definitely *not* a bedtime read over hot cocoa.

The Devil rides out

'There were terrible injuries to her face.'
Dr Thomas Christie: Principal Medical Officer,
Holloway Prison

At about 7:20 a.m., on Wednesday, 1 September 1954, Noreen O'Connor telephoned Peter Tiarks, the son of her former employer Frank. Calmly, she said: 'Please come over. Something terrible has happened to Marie. She's in the power of some evil.'

Peter lived about fifty miles away in the town of Bridport, Dorset. He immediately set out for Loxton, which he reached at 10 a.m. In the meantime, the daily help, Mrs Eva Simmons, had turned up at 8:15 a.m. She observed that the curtains in Marie's upper bedroom window were closed and noticed that Noreen O'Connor was lying, fully clothed, on a sofa in the sitting room. 'Noreen was smiling as if at peace with the world,' she later told police.

Upon his arrival at the cottage, Peter asked Noreen what had happened. She calmly explained that she had seen an 'evil look' in Marie's eyes, adding that this happened regularly whenever Marie looked into a certain corner of her bedroom as if something evil was sitting there. When Peter pressed her further, Noreen asserting that she had not killed the *spinster* Buls – only the *evil* in her eyes.

Peter sent for a doctor. '*A doctor?*' you might ask. If I had witnessed such a terrible scene I would have sent for as many priests as I could lay my hands on. Dr Norman Cooper soon arrived from nearby Winscombe, just five minutes' drive away. Climbing the stairs, medical bag in hand, he found the deceased lying as stiff as a board on the floor between the bed and the wall. She was on her back, fully dressed, with her arms folded. Her eyeballs had collapsed into their sockets – not plucked out as she had told Peter, though she probably believed she had, perhaps following a perceived biblical instruction – just black bloody holes with streaks of orbital fluid and blood drying on her face, which was now as white as plaster cast. The eyelids, upper lip and right nostril were torn. Rigor mortis had long settled in, and the doctor estimated the time of death at some seven to ten hours previously. Cause of death: 'shock following the injuries to the elderly lady's face'.

Now assured that Marie was dead, Dr Cooper went down to the sitting room to talk to Noreen. She explained that on the previous evening there had been a lot of 'evil things about'. As authors Nicola Sly and John Van der Kiste say in *Somerset Murders*: '[Noreen] claimed to have heard the sound of drawers being opened and closed and went to check on her elderly companion. There, she formed the impression that Miss Buls did not look after herself.' They go on: 'As Noreen approached Miss Buls, she had received an electric shock from the old lady's bedspread. She had sat with the woman, whom she felt was in some "kind of grave danger", holding her hands and praying, at which point she heard a strange, disembodied voice saying: "This is my hate". Noreen then realised it was Marie's eyes that were evil and that "she had to get them out!"'

The police were summoned to Gardeen.

Sergeant C. Woodriffe arrived first. He searched Marie's

bedroom, where he found a tooth, some hair and a broken cloisonné hair clip. He took a sample of blood from the bedroom floor. In the bathroom the officer found numerous items of wet clothing, including a dress, an underskirt and a bra. Along with a bloodstained towel and scrapings from beneath O'Connor's fingernails, all of these items were bagged then sent to the forensic science laboratory at Bristol.

One can say that Sergeant Woodriffe was as bright as his policemen's whistle. He had summed up what had happened in an instant, as would all of those thousands of my readers and colleagues who attend CrimeCon UK. Any Agatha Christie or Lieutenant Columbo fan will get it in a heartbeat. This was *not* a suicide, period, not least because there was no note left by the deceased explaining why she had lost the will to live, and in doing so had taken it upon herself to rip her eyeballs out of her own face. Nothing along the lines of: 'I am ending it all. I have taken it upon myself to pluck out my eyes, knock out some teeth, do some damage to my head and leave some of my washing in the bathroom for someone else to hang out to dry.' This was a slam–dunk, blue–chip, gold–plated case of homicide. Noreen was arrested and taken into custody at Weston-super-Mare police station. She was quiet until the evening, at which time a strange turn of events unfolded. Custody officers heard wailing coming from her cell. It was an unholy sound. It made the hairs on their necks bristle. Peeping through the cell peephole, the officers took turns to see her moving a chair and small table around. She was chanting religious sayings, then she knelt down to pray. Oh, what a pitiful sight she must have been, too: an utterly broken woman who had led an exemplary life, mentally well-balanced to a fault, one who'd never crossed swords with anyone. The officers were now very worried about her state of mind, and a police doctor was called toot suite to examine her.

On the following morning, in the presence of Noreen's solicitor, Inspector Leslie Long formally charged her with the murder of Marie Buls. The accused took the news calmly, answering that she had no objection at all in telling them what had happened and why. As is the usual practice, she was brought before local magistrates. At Axbridge she explained to the bench that she and Marie had lived together harmoniously, and revealed that she had been under no obligation under the terms of her late employer's will to lodge Marie in the house. Nor did Noreen benefit from the murder – a fact she was well aware of, having witnessed the old lady's will being drawn up and signed.

The magistrates were told by Peter Tiarks that Noreen had been showing 'signs of a mental illness'. Peter was not a psychiatrist, so in any court of law his opinion was inappropriate. He'd based his premise purely on his chat with her. She'd told him about a trip to Plymouth taken that previous weekend. She'd confessed to 'feeling happy, almost to the point of elation and singing throughout her journey,' he recalled. Then Noreen described a near accident during the outing – an incident she was convinced had been engineered to cause her death by someone whom we might assume was Marie Buls.

As authors Nicola Sly and John Van der Kiste put it: 'At first they decided to take lunch at a French café, but changed their minds opting for the Grand Hotel on Plymouth Hoe.'

They go on: 'Coincidentally, this had been a place at which Noreen had last eaten with her employer, Frank Tiarks, and now when she, Marie Buls and another woman were directed to the very same table, Noreen had taken it to mean that her former employer was with her in spirit and had intervened to prevent her being taken to a French café.' This leaves me to conclude that once-alive, now-dead-facing-east Frank Tiarks had never been a lover of French cuisine.

Based upon what they'd heard thus far, the magistrates committed Noreen to stand trial at Somerset Assizes. She pleaded not guilty. Politely bowing to the chair of the bench, Mrs Greenhill, she said quietly: 'Thank you, madam.' Noreen was totally compos mentis throughout the hearing: simply put, she understood the nature of her crime. She fully comprehended the committal proceedings. As we will see later, this is quite the opposite to the behaviour of someone who has suddenly gone insane and the Devil take the hindmost.

But had Noreen O'Conner suddenly gone completely mad, or was this a case of 'temporary insanity'? We might ask ourselves what dreadful vision came from Marie Buls's eyes? What secret inner voice inside Noreen's head compelled her to commit such a wicked act? There was not even a smidgen of motive; no financial worries due to her income from investments, because Noreen was a shareholder and director of the Callow Rock Lime Company bequeathed to her by Frank Tiarks. Therefore, it seems that Noreen *had* seen or *imagined* something in Marie's eyes, a terrifying entity she needed to extinguish – or as she said in her own words, 'to get out!'

Backing up a tad, the Callow Rock lime quarry is still active. Located between Cheddar and Shipham, it was established by Herman and Francis C. Tiarks in 1919 to manufacture high-purity white lime from the Burrington Oolite. Their altruistic aim was to create employment for returning British troops from World War I. At no cost, the company would later provide the white limestone that is now atop Noreen's grave. Given that the Tiarks were German-born and -raised, I think that in every respect the Tiarks and their quarry were magnanimous to a fault, don't you?

On 25 September 1954, Noreen was transferred to Holloway Prison, London. Here, the chief medical officer, Dr Thomas Christie, examined her. His opinion was that she was suffering from an 'acute mania', which had caused 'defective reasoning'. Whether or not this *was* a correct opinion remains to be seen. Back then, 'acute mania' referred to the manic phase of bipolar disorder, which is characterised by an extremely unstable euphoric or irritable mood with hyperactivity, excessively rapid thought and speech, uninhibited and reckless behaviour, grandiosity and flight of ideas. However, acute mania very rarely leads to murder most foul. Furthermore, mania can occur in cycles over several weeks or months with no predictable triggers. Treatment may involve therapy, hospitalisation and medications. As has already been established, for her entire life right up until the few days preceding her murderous attack on Miss Buls, Noreen O'Connor had been a mentally stable young woman with a straight head and good morals; and a very predictable and loving person at that. There had never been even a hint of *anything* such as a bipolar disorder in her history. Nonetheless, Dr Curran, a psychiatrist based at St George's Hospital, London, supported Dr Christie's opinion, adding in a topsy-turvy, upside-down sort of way, that he felt 'it highly *improbable* that Noreen O'Connor didn't know what she was doing when she murdered the frail Miss Buls' [author's italics], which was precisely the opposite of what Noreen had told everyone. In common parlance, she had 'coughed' the murder from the get-go. She put her hands up and, as it turned out, she would never retract a word of her confession.

The trial

'There was a large bruise on the back of the deceased's head. It is highly possible that Miss Buls was unconscious at the time her atrocious injuries were received. One of her hands was bloodied and swollen and in it were clutched a few hairs.'

Consultant pathologist Dr A.T.F. Rowley

Noreen O'Connor's two-hour trial started on 18 October 1954, at Somerset Assize Court in Wells, with Mr Justice Sir Lawrence Austin Byrne presiding. Born into a wealthy Irish Catholic family at Croneybyrne House, near Rathdrum, County Wicklow, Sir Lawrence had served as a lieutenant in the Queen's (Royal West Surrey) Regiment in World War I. He is perhaps best known, however, as the Crown prosecutor in the 1945 case of William Joyce (aka 'Lord Haw-Haw'). And as a writer, I cannot fail to mention that he was also the presiding judge in the case of *R. v. Penguin Books* under the Obscene Publications Act 1959, for the publication of D.H. Lawrence's *Lady Chatterley's Lover* (1928). God only knows what he would have made of *Fifty Shades of Gray*, or an Ann Summers catalogue, come to that! Odd is it not – *Fifty Shades of Gray* plus sequels cover all of the seven deadly sins and some more... and it has become one of the most bestselling fictional works of all time. Although I have neither the time nor the inclination to read that salacious book, this certainly proves what a funny old world we live in, do you agree? For my part, I rather like sitting up in bed at night with a glass of hot milk and the Bible. The Song of Solomon works for me: 7:4 kicks off with: 'Your neck is like a tower of ivory, your eyes like pools in Heshbon by the gate of Bath-rabbim' and so forth until things get really hot, trust me.

I digressed, silly me.

The Courts of Assize – commonly known as 'Assizes' – were held in the main county towns and presided over by visiting judges from the higher courts based in London (for the US, read: 'Circuit Judges'.). Since the twelfth century, England and Wales had been divided into six judicial circuits, which were the geographical areas covered by said judges.

The jury now learned that Noreen had been a kindly, sympathetic and very efficient woman: 'a pillar of Loxton', as one witness testified. That was until her behaviour had become increasingly strange in the few days leading up the murder.

The former clerk to Axbridge Rural Council, one Mr Bailey, stiffly entered the witness box and took the oath. He testified that he must have been one of the last people to have spoken to Noreen before the dreadful events of the night of Tuesday, 31 August through to Wednesday, 1 September. He explained that she had visited him at his office during that Tuesday, and had asked about her recent jolly to Plymouth. She'd told him of eating at the Grand Hotel and of her sense that the late Mr Tiarks had been guiding her to their favourite table. Although himself not a medical person, Bailey offered his opinion to the court that she was 'mentally deranged'. He went on to say that having left his office, Noreen returned later in the day and had 'babbled about various subjects', which he found 'nonsensical'. She had referred to a member of his staff as a 'good man', saying that 'the goodness of his soul is reflected in his eyes'. Bailey asked if she would see him again the following day. Noreen replied that she didn't know where she would be and that she felt so happy that she '... might go anywhere'.

Called to the bar in 1931, the controversial advocate Sir Norman John Skelhorn, KBE, QC acted for Noreen. He summed up his position for the jury, stressing that no 'earthly motive can be found whatsoever' for the killing. If I had been Sir Norman, I might have said: 'Members of the jury, only the Devil knows the motive' − only to be disbarred for life.

Sir Norman reiterated that it was likely that Miss Buls had not suffered terrible pain from her injuries, since the medical opinion was that she had become unconscious before they were inflicted, 'either as a result of a blow to the head, which was supported by a large bruise found at autopsy, or having succumbed to heart attack or another stroke'. In measured tones, he went on to say that inflicting these injuries was something 'foreign to the accused's nature',

Noreen being a woman who was known as a 'kind, friendly and a devoted, efficient nurse'. Not mentioned, however, were the defensive injuries found on the decedent's hands, nor the hair found clutched in Noreen's hand, which indicated that the victim put up the fight of her life. In any event, perhaps this would have been quite unnecessary, as the defending counsel wanted to gain some sympathy from the jurors. Contrarywise, it could have also been suggested that Miss Buls was initially hit over the back of the head, fell down onto her back and desperately tried to fight off Noreen O'Connor who then went for her eyes. Noreen's fingernail scrapings would have proved that point, with the old lady expiring as the result of extreme shock. This would have upset the jury even more and, in their minds, have alienated Noreen to the nth degree.

Having heard this brief evidence, Mr Justice Byrne directed the jury that if they were satisfied with the evidence, there could be no doubt in their minds that Noreen O'Connor *was* guilty of murder. Then he asked the jurors to consider the second aspect of the case, that according to medical opinion the defendant was unaware of what she was doing, or that if she did know then she did not know her behaviour was wrong. If the jurors thought she was guilty of murder, then he advised them that the correct verdict would be 'guilty but insane'.

According to authors Nicola Sly and John Van der Kiste: 'The jury did not need to retire to further consider the evidence. Nodding affirmatively to each other, in only a minute they delivered their verdict – finding Noreen O'Connor guilty of the murder of Miss Buls but insane, leaving the judge to direct that she be detained at Broadmoor Special Institution at Her Majesty's Pleasure.'

Mr Justice Byrne, was applying the M'Naghten rule – of which more later. Noreen spent her remaining years as an inpatient at St Andrew's Hospital, Northampton, a charitable organisation devoted to the care of patients with mental disorders, learning disabilities and acquired brain injuries. She died there in 1983, aged seventy-six. But *was* Noreen O'Connor 'insane'? Her story is not quite over yet. I am about to turn things on their heads.

Exorcisms and the NHS

'Since the primary motive of the evil is disguise, one of the places evil people are most likely to be found is within the church. What better way to conceal one's evil from oneself, as well as from others, than to be a deacon or some other highly visible form of Christian within our culture?'

M. Scott Peck, MD: *People of the Lie:*
The Hope for Healing Human Evil (1998)

Dr Peck is sensible and he nailed that one down in one. My readers are equally sensible; we like to think outside of the box, do we not, and when needs be we keep an open mind.

During my career as an investigative criminologist I have interviewed many stone-cold killers who are thoroughly evil yet have been labelled 'mad' – that overused throwaway adjective – when in truth they are completely sane. Case in point, the aforementioned Peter Sutcliffe. They are wicked, it's as simple as that. Having said which, solid evidence of satanism goes way back in our history. So, on this delicate issue, I bow to and respect my readers' moral discretions and religious beliefs.

Now, here comes a double whammy.

In article titled 'Dancing with the Devil: Exorcism in the NHS' in *HSJ Heath Check,* published by Wilmington Healthcare on 2 November 2011, Blair McPherson states:

> You would not be surprised to be told that some people with mental health problems claim to hear voices and be possessed by demons. You might be a little surprised to be informed that the church still carries out exorcisms or 'deliverances' (from evil) as they are now known. However, you *would* be surprised to learn that the NHS uses exorcism as an alternative treatment for mental health problems, according to an article by Daisy Greenwell in *The Times* newspaper [of] 1 November 2011.

The reader can find this article online. It is a fascinating read, one that may lead us to believe that there really are demons living among us. So let's consider this point. After many of the world's most prominent forensic head-shrinkers, aka psychiatrists, have tried every remedial mind-calming treatment known to mankind and failed, they resort to bringing in papally authorised priests, some holy water sprinkled crosses, set formulas, gestures, symbols, icons and amulets etc, to set things right. All of which gives Satan the nod, at once confirming his very existence. Indeed, on the internet you can find countless articles that verify real possessions and exorcisms. Noreen O'Connor herself went through an exorcism at Broadmoor Hospital, but her alleged demon was *not* cast out because one could not be found, which raises another question: was it Marie Buls who was possessed?

Wow, that's a chilling thought, even if I say so myself!

Let me try to tidy this up a bit. We have seen that Noreen displayed a charitable character for 99.99 per cent of the time. Therefore, does it not seem almost inconceivable that this loving, caring woman who doted on Marie Buls should rip out her eyes from their sockets? In her statements to police and others, Noreen seems to have started acting strangely, for example exhibiting a fixation on chairs when she dined at the Grand Hotel on Plymouth Hoe, *but up until that very day* she had acted normally, never showing any signs of acute mania or defective reasoning. Remember, though, she had referred to a member of Mr Bailey's staff as a 'good man', saying that 'the goodness of his soul is reflected in his eyes'.

During an acute mania episode, an individual may experience increased impulsivity that causes then to act in a way that is brash, inappropriate or promiscuous. And there *were* reports of Noreen having increased energy, getting over-excited, talking very quickly and jumping from one topic to another. It is also correct to say that acute mania is a mental illness, one where the sufferer can also experience psychosis with accompanying hallucinations and delusions, all of which indicate a separation from reality.

'Once evil is invited in, tremendous effort is required to show it to the door and kick its cloven hoof off the threshold.'

E.A. Bucchianeri: *Vocation of a Gadfly* (2018)

Noreen had explained that she had heard Miss Buls (or something) moving chairs around in the old lady's bedroom, doors and drawers opening and closing, strange chants as if 'Marie was talking to someone who was not in the room'. Noreen also stated that Marie often stared into a corner of her bedroom as if 'something evil was there' and that she heard a voice coming from Marie's eyes saying, 'This is my hate'. Noreen further claimed that when she touched Marie's bedsheets she received an 'electric shock', and that Marie's room was in a mess as if 'she could not look after herself'.

If the reader has watched the American supernatural movie *The Exorcist* (1973) starring Linda Blair as the possessed Regan, you will have noticed that Regan's bedroom became a big mess too. You can watch the trailer online; it's more than enough to make you hide under your bed. Although this movie was partly based on a real-life exorcism, the mentally debilitating effect the film had upon millions of viewers just might give serious pause for thought. It's a fact that many people who saw *The Exorcist* at the flicks came out vomiting their popcorn and fizzy drinks all over the pavement and passers-by.

'Nothing is so firmly believed as that which we least know.'

Michel de Montaigne: *Essays* (1580)

Without going completely off the wall, let the reader imagine being in Noreen O'Connor's shoes back then, or *right now* in the dead of night if you prefer. You hear strange noises upstairs. You find an elderly lady sitting bolt upright in her bed and she is pointing to a corner of the darkened room. 'It's in there,' she says. 'It's there, look!' You reach across to calm her and receive an electric shock from the bedspread. Suddenly, the old lady's eyes glow red, she grasps out at you, and you sense the evil in her, like a possession, and...

Oops, I went off track just there. But might we suggest that after the violent murder, Noreen O'Connor suffered a form of post-traumatic stress disorder? PTSD, as we all know, develops in some people who have experienced a scary or dangerous event, either real or imagined, and it can unbalance the mind for a lifetime. It is natural to feel afraid during and after a traumatic situation, for fear triggers many split-second changes in the body to help defend us against danger, or to avoid it. But in today's more enlightened societies, we do not start labelling sufferers from PTSD as 'mad' or 'insane', do we?

It is also worth noting that immediately after the murder, Noreen O'Connor looked as if she was peace with herself. Maybe the terrifying adrenalin rush had subsided. She admitted and understood the nature of the crime she'd committed. She cooperated fully with the police and the courts; all of which was totally commensurate with her previous good character and which, when taken in the round, is in *total contradiction* of the legal definition of criminal insanity that we'll examine later.

'I can calculate the motion of heavenly bodies, but not the madness of the people.'

Sir Isaac Newton

Mental illness is not a bar to prosecution for crimes. Prisons and jails are full of miscreants who were not taking medication for one mental disorder or another when they committed one. Moreover, proving so-called insanity as a legal defence for a crime is very difficult. There are defence attorneys who will still try it on, yet only a few succeed, as this book will highlight. In the case of *R. v. O'Connor*, it was proven beyond any doubt that Noreen had committed murder. The court, however, was lenient in its sentencing – was, indeed, extremely compassionate I must add.

'In time we hate that which we often fear.'

William Shakespeare: Antony and Cleopatra
(Act 1, Scene 3)

I have noted in some of my previous books that one rarely knows what goes on behind drawn curtains or locked doors; sometimes this may include the true nature of dread secrets and horrors residing within. Perhaps if we think outside the box, Noreen herself may have given us a subconscious, lateral clue as to why she so horrifically murdered a frail old lady. For did she not say that she had heard a voice coming from inside Marie Buls saying: 'This is my hate'? Did Noreen not say: 'I was killing the evil in her eyes'? Given which, is it not feasible that despite the good character attributed to Noreen by the people living in her *outside* world, behind those windows and doors the two women had grown to detest each other? Marie Buls, despite her frailty, had her health and freedom – and her job taken away from her during World War I, when she'd been interned; what she believed was her due had been taken away by the younger, more attractive and vivacious Noreen O'Connor. Did this plant the seeds of a deep-seated jealousy and hatred in her – prompting the words that allegedly came from Marie ('This is my hate?') and in keeping with the quote above, perfectly quilled by William Shakespeare?

Now it's time for us to leave sleepy Loxton. As a favour to me, please look the place up online, for it is a small village that tens of thousands of people pass by each day without giving a thought to its existence – and that's perhaps the way the locals wish it to be. We should respectfully admire them for this.

Lizzie Bordon had an axe
She gave her mother forty whacks
When she saw what she had done
She gave her father forty-one.

Hey, in the US of A, there would be a gift shop selling all of the tat associated with murder most foul. The building where Lizzy Borden gave her parents eighty-one whacks is now a guest house with a 'two-room suite on the second floor that Lizzie and Emma had'. You can also stay in the same room where Abby Bordon was brutally bludgeoned to death, all for the mean sum of $275 per night for two people. Can you imagine Gardeen turned into a B&B? How tasteless.

And, instead of a genteel church warden like Jane with her husband showing one around, one would have some armed-to-the-teeth, overweight redneck sheriff's deputy standing over a grave toting his 'law enforcement tools'. Oh gosh, these Americans do get themselves at it.

So now, dear reader, as a juror it is your 'tick-the-box time'. I respectfully direct you to consider everything you've read thus far with regard to Noreen O'Connor, and decide on your own verdict. Is it to be sad, bad, mad, insane or distilled evil?

Mad as a hatter?

'Mad, adj. Affected with a high degree of intellectual independence; not conforming to standards of thought, speech and action derived by the conformants from study of themselves; at odds with the majority; in short, unusual.'
Ambrose Bierce: *The Devil's Dictionary* (1906)

No nightmares, please, as we move on to becoming as 'Mad as a hatter'. Later on, this will take us into the dysfunctional world of the 'Surgeon of Broadmoor', none other than William Chester Minor, the insane Victorian-era US Army surgeon and extraordinary *Oxford English Dictionary* contributor. First, however, we must take dip into that adventurous book written by Charles Lutwidge Dodgson – better known as Lewis Carroll – *Alice in Wonderland* (1865; originally titled *Alice's Adventures Under Ground*).

A brilliant mathematician, Dodgson had secured a first-class honours degree in the subject at Oxford University, and remained at his college, Christ Church, for the rest of his life, where he lectured in mathematics, published books on mathematics, and amused himself by inventing, mostly word and mathematical, puzzles and pursuing his other great interest, photography.

Alice was one of the children of Henry Liddell, dean of Christ Church, with whose family Dodgson struck up a friendship, having first met them on 25 April 1856 when they came across him and a friend preparing to photograph Christ Church Cathedral. The family, especially the young daughters became photographic subjects of Dodgson, and one of the stories he told Alice and her sisters Lorina and Edith during a boating trip became the children's classic in which the Mad Hatter appears as one of the book's many eccentric characters.

At this early point in this book, I guess the reader will be wondering what *Alice in Wonderland* has got to do with our road trip into criminal insanity. You would be right to question the connection, although if you hail from the valley town of Denton, or the village of Haughton, Greater Manchester, you might already have some idea. Doubtless you will already know a thing or two about hats, because both places were once among the foremost hatting centres in the world. Indeed, felt hatting was recorded in Denton as early as 1702 and gained supremacy in the industry towards the end of the nineteenth century. But hat-making could be a very dangerous business, or let's say – more generously – far from risk free. The business all came about when local farmers supplemented their incomes by making felt hats.

'If you want to get ahead... *get a hat!*'

British hat-makers' slogan (1949)

In truth, the phrase 'mad as a hatter' had been around some time before Lewis Carroll set pen to paper. A 2015 online article by Elizabeth Nix confirms that 'the expression is linked to the hat-making industry and mercury poisoning,' adding that 'In the 18th and 19th centuries, industrial workers used a toxic substance, mercury nitrate, as part of the process of turning the fur of small animals, such as rabbits, into felt for hats.' One of the problems the factory workers faced was during the separation process – removing the fur from the hide – when the hatters were exposed to mercury vapours.

'Workplace safety standards often were lax,' Nix adds, with considerable understatement. Poor ventilation could also be a recipe for disaster, given that solvents were part of the process too. An explosion at the factory of Joseph Wilson & Sons in Denton on 14 January 1901 – caused by vapour from methylated spirits used for dyeing – killed thirteen people and wounded others. Yet, this isn't the end of it by a long chalk. Those who worked in the hatting industry, exposed to mercury for prolonged lengths of time, developed a number of disorders, mental as well as physical, such as moodiness and unpredictable behaviour, hallucinations, speech problems and tremors – commonly known as the 'hatter's shakes'.

To go further into the why and how of the toxicity of mercury . . . inorganic mercury salts are corrosive. Although I have not tried this experiment at home myself, I am reliably told that once mercury nitrate is ingested, gastritis, ulceration and necrosis of the gastrointestinal system can occur. To add a tiny flourish here, the signs and symptoms of mercury poisoning include irritation of the eyes; nausea; dysphagia; vomiting (sometimes haematemesis or vomiting of blood); abdominal pain, and diarrhoea (sometimes haematochezia or rectal bleeding). Death due to fluid and blood loss may result. What's more, mercury is also a neurotoxin. So aside from upsetting up just about every part of one's body, it can cause, as mentioned above, neurological damage that leads to hallucinations and psychosis. There is a very good reason for this, too: the shiny silvery metal is liquid at normal temperatures but droplets of it can turn into vapour at room temperature. The lungs easily absorb this invisible mist and once in the body mercury can pass through cell membranes and the blood-brain barrier (BBB), a semi-permeable border of cells that prevent solutes in the blood as it circulates from crossing into the central nervous system.

I like simple analogies – don't you? – because they can make a complicated matter easier to understand. So to use one here, let's imagine the central reservation along a dual-carriageway. The reservation is the 'semipermeable border' and if one 'non-selectively' drives through it one is bound to smash into another vehicle coming from the opposite direction. And if that doesn't screw up one's central nervous system, nothing will!

So, it should need no further elaboration for you to understand that if one puts some of this mercury on one's head, or breathes in the fumes for any length of time, one will end up seriously chemically unbalanced for decades, if not until a premature expiry date comes about. Even if one is exhumed from one's last resting place several millennia later, mercury nitrate can still be detected in one's skeletal remains. So let's give this mercury stuff some credit: it's a persistent little rascal, wouldn't you agree?

In the 'Constitution State' (Connecticut), tremors caused by mercury poisoning were dubbed the 'Danbury Shakes'. The city of Danbury (once called the 'Hat Capital of the World') had remained a major hat-making hub into the early twentieth century, although by the 1920s few manufacturers survived. The Danbury Shakes were no laughing matter. Many of the sufferers ended up at the Fairfield State Hospital in Newtown, a mental-health facility that at its peak housed over 4,000 mentally upside-down, chained-to-the-walls, bouncing-off-the-ceilings, intractably confused patients.

For the record, back then the treatment at Fairfield included hydrotherapy, insulin shock treatment, application of leeches, electroconvulsive therapy and frontal lobotomy. At one time it was thought that forced vomiting could cure some of the mental ills, too. Can you imagine the following conversation: 'C'mon David, you be a good ol' ex-hatter, now. Stick your fingers down your throat, let's bring up your dinner before we give you some hydro, whack some insulin into you. Look, here are some leeches that we're gonna put into your underpants before we plug you into the electrics while slicing into your brain.'

Levity aside, the majority of Fairfield's staff and utility buildings, along with all of the patient's wards, were connected by a series of concrete tunnels that were used to move the mentally indisposed incumbents and rattling trolleys of equipment between the buildings, especially during the winter months and on rainy days. Said subterranean passages were also used to convey food; even corpses were trolleyed through them en route to the onsite morgue.

So imagine this too, if you please. There you are. Your name is 'David', a mentally disassembled former hatter wheeling some rapidly cooling baked beans on toast through a damp, dimly lit tunnel when, through the gloom your accompanying nurse makes out a colleague approaching from the opposite direction: 'Goodness me, it's Nurse Joyce, and who are you wheeling to the morgue today?' asks your minder. The reply comes back: 'Oh hi, Sister Beneficia. It's "Jack the Hat". Can you scratch him off the dinner list? Thank you.'

So, if you'd been working in hat manufacture during this period, could it have turned you too into a nutty fruit cake? For the answer, please read on.

Thomas H. 'Boston' Corbett

'Understand me. I'm not like the ordinary world. I have my madness, I live in another dimension and I don't have time for things that have no soul.'

> Attributed to Charles Bukowski:
> German–American poet, novelist
> and short-story writer

For a notable example of a mad hatter, we need look no further than a London-born hat-maker called Thomas H. 'Boston' Corbett. His family moved to the United

States when he was a child, and in due course he became apprenticed to a milliner. Over the years that followed he continued working as a hat maker, all the time exposed to noxious mercury fumes. He married and was to become a father, when, tragically, his wife and baby died in childbirth. This drove him to drinking heavily and soon he was unable to hold down any job and became homeless until a street preacher persuaded him to join a Methodist Church. He stopped drinking and became fanatically religious, and soon resumed working as a milliner. The mercury vapours he had inhaled over the years were taking effect – to the point that when he was propositioned by prostitutes, he went to check his Bible and, inspired by the Gospel of Matthew, castrated himself – with a pair of scissors.

Three years later, in April 1861, he enlisted in the Union Army, where his proselytising led to him being court-martialled and almost executed. He was pardoned and enlisted in the 16th New York Cavalry Regiment; three years later he was captured by the Confederate States Army and kept prisoner for five months. On his return to his regiment, he was promoted to sergeant. And on 26 April 1865, he shot and killed President Abraham Lincoln's assassin, John Wilkes Booth.

He was arrested and taken to be court-martialled, but claimed that he was acting in self-defence – though he had earlier declared that 'Providence directed me.' He was absolved as 'a patriot'.

On his discharge from the army, Corbett, now lauded as a hero, resumed work in the hat-making industry; he also worked as a preacher, though his behaviour became increasingly erratic and paranoid. He eventually moved to Kansas, where he lived a solitary existence as a homesteader in Pine County and continued to preach. In 1887, Corbett, by then in his fifties was committed to the Topeka Asylum for the Insane after threatening a group of people at the Kansas Statehouse with a firearm.

This sort of incident is not unique in the US. In fact we will meet a chap just like this later on, by the name of Dr Julio Mora, and if he wasn't criminally insane I know not who is. But, the thing is, you don't get any of this naughty behaviour going on in the UK, mainly because we don't allow our folk to buy and openly carry military-grade firearms, as I point out in my book *Talking with Psychopaths and Savages: Mass Murderers and Spree Killers*.

In 1888 Thomas Corbett escaped from the facility and disappeared for good, in something of a forerunner to the 1975 movie *One Flew Over the Cuckoo's Nest*. There is some indication that Corbett died in a fire, therefore we might say that he went up in smoke. And, at this point, and as we are discussing madness, I have just spotted, by pure coincidence, a sign along Highway 634 SW Mulvane, saying: 'Topeka State Hospital'. So, as Corbett once escaped from there, we really should pay the place a visit during our road trip.

There must be a full moon out there

It is the very error of the moon.
She comes more nearer earth than she was wont
And makes men mad.

> William Shakespeare: *Othello* (Act 5, Scene 2)

The architect of what was then known as the Topeka Insane Asylum, was the majestically bearded John G. Haskell – a frock-coated gentleman who certainly knew a thing or two about designing buildings. It opened in 1879, staying operational for over a century before being abandoned then almost completely demolished – only the gothic, Count Dracula-style entrance remains standing today.

Although I have not yet visited this old asylum in the 'Wheat State' (Kansas), let alone been chained to a bed in one of its wards, this, I stress, *is not* the sort of place that one would want to visit in the dead of night The only sounds are the rustle of small critters among the leaves and the hoot of a lonely owl perched high up in the scudding moonlit branches of some nearby trees. Yes, there is 'Owlbert', waiting to swoop without a screech on one of the aforementioned mice and other diminutive beasts for a late-night snack.

According to some local legend, the old asylum is haunted. Of course, it has to be when you consider how many horror stories exist about this former nuthouse, including one about a journalist who went in there to write a story and saw a patient who had been tied up for so long that his skin had begun to grow around his restraints. There exist records of abuse, neglect and rape, with many lunatics kept chained up naked for months on end – all of which gave our Thomas Corbett a damned good reason to escape, if you ask me.

Lunatic (adj.)

[ad. late L. *lūnātic-us*, f. L. *lūna* moon ...]

Originally, affected with the kind of insanity that was supposed to have recurring periods dependent on the changes of the moon. In mod. use, synonymous with insane; current in popular and legal language, but not now employed technically by physicians.

Oxford English Dictionary

We often categorise serial killers as 'mad men' when they are perfectly sane. For example: Ted Bundy was 'mad killer', but technically he was of sound mind. We never label these serial murderers and rampage killers 'lunatics' or 'moonstruck'. That said, these days in the medical profession, people who are afflicted with serious mental illnesses may be called insane, because 'lunatic' is no longer quite the PC label it once was.

This might seem like a lot of hair-splitting, but I rather believe right now that as our road trip into the minds of men and women who have 'flipped' develops, toe-tagging these individuals correctly will become of some import.

Just think of the phrase 'There must be a full moon out there,' often trotted out to explain odd nocturnal events. It's a theme explored in *Scientific American*'s Mind & Brain: 'Lunacy and the Full Moon – Does a full moon really trigger strange behavior?' by Hal Arkowitz and Scott O. Lilienfeld (published on 1 February 2009). The article reminds us that the name of the Roman goddess of the Moon was Luna: *luna*, from which 'lunatic' is derived, being the Latin for 'moon'. The same paper also tells us that 'the Greek philosopher Aristotle and Roman historian Pliny the Elder suggested that the brain was the "moistest" organ in the body and thereby most susceptible to the pernicious influences of the

36

moon, which triggers the tides.' Indeed, in Europe, through the Middle Ages, it was widely believed that some people could (and did) turn into werewolves during a full moon. The 1897 novel by Bram Stoker, *Dracula*, very loosely based on the legendary fifteenth-century ruler of Wallachia, Vlad III, 'the Impaler' (he had a nasty habit of executing his enemies and insubordinates by impaling them), son of Vlad Dracul, did nothing to dispel the myths. In supposedly more enlightened times, the moon's effect, now also sometimes called the 'Transylvania effect', has been reputed to bring about behavioural and physiological changes in living creatures – there are those who will claim that suicides and murders, erratic outbursts, eruptions of violent behaviour, traffic accidents, and so on, are more widespread when the moon is full. (And did Noreen O'Connor kill Miss Buls during a full moon? Actually, no!)

Let us now return to the Topeka Insane Asylum. To make matters even worse for its incumbents, in 1913 a sterilisation law was introduced aimed at 'habitual criminals', 'idiots', 'epileptics', 'imbeciles' and 'the insane' . As a result, fifty-four people were sterilised during the seven years that followed, and the practice increased before it was given up in about 1950. Unfortunately, a number of patients were involuntarily sterilised when they had been wrongly incarcerated; they weren't mentally ill at all. Others, however, were quite obviously as mad as hatters. Kenneth 'Ken' D. Waddell is a jolly fine example.

In 1992, the asylum was once again in the news when a thirty-year-old music therapist called Stephanie Uhlrig was murdered by hefty 'Mad Ken', who was classified as a high-risk patient. You can find his mugshot online. One glance at his picture will tell you that this chap was not the sort to invite round to watch *One Flew Over The Cuckoo's Nest* on Netflix, with tea and cakes.

While we're on the subject of mugshots, many of my readers will be au fait with the now totally debunked theories put forward by the Italian professor Cesare Lombroso, the so-called 'father of criminology', who once, while getting himself into a bit of a lather, wrote in his 1876 book *Criminal Man*:

> At the sight of that [human] skull, I seemed to see all of a sudden… the problem of the nature of the criminal – an atavistic being who reproduces in his person the ferocious instincts of primitive humanity and the inferior animals. Thus were explained anatomically the enormous jaws, high cheek-bones [and other features] found in criminals, savages, and apes.

Cesare doesn't mince his words. He breathlessly continues, linking this selection of physical attributes with a 'love of orgies, and the irresistible craving for evil for its own sake, the desire not only to extinguish life in the victim, but to mutilate the corpse, tear its flesh, and drink its blood'.

And, to whose head in particular was Cesare referring, you may ask? It had belonged to one Giuseppe Villella, who had gone to prison for theft and arson – nothing more, nothing less.

Well, maybe Lombroso was *almost* onto something. Let's give him a break, shall we? Take a look at the face of gay British serial killer Stephen Port, and tell me that he was *not* descended from the lower classes of the Planet of the Apes. Take a peek at the mugshots of any number of criminals. My book *Love of Blood* has police photos of some of British serial killer Joanne Dennehy's accomplices: Gary John Stretch, Leslie Paul Layton and Robert James Moore. Aside from their somewhat unedifying physical lack of Adonis attributes, one look into their eyes will shout out: 'MORON' from the Latin *morus*, Greek *mōron* meaning 'stupid', the *OED* tells us, and was adopted by the American Association for the Study of the Feeble-minded in the early twentieth century to denote 'one of the highest class of feeble-minded; an adult person having a mental age of between eight and twelve' – suiting Stretch, Layton and Moore to a T: they were not mad, by a long chalk… plumb-dumb stupid would a better description.

Let's now turn our attention back to Kenneth 'Ken' D. Waddell. Mother-of-two Stephanie Uhlrig and another therapist took some high-risk patients out in a bus to watch a movie. After they returned, Waddell, obviously upset with the flicks, strangled Stephanie and left her body in the men's rest room. She had gone there because she was concerned about the length of time he was taking to have a pee. So, was Mr Waddell sad, bad or mad; insane or evil? You can judge for yourself. Never mind that he had been transferred to Topeka State Hospital in 1987, after being given a bed in the Larned State Hospital two years previously. He was sent there after Lyon County jury found him guilty by reason of insanity following the aggravated battery of a nineteen-year-old Emporia State University student.

Court records indicate that the teenager was jogging along a nature trail on the university campus when he attacked her, threw her to the ground and stabbed her once in the back and once in the abdomen with a knife. Since 1996, Waddell has racked up fifteen disciplinary violations, including battery, obscenity and dangerous possession of contraband. At the time of writing he is supposedly locked up in the El Dorado Correctional Facility, where, according to Kansas Corrections Department records, 'He works in a job.' However, a search of the KDOC's inmate locator shows him to be no longer behind bars. Maybe he was granted the parole he had long been seeking?

Oh, and if we have time, and as you have brought your packed lunches and bags of Doritos that taste like reconstituted cardboard with you, we can visit Topeka's cemetery, where no less than 1,157 patients are buried. Alas, there won't be much else to see because only sixteen of the graves have headstones, so God only knows where the remaining remains are. Um, on second thoughts, maybe not. It's getting dark now and I swear to God that I have just seen some glowing red eyes looking at us through one of those windows... who could it be? 'The Gray Lady of Topeka' is one contender, or perhaps it is 'David the Deranged Mad Hatter of Danbury'.

All aboard now.... *let's go!*'
'My lad chewed and swallowed a dictionary. We gave him some Epsom salts – but we can't get a word out of him.'

Leslie 'Les' Dawson: English comedian, actor, writer, presenter

So what else do we know about madness apart from *Alice's Adventures in Wonderland*, mercury-nitrate-impregnated felt hats, shooting at people and mental asylums?

Let's hit the dictionaries

'Integrity without knowledge is weak and useless, and knowledge without integrity is dangerous and dreadful.'

Samuel Johnson: writer and lexicographer

As my wallet and my bookshelves forbid me possession of the twenty-plus volumes of *The Oxford English Dictionary* (*OED*), I usually turn to one of its fine offspring, *The Oxford Dictionary of English* (*ODE*); this politely informs me that madness means: 'the state of having a serious mental illness ... extremely foolish behaviour ... a state of wild or chaotic activity'. That mad is '*Chiefly Brit.* mentally ill; insane ... extremely foolish ... in a frenzied mental or physical state ... *informal* very angry ... very enthusiastic ...'

Among 'phrases', the *ODE* does mention 'as mad as a hatter', explaining solemnly, 'the allusion being to the effects of mercury poisoning from the use of mercurous nitrate in the manufacture of felt hats'.

On the subject of Oxford dictionaries, it just so happens that one of the original volunteer contributors to the *OED* was himself a mental asylum resident and truly as mad as a hatter – as we'll see.

Next off my burgeoning bookshelves comes a fat copy of *Roget's Thesaurus* in which political correctness is thrown completely out of the window. Under 'insanity' one finds a whole raft of synonyms such as: 'unsoundness of mind; lunacy; certifiability; intellectual imbalance; mental derangement; disordered reason; imbecility; cuckoo; dippy; whacky; barmy; bonkers and pea-brained'.

Um, please 'scuse me for a moment: I have just received an urgent telephone call from a member of my church knitting circle advising me that a minibus of green Wellington-booted blue rinses from the Budleigh Salterton Mentally Disintegrating Minds Group is on its way to my home to demand that I repent. But I don't do redemption unless I am redeeming some Co-op vouchers at a till. I'll be back as soon as I have barricaded the garden gate and moved my family of red-nosed gnomes and the pink windmill fairground prize to safety.

Phew, that was a close call, but at least now we are getting down to Roget's nitty-gritty: loony; nutty as a fruit cake; nuts; bananas; daffy; idiot; scatter-brained; crack-brained, and – yes, yes! – there is a reference to hats ('as mad as a hatter'), followed by 'mad as a March hare' ('mad' because in March, their breeding season, hares go, um, bananas), the latter, a cousin of the somewhat unfortunate American jackrabbit. I say 'unfortunate' because back in the nineteenth century, after the brightly named Zadoc Benedict accidentally, and quite literally, stumbled on a technique to create felt by adding heat, moisture and pressure and mercury chloride to jackrabbit pelts – guess what he did next? He used his bedposts to shape the malodorous damp jackrabbit felt into hats – all of which must have made Mrs Benedict madder than hell because it would have stunk the house out.

But how did that idea pop into Zadoc's head?

The facts of the matter are, our Zadoc had stumbled while out walking, so he plugged the hole he'd made in the sole of his shoe with jackrabbit fur – as one does, I suppose. Over time, the fur turned damp (ugh) and metamorphosed into felt. Thereafter, scores of his hat-making employees went stark raving bonkers, as did Ma Benedict, who had to darn his socks.

'So, Christopher, what does "mad" mean in American-English', you might ask? Well, to our alleged cousins across the Pond, 'mad' simply means 'angry'. And what do American psychiatrists/psychologists – aka 'head shrinkers' or 'mind probers' – have to say? Keeping it short and sweet, the American Psychological Association opts for: 'madness *n.* an obsolete name for mental illness or for legal insanity'.

Let me assure you that as we march steadily on through this book a certain amount of psychiatric gobbledygook, of excessive, generally unintelligible shrink jargon, will follow for reasons that *will* become patently clear.

Now, however, it's time to return to a gentleman that I mentioned right at the start and ask: who was Daniel M'Naghten? Step forward 'Danny Boy', you're up next!

Daniel M'Naghten:
the M'Naghten rule

'Passion makes idiots of the cleverest of men, and makes the biggest idiots clever.'

FRANÇOIS, DUC DE LA ROCHEFOUCAULD

By way of an introduction, the M'Naghten rule (the names is pronounced and often spelled 'McNaughton' – a search of the family's genealogy also shows it as 'McNaughtan') – dates back to the 1840s, and is based on a jury instruction in a criminal case where there is a defence of insanity. Under this ruling, a defendant is considered to have been insane at the time of the act – in the context of this book, a murder – if he or she *did not know* right from wrong or, *did not understand the moral nature* of the act because of a mental disease or defect. But here is the thing: one never finds the M'Naghten rule applied to a bank robber, a common thief, a conman or a shoplifter for pinching a tube of toothpaste. I wonder why!

The M'Naghten rule is one of the main planks, or raisons d'être, for this book, because although initially well meant, it is a legal standard, albeit a tad tweaked in many jurisdictions, that has been abused by countless defence and prosecution lawyers and their appointed forensic psychiatrists from its inception right up 'til the present day. Strong words and accusations indeed, but when the reader starts examining the murder cases that we'll examine here, I hope all will become as clear as day. Hence my opening quote by the Duc: had Daniel M'Naghten been blessed with the great gift of 20-20 hindsight, he ought to have heeded it well.

> 'Is not this the carpenter's son? Is not his mother called Mary? And are not his brothers James and Joseph and Simon and Judas?'
>
> Matthew 13:55 (Bible, New Revised Standard Version)

Um, not exactly. Although he was indeed the son of a carpenter/wood-turner/landlord (after whom he was named), Daniel M'Naghten was hatched in broad daylight in Glasgow in 1813, not in a stable at night under a wandering star with some attending wise men holding perfumes and stuff.

After the passing of his mother Ada, 'Daniel the Younger' went to live with his dad's family and became an apprentice wood-turner. Later he became a journeyman at Daniel the Elder's workshop in Stockwell Street, Glasgow – a site more recently remodelled into an Argos store. For the benefit of my British readers, and from every other country in the world for that matter, in the US 'remodelling' means some botoxing, or lots of botoxing,, and/or, slapping makeup onto faces using a trowel. Here in the UK, we get 'Bob the Jobbing Builder' around to knock up some shelves. Different cultures, I am sure you will agree.

For reasons unknown to us, Daniel the Elder refused to give his son a partnership in his wood-turning business, so for the next three years he took to acting, returning to Glasgow in 1834 to set up a wood-turning firm on his own account. For the next five years Daniel was successful; first in Turner's Court off Church Street, where he turned a lot of wood, then back to Stockwell Street, where he turned even more trees into things such as newel posts, spindles and just about anything that might be worked on a lathe.

As with many alleys, Turner's Court got its name from a past occupant of the 'front house' and has zilch to do with wood-turning. There were five houses in the court, which still exists to this very day. Somewhat ironically, the front house was occupied by a Mr Turner, a stocking knitter by trade, though some say that an artist called William Turner (not the famous J.M.W. Turner) periodically stayed there too. And here's a thing – the etymology of 'Turner' is a name for a lathe turner. Originally derived from the Norman Old French verb *tournoieur*, it came to England following the Norman Conquest, and dates to the twelfth century. Today it's the UK's twenty-eighth most common surname. It's kind of like the surname 'Fletcher', derived from men who originally fletched (feathered) arrows in the Middle Ages, the heyday of the longbow as a battle-winning weapon.

According to trial records, Daniel M'Naghten was

teetotal, industrious and lived the most frugal of existences. In his spare time, he attended the Glasgow Mechanics' Institute, and the high-brow Athenaeum Debating Society. It's worth digging a little more deeply here, for it will carry much weight when we later try to assess M'Naghten's state of mental health.

At the Glasgow Mechanic's Institute, men paid a quarterly subscription fee for the new model of technical education giving classes, access to libraries as well as apparatus to be used for experiments and technical work. Indeed, there were mechanics' institutes worldwide. The first-ever such institution was also in Scotland: Edinburgh School of Arts, founded in 1821. Its stated purpose was to 'address societal needs by incorporating fundamental scientific thinking and research into engineering solutions', and it was a breakthrough in teaching laypeople about science and technology. Clearly then, our Daniel M'Naghten was industrious, to say the least. But it was the Athenaeum Debating Society that really caught my attention. This was definitely not one for the hoi polloi; its early members were the elite. It was founded in 1824 by the statesman John Wilson Croker, then Secretary to the Admiralty.

Then comes chemist Sir Humphry Davy, 1st Baronet, PRS, MRIA, FGS – the inventor of the 'Davy Lamp' – who became the first chairman.

There is scientist Michael Faraday FRS – famously known for his contributions to the understanding of chemistry and electrochemistry. He was the first secretary.

An impressive fifty-one members of the Club have won the Nobel prize, including at least one in each category.

There's first the Athenaeum Club; so wise there's not
a man of it
That has not sense enough for six (in fact that is the
plan of it);
The very waiters answer you with eloquence Socratical,
And always place the knives and forks in order
mathematical.
Theodore Edward Hook: man of letters, composer
and one-time civil servant in Mauritius

Hook was known as a playboy and a practical joker – look
up the 'Berners Street Hoax'. He received the world's first
postcard in 1840, and is believed to have posted it to himself.
In 1820 he launched the high Tory, and then Sunday,
newspaper *John Bull*.

Daniel M'Naghten was at one time a member of this
debating club, so no mental slouch was he! Furthermore, he
did a lot of walking, a lot of thinking and more than a lot
of reading. He even taught himself French so that he could
read François, Duc de La Rochefoucauld's, *Maxims and Moral
Reflections*. And this high-born French moralist's thinking
appears to have started to turn Daniel's head.

The Duc de La Rochefoucauld was a great writer, and
occasionally his words make a lot of sense; there are welcome
smatterings of tongue-in-cheek humour thrown in too. He
also comes over as being well-over-the-top vainglorious, full
of airs and graces; a peacock, a smug smarty-pants; the noun
'modesty' clearly never entered his toffee-nosed vocabulary.
In today's lingo one might call him a self-opinionated,
swollen-headed prick – and here's the evidence.

49

The Duc's literary debut was his penned self-portrait, in which he describes himself as one might when 'Desperately Seeking Joséphine', or for that matter a potential paramour on a dating site, such as bornlosersmatchmaking.fr.og:

I am of a medium height, active, and well-proportioned. My complexion dark, but uniform, a high forehead; and of moderate height, black eyes, small, deep set, eyebrows black and thick but well placed. I am rather embarrassed in talking of my nose, for it is neither flat nor aquiline, nor large; nor pointed: but I believe, as far as I can say, it is too large [rather] than too small, and comes down just a trifle too low.

What a self-admiring jerk-off. Don't you think that this clown needed to have his nose rearranged with a smack in the face, to be gifted, gratis, even blacker eyes than he already has? But wait, the Duc hasn't finished quite yet:

I have a large mouth, lips, generally red enough, neither shaped well nor badly. I have white teeth, and fairly even. I have been told I have a little too much chin. I have looked at myself in the glass to ascertain the fact, and I do not know how to decide. As to the shape of my face, it is either square or oval, but which I should find it very difficult to say. I have black hair, which curls by nature, and thick and long enough to entitle me to lay claim to a fine head.

And probably a very big head too, methinks; the French word *crâneur* springs to mind.

Having now had a dig at les Français, let's return to Daniel M'Naghten who for a while employed a Chartist activist named Abram Duncan in his workshop. For further information on the Chartist movement, the reader might wish to look elsewhere, but I betcha that you won't!

We now find ourselves in December 1840. For the benefit of any readers who were not born back then, a few highlights. This was a leap year! The UK introduced the Uniform Penny Post that year – the very reason why Theodore Hook was able to post the first ever postcard to himself. This was also the year when the steamship *Lexington* caught fire and sank off Long Island – the lesson to be learned here is that steam, fire and icy water combined with a mind-bending amount of utter incompetence do not make for an ideal mix. Perhaps more important for us, M'Naghten sold his wood-turning/head-turned business that year and spent the next two years travelling between London and his home city, with a brief trip to France. He is known to have attended lectures on anatomy in 1942. By then, though, things had started to sail south. In 1941 Daniel started complaining to various people, including his father and the local commissioner of police *and* a Labour MP, that he was being persecuted by the Tories and followed by their spies. No one took him seriously; he simply seemed deluded.

But was he deluded – or, to use another term, 'off his rocker?'

Date: 20 January 1843. Location: Whitehall, London. Plan: murder.

Poor Drummond is universally regretted.
Queen Victoria: letter, with more than a touch of
regal hyperbole, to Leopold I of Belgium

A handsome blue-blood cut of a man, Sir Robert 'Bobby' Peel, second baronet – a Conservative statesman who served twice as prime minster of the United Kingdom and was also chancellor of the exchequer and two-time home secretary – is regarded as the father of today's modern policing. Yet, as all we true-crime buffs know, London's first professional police force is generally assumed to have been the Bow Street Runners; they originally numbered just six men and were founded in 1749 by magistrate Henry Fielding, who, unlike myself, was a well-known author. For his part, Sir Robert Peel founded the Metropolitan Police Service; his officers becoming known as 'Bobbies' or 'Peelers' – although the phrase keeping one's eyes 'peeled' – perhaps for signs of mischief-making, with skulduggery committed on the side – has a different origin. On that day in 1843, Sir Robert was very nearly at the wrong end of a bullet fired by M'Naghten. But instead, it struck…

Edward Drummond, a member of the family that owned Drummonds Bank. Aged twenty-two, he became a clerk at the Treasury. Later, he served as private secretary to a succession of prime ministers – George Canning, Frederick John Robinson (first Viscount Goderich), Arthur Wellesley (first Duke of Wellington) and, in his terminal role, Sir Robert Peel.

Why 'terminal role', you might ask. Well, on the wintery afternoon of 29 January 1843, Drummond, with a spring in his step, was making his way along Whitehall to Downing Street after visiting his brother at the family's bank in Charing Cross when M'Naghten came up behind him, drew a pistol and point-blank fired into Drummond's back. A police constable immediately overpowered the assassin before a second shot could be discharged and M'Naghten was taken into custody. Whether or not Drummond was the intended victim remains unclear. Certainly, the Tory Sir Robert Peel's extreme-right stance, political achievements and ideology were polar opposites to those of the wood-turner's Chartist views. Sir Robert had been a 'top cop' and M'Naghten believed that Tories had spies watching his every move. So all of this could most likely have added more fuel to his fiery, agitated state of mind. We might also recall M'Naghten's visits to France and that he was an avid reader of François, Duc de La Rochefoucauld's moralistic writings. Having said which, that M'Naghten – who was not short-sighted by a long chalk – had shot a lead ball into the wrong man at such close range is a scenario that does not fly with me.

Remarkably, Drummond managed to stagger back to his house:

> The ball has been extracted. No vital part is injured, and Mr Guthrie and Mr Bransby Cooper [the attending surgeons] have every reason to believe that Mr Drummond is doing very well.
>
> *John Bull* periodical, 21 January 1843

Yeah, right. Indeed, dear Mr Drummond was doing *so* well that complications set in and he finally fell off his perch and shuffled off this mortal coil five days later. He was buried in the family vault at St Luke's Church, Charlton, where his brother Arthur was rector. Coming from a banking family, the Drummonds knew a good few things about vaults, I can tell you that much.

Just seven years later, on 29 June 1850, Sir Robert himself was thrown from his horse while riding on Constitution Hill in London, with tragic consequences. It was about five of the clock in the late afternoon. Although a competent horseman, Sir Robert was not fully accustomed to riding the eight-year-old hunter he'd acquired a few weeks before. Unknown to him it had an evil reputation for bucking and kicking; his coachman did not like the look of it, but his opinion was ignored. Sir Robert had just left Buckingham Palace, where he'd signed the visitors' book and, when in sight of St George's Hospital, he met a Miss Ellis, one of Georgiana, Lady Dover's daughters, who herself was on a skittish horse. Sir Robert advanced to greet her; his horse resisted and while he was gently quieting the animal it suddenly shied again and threw Sir Robert over its head. He died in terrible agony three days later at the age of sixty-two due to a broken collarbone rupturing his subclavian vessels:

All physical pain troubled and agitated him strangely. After this fall, this disturbance, agitation, and aversion to pain, became so strong, that his physicians were unable to succeed in clearly ascertaining all the effects of the accident, and the full extent of the injury. Sir Robert objected to any examination, to any sort of contact; and fell into a state of alarming irritation when his medical attendants insisted. It was not until after the death of Sir Robert Peel, that it was discovered that the fifth rib on the left side was also fractured, and had pressed upon the lung, and produced a congestion of that organ which, it is said, was the determining cause of death.

F.P.G. Guizot: *Memoirs of Sir Robert Peel* (1857)

The trial

'Justice is like a train that's nearly always late.'

Yevgeny Yevtushenko: *A Precocious Autobiography*, 1963

Daniel M'Naghten appeared at Bow Street Magistrates' Court the morning after the shooting. Here he made a brief, mumbling statement in which he described how being hounded by the Conservatives had driven him to his desperate act. As related in Richard Moran's *Knowing Right from Wrong: The Insanity Defense of Daniel McNaughtan* (1981), he claimed: 'The Tories in my native city have compelled me to do this. They follow, persecute me wherever I go, and have entirely ruined my peace of mind... It can be proved by evidence. That is all I have to say.' And he was as good as his word, for he never spoke about the assassination attempt again, apart from a few words when asked to plead guilty or not guilty at arraignment.

Upon his arrest a bank receipt for £750 was found in his possession – a very considerable sum in those days; it would be worth some £122,000 today. M'Naghten's father arranged for the court to allow this to be used for his son's defence and for the case to be adjourned in order to hoover up evidence relating to Daniel's state of mind. A trial date was set, but the efficiency with which the defence organised itself subsequently led to conjecture that leading figures in the fields of law and medicine were using the case to institute changes in the law regarding criminal insanity.

M'Naghten's trial took place at the Central Criminal Court, the Old Bailey, on 2–3 March 1843, with Chief Justice Tindal, Justice Williams and Mr Justice Coleridge presiding. When asked for his plea, the defendant replied: 'I was driven to desperation by persecution... I am guilty of firing,' which was taken to mean 'Not Guilty'.

M'Naghten's defence was led by a bigwig, one of London's best-known barristers, none other than Sir Alexander James Edmund Cockburn, 12th Baronet, a jurist and politician who later served as the lord chief justice for twenty-one years. In 1847, Sir Alexander had decided to stand for parliament, and was elected unopposed as Liberal member of Parliament for Southampton. Lord John Russell appointed him solicitor general in 1850 and attorney general in 1851 – a post that he held until 1852. This somewhat begs the question: why would such a distinguished legal eagle take on this sort of case, which amounted to the attempted assassination of a Tory prime minister? The answer may well rest in the fact that Sir Alex was a dyed-in-the-wool lefty – his political leanings swinging more towards the Chartist Movement than the Conservatives, who were hard-line right-wing at that time.

The prosecution was led by the solicitor general, Sir William Follett – the attorney general himself being too busy in Lancaster prosecuting Feargus O'Conner and fifty-seven other Chartists following the 'Plug Plot Riots', with which Daniel M'Naghten was well acquainted. More formally known as the 1842 General Strike, the riots started among Staffordshire coal miners and soon expanded to take in mills in Yorkshire, and mines from Scotland to south Wales and the West Country. It was a movement of resistance to the imposition of wage cuts, and would involve nearly 500,000 people. The Tories had spies everywhere and potential troublemakers, such as M'Naghten with his Chartist sympathies, were closely watched.

At M'Naghten's trial, *both* prosecution and defence based their case arguments on what constituted a legal defence of insanity – effectively ensuring that no one would lose face, so to speak – with each side agreeing that M'Naghten was under the delusion that he was being persecuted. The Crown claimed that in spite of M'Naghten's' 'partial insanity' (note that) he was 'a responsible agent capable of distinguishing right from wrong, and was conscious of committing a crime'. To bolster this point, witnesses as diverse as his landlady and a lecturer in anatomy a testified to his apparent sanity. They had a point. Having attended the Athenaeum Debating Society, taught himself French, avidly read François, Duc de La Rochefoucauld's works and run a successful wood-turning business, M'Naghten could hardly have been labelled stark raving bonkers.

In his opening statement, Sir Alex Cockburn admitted that there were difficulties in the practical application of the English law that stated that a person deemed insane is unable to know right from wrong and should be exempt from legal responsibility and legal punishment. Here, he was defending an apparently intelligent, rational and sane man – his argument was that his client had acted under the influence of a 'morbid passion' that, medical experts agreed, had left him subject to 'ungovernable impulse' and no longer a 'reasonable and responsible being'.

Cockburn also quoted extensively from Scottish judge David Hume (Baron Hume of Ninewells FRSE) and American psychiatrist Isaac Ray (the latter is still regarded as one of the founders of the discipline of forensic psychiatry).

The defence then called some top-gun witnesses, including Dr Edward Thomas Monro. Sir Alexander Morison and Dr Forbes Winslow, all leading figures in medicine. Each of the trio stated that M'Naghten had lost 'all restraint over his actions' because of his delusional state of mind.

For the reader interested in genealogy, Dr Monro of Fyrish, of the ancient Clan Munro, was from a dynasty of doctors who, in the eighteenth and nineteenth centuries, specialised in seeking a cure for 'insanity'. Like his great-grandfather, grandfather and father, Edward Monro held the post of principal physician at London's notorious Bethlehem or Bethlem Hospital (more familiarly known as Bedlam and from which the word 'bedlam' derives).

For his part, Sir Alexander Thomas Morison MD was a Scottish physician who also worked in the emerging field of what would become psychiatry. Ironically, in 1852 his portrait was painted by the insane murderer Richard Dadd, a patient of his, although it is not one of Dadd's better works, it has to be said, more of a 'pot-boiler' in my humble opinion. This leaves us with Forbes Benignus Winslow DCL, FRCP

Edin, MRCP, MRCS, MD, a British psychiatrist, author and an authority on lunacy during the Victoria era.

With that large battery of silver-spoon-fed psychiatric experts pointing their richly embroidered heritages and psychiatric qualifications in his direction, it was hands-up time for Sir William Follett. He was able to offer up no medical witnesses who might challenge their evidence. Consequently, the trial ground to a halt after he half-heartedly apologised to the bench, adding: 'I cannot press for a verdict against the prisoner.' Thereafter, Chief Justice Tindal made it clear that the case had indeed been one-way traffic and advised the jury that M'Naghten would be properly taken care of if they found him guilty of murder on the grounds of insanity Which they did. His acquittal prompted a debate in the House of Lords, informed by discussion with a selection of judges, over the whole issue of how insanity could be defended in a court of law. In turn, this gave rise to the establishment of the so-called M'Naghten rule (or 'rules'), a set of criteria by which criminal culpability might be assessed and the verdict 'guilty but insane' might be returned.

For me, this is where issues arise. In his 1981 book *Knowing Right from Wrong*, Richard Moran, professor of sociology at Mount Holyoke College, South Hadley, Massachusetts, argues that there are certain aspects of the M'Naghten case that have never been explained. Moran doubts that the sizeable bank receipt found on M'Naghten at the time of his arrest could have come from his wood-turning business, and this seems reasonable enough. He also tells us that the court ignored M'Naghten's political activity, and the possibility that there may have been a strong element of truth to his complaints of persecution. More recently, Moran has said that M'Naghten was a 'political activist who was financed to assassinate the prime minister', and who subsequently feigned insanity to avoid more serious punishment.

Somewhat impertinently, I take a slightly different view. M'Naghten didn't explain what form his persecution had taken to either the Bow Street magistrates or the trial court – he simply said that he had been persecuted, giving no further details. Admittedly, it's puzzling that he was found to have recently deposited such a huge sum in a bank. For that amount of money I am sure that the Chartists (if they *were* behind the assassination attempt) could have found a professional hitman.

For those of you keen to find out about subsequent modifications to the M'Naghten rule, there is an excellent article by Shruti Mishra titled 'Applicability of M'Naghten Rules in Contemporary Situations' – to be found online. It is a must-read for anyone studying the law in the context of insanity, as is the online Law Dictionary's 'The Four Tests Used for Determining Legal Insanity'.

I hazard a guess that by now the reader will be wondering what all of this psycho-legal stuff is leading up to – it sounds frightfully long-winded, does it not? But it's worth bearing in mind that forensic psychiatry and forensic psychology are 'disciplines' and most certainly *not* 'sciences'. As this book develops, and while using the O'Connor and M'Naghten cases as our starters for ten, the reader will soon discover that, more often than not, the shrinks are often as mad as the patients they treat.

'Men will always be mad, and those who think they can cure them are the maddest of all.'

Voltaire, aka François-Marie Arouet: letter (1762)

Moving steadily on, the noun 'forensic' means 'an argumentative exercise'. So far as we are concerned, in its broadest sense this means the *scientific* tests or techniques used in connection with the detection of crime; to be used in, or suitable to, courts of judicature inter alia: forensic medicine; forensic science; forensic pathology; forensic experts, etc. So the question to be asked is: do psychiatrists – forensic or otherwise – really deserve a place in the criminal courts when attempting to judge the state of a defendant's state of mind? To help us along our way, and as a gun played not an insignificant part earlier in this chapter, allow me to use ballistics as an example of *real* forensic science. And if you think am going off target here, please bear with me.

A shot in the dark

'The function of an expert is not be more right than other people, but to be wrong for more sophisticated reasons.'

Sir David Butler, psephologist:
The Observer (1969)

For a real, tangible, pretty-easy-for-a-jury-to-understand science, we can briefly consider 'forensic ballistics', and see how this stacks up against forensic psychiatry. In my humble opinion, the latter often boils down to merely supposition based upon educated or uneducated guesswork – oft-times a Woolworths pick-and-mix of over-optimistic opinions and conclusions.

Most of us have watched at least some of the many CSI documentaries on television or online, and therefore we know that forensic ballistics (firearms evidence) is a complex field of study with many technical facets. For which excellent reason it is the province of the firearms expert, whose skill and knowledge at every stage will be of the greatest importance. There is no room for guesswork at all. Moreover, a successful prosecution in a murder case may depend on the thoroughness with which the physical firearms evidence is prepared – what the eye *can* see, in other words. This is illustrated by an early murder investigation that helped to establish the firearm specialist's professional standing in Britain. It is a case very close to my own heart because my grandfather, Oscar Berry Tompkins, a former captain in the Machine Gun Corps during World War I, was the defending solicitor in the related case, acting for one William Henry Kennedy.

The facts in the matter were as follows. Early in the morning of 25 September 1927, the body of a PC 489 George William Gutteridge was found in a country lane at Stapleford Abbotts in Essex. He'd been shot four times, including one shot through each eye, and it was assumed by police that he had been gunned down while questioning two motorists. On the previous night, a Morris Cowley car had been stolen from a certain Dr Lovell, who lived in Billericay. This car was later found abandoned in Brixton, London, and on its floor lay an empty cartridge case bearing the headstamp 'R.L.IV', which identified it as Mark

IV ammunition manufactured at the Royal Laboratory, Woolwich. This was special flat-nosed ammo issued only to British troops in 1914. Although badly misshapen, one of the bullets extracted from the dead police officer at postmortem – carried out in the cart shed of a local pub, no less – was proven to be a Mark IV, which suggested that the murder weapon was a .455 Webley revolver. More significantly, this was the first case in British criminal history where a comparison microscope was used and this cartridge case showed a clear mark on its base imprinted by the revolver that had fired it. It was thought that the gun had been roughly cleaned at some stage with a metal rod that had marked the breech face. Because of this particular characteristic, the indentation became known as the 'Jockey Cap'. Furthermore, this meant that the gun that fired that round would leave a unique mark on every other cartridge fired from it.

Sometime later, William Henry Kennedy and Frederick Guy Browne were arrested and found to be in possession of two .455 Webley service revolvers. Using his comparison microscope, gunmaker Robert Churchill (no relation to the political Churchills) corroborated the earlier findings concerning the distinctive 'Jockey Cap' mark on the cartridge case from the car. It was demonstrated beyond doubt that this matched a tiny flaw in the breech of one of the revolvers. The gunsmith also tested fifty other .455 Webleys to see if they made similar breech marks on the cartridges fired in them. No comparable marks were made. War Office experts tested over a thousand .455 revolvers in the same way, with the same result. Both criminals were hanged; my book *The Long Drop*, based on secret 5(1) extended closure documents, is the definitive account of the case. One of the Webley revolvers is in the collection of the Essex Police Museum at Chelmsford. I believe the other revolver is in the Black Museum at Scotland Yard.

The reader will know that by using different, solidly proven forensic sciences, tests can be carried out on anything 'physical' that has been carefully collected at crime scenes. This includes: DNA; fibres; glass fragments; paint; hair, and so on. Indeed, these days the list is almost endless. But to return to the point that I made earlier, there is *absolutely nothing* 'physical' about forensic psychology or psychiatry; it is all about forming 'opinions'. As Austrian journalist, satirist, essayist, playwright and poet Karl Kraus writes in *Half-Truths and One-and-a-Half Truths* (1976): 'Sound opinions are valueless. What matters is who holds them.' And he is correct.

In all cases, an argument is made by a forensic psychiatrist, such as myself, for the defence. It is up to the court (judge) to decide whether he accepts it or not. If it is a clear-cut case, the judge will accept the psychiatrist's evidence. If there is doubt, the Crown Prosecution Service will often instruct their own psychiatrist. Both teams of psychiatrists are then called to give expert evidence during the trial. Usually, whoever makes the stronger argument tends to win.

Forensic psychiatrist Dr Sohom Das: email to the author, 26 January 2022

'Whoever makes the *strongest argument* tends to win.' Which could be interpreted as 'the better side tends to win'. But this is not a competition designed simply to win, it is supposed to be a search for the truth, is it not? This prompts the question: what if a defence hired two or three forensic psychiatrists and none of them can fully agree with each other? Or, what happens if the prosecution hired two or three forensic psychiatrists and they end up bickering among themselves – let alone with all six shrinks from both sides disagreeing with the opposing team? To coin the famous Laurel and Hardy catchphrase: 'Well, here's another nice mess you've got me into, Stanley.' That may sound a tad glib, but later in this book we will see more real-life 'fine messes' and our examination of these will prove that the very raison d'être for this book's foundations are hopefully dug deep.

I'd like to expand on this point to tackle the utter duplicity of so many US forensic psychiatrists and psychologists. There can be no better illustration than when a psychiatrist is called on behalf of the defence to provide an 'opinion' in an attempt to mitigate the prisoner's state of mind. In the hope, of course, of having a more severe and lengthy sentence – perhaps for life, or even the death sentence, in a mainline 'big house' – reduced to a term in a secure psychiatric hospital from which the person may well get released someday. Echoes here of the M'Naghten rule. There are so many instances where the very same defence psychiatrist will have also consulted for the prosecution on some previous occasion. In these cases, which are innumerable, if the coin were to be flipped over, the same shrink could be arguing that the very same man in the

65

dock was completely sane. And, if that is not professional hypocrisy, I do not know what is.

Therefore, in most if not every case of murder where the defendant's state of mind comes into the equation, usually it rests in presenting to a court the possibility of insanity or some other overwhelming mental issue as a mitigating factor in efforts to have a person's sentence reduced, or to have the person committed to a mental hospital rather than incarcerated in a penitentiary. We have already seen this in the case of Noreen O'Connor, who was committed to a mental asylum. And in the Daniel M'Naghten case, the psychiatric evidence brought by his defence team far outweighed the Crown's argument in a case of the better side 'winning' with no real attempt to find out what actually happened. As Sherlock Holmes might have put it: 'Precisely, Doctor Watson, there was no need for a search for the truth. M'Naghten admitted the shooting, which had taken place right in front of a police constable. The facts stare us straight in our faces.' And as Dr Sohom Das implies above, having heard all of the psychiatric evidence, the judge decided that M'Naghten – as with Noreen O'Connor – was not mentally fit to stand his trial; it was believed that he would not have understood the proceedings, and would thus have been unable to provide any reasonable mitigation in his defence. However, is it not patently obvious that both M'Naghten and O'Connor fully understood the nature of the charges before them and, furthermore, were fully au fait with the proceedings? The fundamental problem in both cases lies in the fact that the two defendants knew *exactly* what they had done was wrong and understood the legal proceedings.

Therefore, I would suggest that in both cases these were very fine examples of temporary insanity at best, if at all. In ballistic terms, Daniel M'Naghten found himself in an unfortunate position somewhat akin to that of a man facing Captain Oscar Berry Tompkins's machine-gun battery armed only with a bow and a few half-fletched arrows.

I suppose one could hypothesise about the upshot of the M'Naghten case until the cows come home, but for the purposes of this book and using the immortal words of Chris Tarrant, host of a certain award-winning TV quiz show of yesteryear, we might say: 'Here's a cheque for £80,000... but we don't want to give it to you just yet', to be followed soon after by: 'Is that your final answer?' So now the question *we* must try to answer is: who gave M'Naghten such a large amount of money? It could have been the case that he shot at Mr Drummond because he was indeed his intended target all along.

We know from M'Naghten's narrative that he was educated, careful, teetotal, well-read and a well-travelled, hard-working industrious bachelor with no prior criminal record. Yet there was no way in several dozen lifetimes that he could have accumulated such a large sum on his own account. Furthermore, is it really feasible that earlier in the day of the shooting he could have wandered into Drummond's Bank with that large sum of money, deposited it and got a receipt without raising the staff's suspicions? This money might well have come from the Chartist movement, and it has to be at least a possibility that he was secretly depositing that money on their behalf. If you have a spare £80,000 to hand today, try going into any bank and spilling the grubby notes onto a clerk's counter. Then stand back to wait for a reaction.

I suggest, with a red flag now metaphorically hoisted at Drummond's Bank – and I know that the reader will think that your author is going crazy now – that we cannot rule out that Mr Drummond had words with M'Naghten, perhaps telling him in no uncertain terms that he would be making further enquiries. Rightly so, in the heated political climate of the day. And maybe he intimated that he might contact the police, too. Now caught between a rock and a hard place, M'Naghten grabbed his receipt, followed Mr Drummond after he left the bank and upon seeing him walking up to a police constable in Whitehall drew his pistol and fired.

There's another factor to consider here. I want you, dear reader, to picture this hypothetical situation. Imagine that your political leanings demanded that you assassinate one of this country's more recent prime ministers, the aforementioned Boris Johnson. Well, you would certainly know what Boris looked like, wouldn't you – I mean, who else in the UK government has a similar flyaway hairstyle? And, if today you followed him along Whitehall, just as M'Naghten followed Drummond on 20 January 1843, I am sure that you would know if the man you were about to send to his grave *was* the PM and not some mere pen-pushing suit. But of course I am *not* suggesting that such a wilful act will have ever crossed your mind. God forbid. (And of course we've had other PMs since …)

I stress again: M'Naghten wasn't a bumbling village idiot. He read, he travelled and he was a card-carrying member of the Chartist movement, which had been under pressure from the Conservative government for some a while. Let's recall the highbrow lectures he attended too. That he and countless other Chartists were being watched, followed, or even 'spied upon', should really come as no surprise to anyone. Upon reflection, I feel that the court's decision that M'Naghten was mad as does not float. It was an establishment cop-out. The last thing that it wanted was for him to be hanged and become a Chartist martyr, which was on the cards from the outset.

To try to finally get to grips with M'Naghten's state of mind, we can look a little into his life after the trial. And what do we discover? Following M'Naghten's acquittal for intentional murder, he was transferred from Newgate Prison to the state criminal lunatic asylum at Bethlem under the 1880 Act for the Safe Custody of Insane Persons Charged with Offences.

Let me now dip into P. Allderidge's essay 'Why was McNaughton sent to Bethlem?' (which you can find in *Daniel McNaughton: His Trial and the Aftermath* [1977], edited by D.J. West and A. Walk). Therein, we discover that his admission papers state that M'Naghten 'imagines the Tories are his enemies' and is 'shy and retiring in his manner'. Yet, apart from one hunger strike, which ended with force-feeding, M'Naghten's twenty-one years at Bethlem appear to have been uneventful. There was no regular employment for the men on the criminal wing at Bethlem, but they were encouraged to fill their time with occupations like painting and drawing, playing musical instruments, knitting, carpentry and playing board games and they even decorated the hospital.

During his later years at Bethlem, M'Naghten was classified as an 'imbecile'. Let's address this word 'imbecile'. Its origins are in the Latin word *imbecillus*, meaning 'weak or feeble'; the usual original meaning in English, the *OED* tells me, is 'Weak, feeble; esp. feeble of body, physically weak or impotent' — and it could be argued that M'Naghten was indeed physically imbecile as he had by then developed diabetes and heart problems. The term, however, came more and more to mean 'mentally retarded' — of low IQ, while among lawyers and criminologists such variations as 'moral imbecility' came to be applied to those who were of normal intelligence but who were devoid of 'moral feeling' –perhaps this is what was meant.

Be that as it may, M'Naghten's mental narrative was once at least well above average; I'd argue that being locked up among a large number of genuinely insane patients for so many years could unhinge anyone previously of sound mind. Evidence that we have seen of M'Naghten's life before he murdered Edward Drummond, suggests that he was an intelligent, well-balanced professional, and without a criminal record. In 1864, on his transfer to the then newly opened Broadmoor Asylum, he was recorded on his admission papers, not as an imbecile, but as 'an intelligent man'. When asked at the time if he thought he must been out of his mind when he shot Edward Drummond, he answered carefully — and truthfully as far as it went — 'Such was the verdict — the opinion of the jury after hearing the evidence.'

His physical health continued to decline and on 3 May 1865, Daniel M'Naghten died aged fifty-two,

The Present

Here we are back in the present day with the age-old M'Naghten rule still ringing in our ears. So how did we get from back then to where we are now? The verdict in M'Naghten's trial provoked an outcry in the press. Queen Victoria, who herself had been the target of two assassination attempts prior to Drummond's shooting (six more were to follow), wrote to the then prime minister expressing her concern at the verdict. As a result, the House of Lords revived an ancient right to put five questions to judges relating to crimes committed by individuals with delusions. These were addressed to the twelve judges of the Court of Common Pleas. Chief Justice Tindal delivered the answers of eleven judges (Mr Justice Maule dissented in part) to the House of Lords on 19 June 1843, and stated:

> Every man is to be presumed to be sane, and ... that to establish a defence on the ground of insanity it must be clearly proved, that at the time of committing the act, the party accused was labouring under such a defect of reason from disease of the mind, as not to know the nature and quality of the act he was doing was wrong.

Well, there is no record of any hereditary mental problems within M'Naghten's family: one of his half-brothers, Thomas, was a doctor, a mayor of Blackpool and a magistrate. Added to which we have the evidence of his Broadmoor admission papers, which state that he is intelligent. I firmly believe that M'Naghten shot Edward Drummond with malice aforethought.

The M'Naghten rule dominated the law on criminal responsibility in England, Wales and many other countries throughout the British Commonwealth for over a century. In England and Wales, the defence of insanity to which the rule applies has now been largely superseded, in cases of murder by the Scottish concept of 'diminished responsibility' following the passage of the 1957 Homicide Act.

Daniel's defence had argued that he was not legally responsible for an act that arose from a delusion; indeed the M'Naghten rule represented a major step backwards from the traditional 'knowing right from wrong' test of criminal insanity. Had those previous rules been applied in M'Naghten's case, the verdict might have been different, with him swinging from the end of a rope.

But now, dear reader, what decision have you come to? Having read all of the above, what is your verdict. Was Daniel M'Naghten: sad, bad, mad, insane or truly evil?

Pedro Alonso López: aka the 'Monster of the Andes'

'I am the man of the century, but I knew from the age of eight I was going to be a killer.'

PEDRO ALONSO LÓPEZ

Here is a teaser for my reader: how is it that a car thief, child molester, deranged serial murderer and rapist with a minimum kill tally of about a hundred young girls – yet who proclaims to actually have murdered over three hundred victims across vast swathes of Colombia, Peru and Ecuador between 1969 and 1980 – ends up being diagnosed as insane, only to be released back into society after a handful of years behind bars, with his present whereabouts unknown?

Let us start from the beginning.

López is one of thirteen unlucky children, born in Tolima, Colombia, in the late 1940s, the seventh child of a penniless prostitute called Benilda López de Castañeda and father Megdardo Reyes – who was married to another woman at the time. Reyes was shot and killed six months before Pedro was born, when a rebellious mob attacked the grocery store he was in. This incident occurred at the beginning of the civil war in Columbia known as *La Violencia*. In fact, Colombia would have been last place on earth that anyone would want to have been born; at the time, the country was overwhelmed by riots and unthinkable acts of violence. The problems had started on 9 April 1948, when a popular politician, Jorge Eliécer Gaitán Ayala, was assassinated, prompting the outbreak of civil war. *La Violencia* continued for the next ten years and over 100,000 people died before it was over.

Benilda later claimed that she'd been a loving and caring mother; López maintained that she was cruel and abusive, a domineering woman who ruled with an iron fist. He was brought up in a country ruled by the mob and with a crime rate fifty times higher than anywhere else in the world. According to López, he would watch his mother have sex with clients from a young age, and she beat him on occasions. His early years can be described as anything but joyous – if we are to believe him, that is. My book *Talking with Psychopaths and Savages – Beyond Evil* (2019) goes into some depth about the dangers to vulnerable young children raised in dysfunctional homes.

Aged eight, he was thrown out of his family's home after his mother caught him fondling his younger sister's breasts. He fled, and, soon after, a paedophile lured young López to an abandoned house with the promise of a hot meal then repeatedly sodomised him before throwing him out onto the cold streets. After that incident, López lived and slept in alleys and abandoned buildings, scavenging food from dumpsters, slowly gaining his confidence to travel further afield to end up in Bogotá, Colombia's capital city where he also lived off of the streets.

When López was around ten or eleven years old, an American immigrant couple approached him. They were distressed by his skeletal appearance. Godly people, they provided him with a warm meal and invited him back to their home, where he was given free room and board and enrolled in a school for orphans. However, despite this temporary turn of good fortune, he absconded at the age of twelve after being sexually molested by a teacher. Now all of his previous fears and uncertainty were reborn. He stole money from an office in the school and ran away to the only place that he felt safe — the violent streets of Colombia.

The civil war was now almost over, The country was rebuilding, businesses were beginning to reopen, the economy on the up. Sadly, López had never been skilled in any trade and had had only a minimum education. He spent the next five or six years begging for food and committing petty theft in order to survive. In his mid-teens he joined a gang of street kids for protection. The gang — very much like Britain's real-life 'Peaky Blinders' — fought rival gangs for turf using knives and belts, and for food and places to sleep. They would also smoke 'basuco', a type of drug derived from cocaine.

Aged eighteen, López was stealing cars and making good money selling them to local chop shops — businesses, often mimicking a body shop, that illicitly disassemble stolen motor vehicles to sell their parts. Then he came unstuck.

He was arrested by the authorities for car theft and sentenced to seven years in prison.

López had spent just two days behind bars before being brutally gang-raped by four older inmates. Following this attack, he swore to himself that no one would ever touch him again. In retaliation, he fashioned a crude knife (or 'shiv') out of prison utensils and spent the next fortnight getting his revenge: one by one, he killed each of the four men, the ringleader with his bare hands. This gained him the grudging respect of his convict peers, who never dared disturb him again. His in-house murders were considered acts of self-defence by the local Colombian justice department and because of this only two years were added to his previous prison tariff for the crimes. Nonetheless, the gang rape had deeply traumatised López. After his release he commented: 'With what sanity I had left, and due to the abuse that I had suffered at the hands of my mother, I became fearful of women.' He claimed that with social intercourse with women now psychologically impossible for him, he fulfilled his sexual desires through reading pornographic books and magazines. To his mind, his mother was to blame for his life's sufferings and heartbreaks.

'I then decided to do the same to as many young girls as possible.'

Pedro López: upon his release from prison

López now moved to Peru, where he began murdering young girls between the ages of nine and twelve. By 1978, now aged twenty-one, he had probably killed over a hundred girls from various indigenous tribes before being captured by members of the Ayacucho tribe in northern Peru after he tried to kidnap a nine-year-old girl. Up there in this hauntingly scenic area, often cloaked in mist, these ancient people stripped him and tortured him for hours. López, later told a journalist: 'Indians in Peru had me tied up and buried me in sand up to my neck. They had placed syrup on me and were going to let me be eaten by ants, but a lady missionary came by in her jeep and promised them she would hand me over to police.' She persuaded his captors to allow her to hand him over to the Peruvian authorities, and, he added: 'They tied me up in the back of her jeep and she drove away. But she released me into the hands of the police at the border of Colombia … ' The Peruvian authorities didn't want to waste their time investigating what they saw as petty tribal complaints, so he was deported to Ecuador.

Ayacuchoans

'I like the girls in Ecuador; they are more gentle and trusting. More innocent.'

Pedro Alonso López

According to CNN, during his time in Ecuador, López travelled extensively throughout the region and was killing around three girls a week. Police were concerned about the reports of so many kids going missing but put this down to the ever-growing South American sex-slave rings, so López was never considered as a suspect, at least until April 1980. A flash flood near the mountain town of Ambato, Ecuador, uncovered the bodies of four missing children, prompting the authorities to take a second look at their missing person cases. Police concluded that the girls had obviously met foul play, since someone had taken the trouble to hide their bodies from prying eyes.

> 'He won't live long. It will be a kindness to the world for someone to murder this fiend.'
>
> Carvina Poveda, mother of Maria Poveda:
> a close-call victim

Shortly after the floods, Carvina Poveda was shopping at a local market place in the Ecuadorean city of Ambato, which lies in the Andes Mountains along the Ambato River. With her was her ten-year-old daughter (some sources give her age as twelve years), whom an unknown man attempted to abduct: Carvina saw a man walking away hand-in-hand with Maria and screamed for help as she ran after them. soon the man was trapped by an angry mob of market traders. They held him down and police arrived to find the man rambling incoherently, and assumed he was mad.

At the police station, López refused to talk, and remained for days in his cell, saying nothing, so the cops changed tactics. They persuaded a priest, Pastor Cordoba Gudino, attached to the station to discard any priestly garments and allow himself to be manhandled into López's cell under the pretext that he was guilty of rape – the plan being to gain the man's confidence and get him to discuss his crime. It was days before Pedro opened up but when he did it was like opening a floodgate: confessed to 110 murders in Ecuador, including 53 whose bodies would soon be found in shallow graves in the Andean provinces of Tungurahua, Cotopaxi, Chimborazo, Pichincha and Imbabura. The padre was horrified as López went on to reveal the sickening details of his horrible crimes until eventually the priest could stand no more. He asked to leave the cell and never returned.

In January 1981, López, was convicted of just three homicides, but had confessed to sexually assaulting and/ or strangling 300 victims. Police believed that he'd only confessed after the flash flood that uncovered a mass grave containing many of his victims and because he'd been caught after he had tried to abduct Maria Poveda. At this point, one might have imagined that the authorities would have locked him up for the remainder his days. Ecuadorean law, however, has other ideas about sentencing guidelines. It sets sixteen years as the *maximum* punishment for murder and prohibits consecutive sentences, even though its serious-crime rate is one of the worst in the world. This means that if Ted Bundy had committed his serial killings in Ecuador, he would have been freed to kill again and again in just over a decade, with parole given for good time served. There ya'll go, 'Teddy Boy', you should have done your homework, you homicidal mug!

So with this in my mind, during my research for writing this chapter back in 2021, I thought that it might be a jolly good idea for me to fly out to Ecuador and see the place for myself. Not least because Amnesty International had excoriatingly trashed Article 19.1 of the Constitution of Ecuador, which stated (wait for it): 'The State guarantees the inviolability of life and physical integrity. There is no death penalty. *Torture and all inhuman or degrading treatment are prohibited'* [author's italics]. When I say that Amnesty International 'trashed' this document, perhaps they were being diplomatic. For I would argue that that is one of the most inventive claims of adhering to human rights that any totally corrupt system of law and justice has ever come up with. This, I felt, was a place that I had to visit.

Bienvenidos todos a Ecuador

By way of preparation, I spent some time reading up about the wildlife-rich Galápagos Islands (the name is Spanish for 'saddle', inspired by the giant tortoises found there), and the country's diverse landscape encompassing the Amazon jungle and Andean highlands. I would travel alone and not enjoy the protection afforded to, say, an international film crew: 44 bent-as-paperclips eminent dignitaries; 26 off-road Mitsubishis; 235 heavily armed, working-off-the-books *soldados*; a field hospital; a field kitchen run by a Michelin 4-star chef; a handful of translators; a mile-long string of pack mules with a few off-the-books government Huey helicopters hovering in reserve and 785 indigent poor people paid 10 cents a day to haul around the kit. I mean where is the fun in all of that? No, I like to work alone. It makes life more exciting, don't you think?

Nevertheless, being charitable, I would bring some new, crispy US dollars which would help me in bribing officials; decades later, a cent or two of it just *might*, on a wing and a prayer, drip down to the poor people. According to some estimates, 35 per cent of Ecuador's population are pot-less, with the national increase growing at an average annual rate of 2.28 per cent. I truly wanted to get among these poor people and ask them what they thought about Pedro López's prison sentence for sado-sexual serial homicide – a killing spree sure to guarantee he'll burn in hell and suffer eternal damnation.

I decided to use the historic capital, Quito, as a base. Not wanting to over-egg things, my idea was to stay somewhere modest; a place where at least the water coming out of the taps was not brown. At £153 per night, with a sink plug, and intermittent wi-fi thrown in, the five-star Hotel Plaza Grande sounded great. But when I looked at photos of the place online, I noticed that there were no other guests visible anywhere, not even in the dining areas or bedrooms or bathrooms.

Being a foodie, I looked up the menu for dinner and breakfast. The Café Plaza Grande's eatery boasted an 'environment full of culinary delights typical of Quito of yesteryear and the unique flavors of Ecuadorian cuisines. Capacity 56 people'. Then, when I tried to download the full menus I was confronted with 'Desayunos Break' (*desayuno* is Spanish for 'breakfast) and its '56 covers', for God's sake; give Christopher a break, will ya? And the prices? I couldn't see any on the menu either. Checking out the cost of anything and everything before making any sort of purchase is an essential exercise for us penny-wise folk. No prodigal son is your author, to be sure.

Undeterred, I took a look at the front of this neoclassical Spanish edifice. It has the sort of balcony one sees when a soon-to-be deposed (then shot), heavily medalled dictator addresses a crowd of six million starving people, telling them that 'Todo está bien en el nombre de Dios' ('All is well in God's name'), when it clearly ain't!

Taking all of that into consideration, and being of an inquisitive nature, I carefully studied my international insurance policy, then asked my PC if Ecuador was a safe place to visit. To be frank with you, there are reams of info telling one that it isn't. Ecuador's crime rate is *very high*. Drug trafficking, violent attacks, petty theft and scams occur pretty much each day, with violent crime on the rise year after year. If one's thinking of risking a visit to an ATM, it might be comforting to know that the police offer the services of an armed escort, for a hefty fee (I kid you not). As for the nightlife? From what I can gather, in 2015 no fewer than six Quito hotels were closed down by the authorities in an effort to reduce prostitution, with around a thousand sex workers 'licensed' in Quito alone. And here's another thing. Following protests by these ladies of the night, the administrator of the Central Zone, one Joffre Echeverria, pledged to set a new 'zone' for them to work in (no doubt, we pray, with running water in the brothels – aka 'Chongos', aka 'licensed centres of tolerance'). On top of that, there is the mega high risk of natural disasters – earthquakes, volcanic eruptions, landslides, flash floods that sometimes reveal decaying corpses, and tsunamis – to take into account. Oops, I almost forgot to add 'kidnapping for ransom'. That, I reckoned, would be the least of my worries, because I would sternly tell the bandidos that my publishers wouldn't stump up a dollar for my safe return. ''Tis best, Christopher, that you stay at home, where your carer can keep an eye on you.' So I did.

Travelogue done and dusted. And yes, I have digressed.

'Yes he was released quite quickly. Yes, it sounds strange, but that is our law.'

> Prisons Minister Pablo Faguero: on López's release
> back into society

Still terrified that he would be executed by firing squad, López breathed a *grande* sigh of relief when he was freed from prison on 31 August 1994… only to be rearrested as an illegal immigrant. Now the authorities charged López with another murder, dating back twenty years, but psychiatrists diagnosed him as being insane and committed him to the psychiatric wing of a Bogotá hospital. Four years later, with his insanity (insert: homicidal psychopathy) having been 'cured', López was released on $50 bail, subject to conditions. His first port of call was visiting his elderly mother. She later told a reporter that he had asked for his inheritance. When she told him she was impoverished, López did the decent thing – he *sold* her only bed and chair to even poorer people on the street – which, taken in the round, was not the most magnanimous gesture of all time. He has not been seen since, but this monster of unimaginable wickedness is now wanted by police about his possible connection to another murder, this time dating from 2002. If I were advising the cops, I'd suggest that they return to the Ayacucho tribe in northern Peru, and to try to find his head, covered in raspberry jam, sticking out of the sand.

Confessions

'There is a wonderful moment, a divine moment, when I have my hands around a young girl's throat. I look into her eyes and see a certain light, a spark, suddenly go out.'

Pedro Alonso López: prison interview 1994

Through exclusive interviews with López by various news outlets, including CNN and *Scotland on Sunday*, perhaps we can gain a better insight into this sexual psychopath's depraved mindset. And, in the context of the theme of this book, ask ourselves: was this monster ever insane? Or was he pulling the wool over everyone's eyes?

In a 1994 interview with photo-journalist Ron Laytner, in his Ambato prison cell, the cocky killer boasted, 'I will soon be a free man again. They are releasing me on good behaviour... I'm the man of the century and no one will forget me.' He compared himself to spectators who attend bullfights as they watch in fascination for the kill: 'The moment of death is enthralling and exciting. Only those who actually kill know what I mean. Someday when I am released, I will feel that moment again. I will be happy to kill again. It is my mission.'

López's signature modus operandi was simplicity itself as far as serial killers go. Young, trusting, innocent girls, some as young as nine, fell easy prey to a man offering them trinkets such as hand mirrors, and who then took them to hideaways where he had prepared their graves, some with bodies already in them.

Yes, yes, I know that I have been a tad glib with the levity thus far, but allow me to note: *what follows is not for the faint of heart!*

Once at the body disposal sites, this 'Monster of the Andes' recalled that he would lull his victim – 'with cuddles'! – before raping her at sunrise, then:

When the sun rose I would strangle her. It was only good if I could see her eyes. I never killed anyone at night. It would have been wasted in the dark. I had to watch them by daylight… it took the girls about five to fifteen minutes to die. I was very considerate. I would spend a long time with them making sure they were dead. I would use a mirror to check if they were still breathing.

López added that he would then carry out gruesome 'parties' with his victims, propping them up in their graves and talking to their dead bodies.

My 2020 book *Talking with Serial Killers: Stalkers* was written specifically about the stalking element of a killer's modus operandi, and the thrill these predators get knowing that, given time, it's the end of time for their selected prey. With López we have paedophile serial killer of terrifying proportions. Here, he described part of his technique: 'I walked among the markets searching for a girl with a certain look on her face, a look of innocence and beauty. She would be a good girl, always with her mother. I followed them, sometimes for two or three days, waiting for the moment when she was left alone.'

If you ever intend to visit these South American cities and towns with a young child, where it is quite obvious that on the whole life is cheap – reflected in the fact that even a triple child killer can only serve a maximum of sixteen years in jail (in Ecuador, anyway) – what now follows could be your early morning wake-up call. The children of tourists were fair game to López. He states: 'I spent many days following English and Scottish families and their beautiful young daughters. But I never got the chance to take some. Their parents were too watchful.'

So the question is now asked: was Pedro López sad, mad, insane or evil? He had been diagnosed with a mental illness of sorts – 'avoidant personality disorder' (AVPD) – denoting that he was a socially awkward person with a hypersensitivity to rejection and feelings of inadequacy. People with AVPD spend a lot of time focusing on their shortcomings and are very hesitant to form relationships in case they are hurt. This often results in feelings of loneliness and their disengaging from relationships at work and elsewhere.

Researchers do not completely understand what causes AVPD, but they believe it is a combination of genetics and environmental factors – or a case of nature and nurture, as your author prefers to put it. However, there is much evidence to support the hypothesis that early traumatic experiences and childhood neglect may be linked to the development of this disorder. Research shows that children who see their caregivers as lacking in affection and encouragement, and/or experience rejection from them, may be at increased risk. So do children who experience abuse, neglect and a lower level of care overall, go on to avoid socialising with others?

Undoubtedly, López suffered from AVPD. Yet while it is not classified as *true* psychopathy, it cannot be cured any more than fully emerged psychopathy can. So when the psychiatrists at the Bogotá hospital released him after four years claiming that López was 'cured', they were, in fact, unleashing a child-molesting serial killer back onto the streets. Did any of those shrinks get even a slap on the wrist? I think not.

What else can we say with a degree of certainty about López's psychopathology? He was/is a sexual paraphiliac, that much is plain, for he had persistent and recurrent sexual interests, urges and homicidal fantasies that he acted out in real time with very young girls. Yet I find it a very big leap for him to have decided upon his release from prison for car theft offences to specifically target this kind of young victim (his victimology). And I struggle to believe him when he blames his mother for all of his later sex crimes, or for that matter the paedophile who anally raped him, or the trauma he suffered from the gang rape in prison and which he responded to with murderous revenge.

Millions of young boys suffer from the most godawful childhoods and they don't turn into serial child killers, do they? So, I cannot say with my hand on my heart, or anywhere near it, that his AVPD had much to do with this paedophile's actions. Nor can I say that the gang rape had anything to do with it.

I would say that in Pedro López we find a first-rate example of transfer of blame psychology. Like most lust serial killers, especially the ones I have interviewed or corresponded with over many decades, there is always 'blame-shifting'. The term was originally coined by psychologist Anna Freud in 1936 to describe a kind of self-defence mechanism via which a person attributes their own unwanted thoughts, feelings or motives to another person. López blamed others because he was never able to exhibit one iota of remorse for all of the pain and suffering he caused.

In Pedro López, I find grim echoes of the murderous mindset exhibited by the American sexual serial killer Michael Bruce Ross, who could only ejaculate when he saw the 'light' in his victims' eyes go out. While on death row prior to his execution by lethal injection, Ross told me: 'Chris, strangling someone ain't like on TV. They writhe around and I had to reapply my grip several times, 'cos my hands cramped up. Then they could breathe for a moment or two. There was a glimmer of pleading hope in their eyes. Ya know what, I could only ejaculate when I saw the light of life go out in their eyes. What more do ya'll want to fuckin' know?'

López, abducted his young victims and kept them alive throughout the night cuddling them, talking softly; all of which increased his sexual urges until the sun came up. It's a terrifying scenario, is it not? A small child crying for her mother out there in some dark lonely place with a strange man, perhaps with the twinkling lights of her mountain town not far distant.

Yet there is every chance that he has been killed out of revenge. Life seems to be dirt cheap in certain South American countries. And López buried his victims under a lot of dirt.

So, is (was?) he mad, bad, insane, or plain evil? His actions were, without a doubt, plain evil.

Pawel Ałojzy Tuchlin: nicknamed 'Scorpion'

'From the world of darkness I did loose demons and devils in power of scorpions to torment.'

CHARLES MILLES MANSON: AMERICAN CULT LEADER WHOSE 'FAMILY' COMMITTED A SERIES OF NINE MURDERS IN JULY AND AUGUST 1969

At about the same time as Pedro Lopez was active, but right across the globe, in Poland, another serial killer was stalking women. Pawel Tuchlin is of interest to me because his lust-killer psychopathology is quite unlike that of any other serial murderer I have studied. To me, he is quite unique in the annals of criminal history.

Góra, Kościerzyna County

To try to put this case into some historical context, we should remember that in the aftermath of World War II, Poland was struggling to get back on its feet after being ravaged by the Nazis. Opportunities were few under the communist government instituted by the Soviet Union, whose policy of collective farming – with small farmers running their holdings as a joint enterprise – created further hardships for the farmers, who like all their countrymen were struggling to earn a living.

Fifty kilometres or so south-west of the port city of Gdańsk, capital of the province of Pomerania, lies the small village of Góra, the birthplace of Paweł Alojzy Tuchlin. He was hatched in a rundown farmhouse on 28 April 1946, the eighth of eleven children born to Bernard Tuchlin, a small farmer from the tiny village of Tuchlin in the administrative district of Gmina Orzysz, in northern Poland, and his wife Monika, who seemed to be constantly pregnant.

As Jerzy Pobocha, lead forensic psychiatrist in the Tuchlin case, remarked while discussing his team's research into the killer:

> We fully realised the seriousness of the situation, and whether he would be sentenced to death or not depended on our assessment. ... To discover what drove Pawel to commit such horrific crimes, the team must go back to his childhood. Tuchlin's biography is extremely important because it explains the genesis of his criminal activity.

Like Pedro Alonso López, whom we met earlier, Pawel Tuchlin's formative years were at best dysfunctional: his father was an abusive alcoholic, who seems to have harboured an extreme dislike for his eighth child and would beat him

90

without mercy, while his mother stood by and did nothing to intervene This might well have led to the child's bed-wetting – and that only led to further beatings. Journalist Zbigniew Żukowski, says: 'It was continual beatings to the extent that [Tuchlin] cut his mind off from reality... the greater the beating the more he became reluctant to make human contact.'

As the FBI will confirm, growing up in such an environment *could* have led the lad's psychological under-standing and personality to change and foster extreme aggression in his adult life. We see distinct parallels here with the US serial killer Henry Lee Lucas, British serial killer Frederick 'Fred' Walter Stephen West and German sado-sexual serial murderer Peter Kürten, aka the 'Monster of Düsseldorf'. My book *Talking with Serial Killers and Savages: Beyond Evil* focuses on this very sensitive subject, but of course this is not social rocket science. Suffice it to say that Polish crime scientist Kacper Gradon's observation that 'the abuse and cruelty Tuchlin experienced as a child would play a key role in his future and his bed-wetting right into his teens' is right on the money. As with so many young boys who later metamorphose into serial sex killers, Tuchlin suffered from enuresis. The *Diagnostic and Statistical Manual of Mental Disorders* (DSM-IV) describes this as a disorder marked by loss of bladder control continuing after the age of five years. If it persists after the age of ten, it can be a very serious sign of neurological issues and stress. In Tuchlin's case it persevered until he was fifteen or sixteen. Everyone in the village knew about his problem, because they could always smell urine on his clothes. Even his teachers knew it and girls kept well away from him .

In his own words, Tuchlin later told his trial court:

My illness was that I soaked the bed in my sleep during the night. And the only medicine available to me was 'pyda' [a woven switch or small whip]. When morning came, my mother or father checked the bed. When it was wet, I got a dose of the 'medicine'. The next day, the scene would be repeated because my father was of the opinion that I was staying in my bed maliciously or out of laziness.

They disliked me, especially when Dad drank himself, which happened often. Then it was not 'Paweł': I was 'dujcok', 'piss' and 'skunk'. For this reason, I did not get, for example, money for the cinema.

As I grew up, from time to time there might be some kind of fun social event .... You want to dance? Good, you go ask a girl but she knows you – I do not know, but I think it's a shame to dance with someone who is soaked [in pee] – [and she] says: 'Stinky, I do not want to dance with you,' or something like that.

At the age of eighteen, Tuchlin left his village and joined the Polish Armed Forces – his service ending after a few months because he turned out to be slightly deaf. Being even a bit deaf in the military is not a good thing, as I am sure the reader will agree, especially when someone shouts out: 'Duck, there is a Stinger missile coming our way!' Thereafter, he took himself off to Gdańsk, where he found work as a truck driver.

In 1973, he married and the couple had a child. Clearly, at this point he might have had a chance of enjoying a normal life, but by then, as criminal psychologist Professor David Holmes notes of Tuchlin in the TV series Killers: Behind the Myth: 'Unfortunately his predilection was such that he wanted a lot more than was on offer.'

At the same time, he was getting into trouble with the law for engaging in petty theft. So, it will come as no surprise that this marriage failed and in 1975, they divorced. The exact reasons why the couple untied the marital knot will always elude us; however, it is highly likely that they walked up the aisle praying they'd get the best out of each other and ended up getting the worst – a common theme running through *all* botched-up marriages since time began.

The killer, soon to be named 'Scorpion' by the Milicja Obywatelska (Citizens' Militia), is now about to strike for the first time.

Knockout blows

I heard through the night
The rush and the clamour;
The pulse of the fight
Like blows of Thor's hammer;
The pattering flight
Of the leaves and the anguished
Moan of the forest vanquished.

Henry Jackson Van Dyke Jr: author,
diplomat and Presbyterian clergyman, in
'The Fall of the Leaves' (1874)

We all know about the so-called 'noble art' of boxing and the knockout blow. But what happens if one is hit hard over the head with a hammer, rather than a gloved fist? Because the brain is very fragile, almost entirely made out of blood vessels and nerves and lots of other things. A soft, mushy grey mass of tissue that controls all neural high functions.

Our spongy brain mass is floating in a clear, colourless liquid called 'cerebrospinal fluid', which protects the brain from coming into contact with the inner wall of the skull. Think of a hen's egg, with the yolk being your brain: the shell (your skull); inner and outer membranes, the air cell and albumen etc. That blow could cause your brain to slam into your inner skull. Not surprisingly, you get instant trauma – your brain cells would literally start dying from the physical impact, your brain bouncing on and off the walls of the inner skull until all of the energy from the blows had dissipated. This trauma causes an overwhelming number of neurotransmitters that were previously fast asleep to wake up and fire simultaneously, a system overload if you like, causing a system crash in the form of temporary paralysis – instant unconsciousness. Such 'blackouts' act like a sort of defence mechanism in this respect.

Of course, if one survives a violent hammer attack, one would be relieved to have woken up in hospital. The doctors would advise you that within a few years your headaches *might* cease, and that the hole in your skull will be covered by your hair, that's if you have any hair left at all. But many of Tuchlin's victims never woke up.

It is now Friday, 31 October 1975. Tuchlin is out on the hunt for his first victim. He spots a twenty-one-year-old woman, follows her, and when the moment is right for him – and tragically wrong for her – he strikes her on the back of her head with a hammer. 'He then fulfilled his perverse desires, settling into a grim routine which he will follow for the next eight years. Somehow, some inner power pushed him out onto the streets,' says journalist Zbigniew Żukowski. 'And he got a taste for it. After the first attack he needed more because he enjoyed it. What was once out of his reach, now he could obtain in a simple way.'

But why the use of a hammer? As a kid growing up, Tuchlin had watched as village farmers killed their pigs using a hammer. This is a brutally effective method, particularly when used on human beings, and was one used by Peter Sutcliffe and Harvey 'The Hammer' Louis Carignan, among others. Forensic psychiatrist Jerzy Pobocha calls this 'hammer anaesthesia': Tuchlin instantly knocked his victims unconscious.

One of the most interesting aspects of this man's psychopathology is that he was a compulsive thief with a 'magpie' attitude. He would steal something just because it looked 'pretty' or 'useful', and drop it into his own nest – that being his rundown farmhouse, a place that looked as if it had been picked up by a twister in southern Poland and dropped from a great height into a muddy field hundreds of kilometres north. Indeed, so ingrained was his light-fingeredness that it would be the basis for his final arrest years later, literally resulting in his downfall through the hangman's trap.

Now divorced, in 1980 Paweł married again – a woman called Regina. The couple moved back to his home village

95

of Góra and eventually had a child. His neighbours thought him a well-balanced and caring father and husband, though they noticed how introverted he could become too. I have written previously about this mask of normality that most serial murderers wear to protect the evil entity living within. We see it time and time again with repeat sex killers such as the outwardly respectable Dennis Rader, the gay British murderer Dennis Nilsen, Ted Bundy and even John Reginald Christie. Indeed, it would be hard to find any serial killer *or* mass murderer who didn't wear this false façade to conceal the true beast, their homicidal wickedness quietly breathing within. Theodore John Kaczynski, aka the 'Unabomber', is an American domestic terrorist and former maths professor. He was a mathematics prodigy who, in 1969, went to live a solitary existence, becoming almost a hermit. Seemingly harmless to a fault, he nevertheless blew to pieces three people and injured twenty-three more in a nationwide bombing campaign. But as mass murderers go – and this might sound awful – his kill toll pales in comparison with the tally of many of his type. If the reader wishes to know more, search on statista. com for 'Worst mass shootings in the US'. You will quickly discover that Kaczynski was something of a lightweight in this dreadful field.

At around this period, Tuchlin was again having problems with his high libido – or hypersexuality – and had turned to exhibitionism, the perversion in which sexual gratification is obtained from the indecent exposure of one's genitals to a stranger. In the UK we call this 'flashing' – in Poland I think they call it 'błyskowy', but I am sure any astute Polish readers will be happy to correct me. When he entered his teens, like so many emerging multiple sex killers, he had begun to stalk women and voyeuristically spy on them; watching them sunbathing in the woods or making love. We see this voyeuristic activity in Peter Sutcliffe's early narrative, as he visited the red-light districts to spy on the prostitutes plying their nocturnal trade. This was an early stage in the development of Tuchlin's perverse sex life, which would lead, in time, to his murder sprees. My book *Talking with Serial Killers: Stalkers* deals with this type of paraphilia.

Initially Tuchlin was a 'peeping Tom', one who becomes sexually aroused by observing an unsuspecting and non-consenting person who is undressing or unclothed, and/or engaged in sexual activity. The behaviour may conclude with masturbation by the voyeur who does not seek, or *cannot seek*, sexual contact with the person he is observing. Psychiatrist Jerzy Pobocha observes: '[Tuchlin's behaviour was in keeping with] the saying, "Necessity is the Mother of invention". He desired to engage with women. In practice, it was impossible. So he found another way, not directly but indirectly *at a distance*. But at least he could see them.' As criminal psychologist David Holmes eloquently puts it: 'He seems to have become progressively attached to the idea of a completely passive, almost unconscious female,' and this certainly became the case as Tuchlin's paraphilia started to spiral out of control.

He assaulted two more women over the next few months; as with his first victim, they were left unconscious and seemingly unable to help in identifying their attacker.

I might add, in an attempt to delve a little deeper into

Paweł's mind, that this initial 'distancing phase' in his criminal narrative might well have formed its roots from having been rejected so many times by young women in the past because of the smell of stale urine on his body and clothes. A learned 'shyness', if you will.

The stalker

Stalk 1.: to follow or approach (game, prey, etc.) stealthily and quietly. 2.: to pursue persistently and, sometimes, attack (a person with whom one is obsessed, often a celebrity)... 5. to search or draw a piece of land (for prey).

Collins English Dictionary

Voyeurism: the practice of gaining sexual pleasure from watching others when they are naked or engaged in sexual activity... enjoyment from seeing the pain or distress of others.

Oxford Dictionary of English

Consider those two definitions in the context of Paweł Tuchlin's car-wrecked formative years and you have one human bomb just waiting for a murderous fuse to be lit. The majority of serial killers do *not* begin rampaging at the drop of a Mad Hatter's hat; they 'graduate'. They go through a sort of sexual-deviancy apprenticeship beforehand.

Although the way Paweł Tuchlin was raised should arouse our sympathy – a lone figure who so needed his parents' love, as we all do – we have to ask whether at the stage of his life that we are now discussing, he knew that what he was doing was morally and legally wrong. Yes, he had a paraphiliac condition, an unsavoury attraction to stalking and voyeurism, but how would this stand in relation to the M'Naghten rules and their variations?

Crossing the Rubicon

Between December 1976 and June 1979, most of Tuchlin's time was spent serving prison sentences for theft. Nobody seems to have noticed that while he was incarcerated the attacks on women stopped. That was to change in 1979.

Some psychiatrists would argue that by now something had *changed* in Tuchlin's personality. I say that there was no change as such, more the completion of a gradual process, one that had been building up for several years.

By way of an analogy, let's imagine one of those old steam engines with a fire underneath the boiler. As the water heats up, a safety release valve automatically opens when the steam pressure gets too high. I liken this to the human mind. Tuchlin's sexual deviancy had been simmering away inside his head since his early teens. Factor in his sexual frustration, his dysfunctional childhood and the shame heaped upon him by local villagers and young girls. Something had to blow. If one enjoys good mental health, when stress becomes overwhelming one might react with an emotional outburst, such as a flood of tears, a bout of swearing. We call this 'getting it out of our system'. Tuchlin, however, would blow all of his fuses at once, led by his overriding needs. He had become a cold-blooded sexual psychopath, a person with no conscience. He decided that if he wanted a woman he would go out and get one, and fuck the consequences to her or himself.

Throughout his later interviews with Tuchlin, the forensic psychiatrist Jerzy Pobocha learned that the murderer had a 'general plan in his head... it had to be a single woman... the place... the murder crossroads... must be safe in the sense that there shouldn't be any people around. The idea was to act effectively and safely.' Well, that sounds pretty obvious to me: surely all serial killers selectively kill their prey out of the sight of prying eyes?

Professor David Holmes likened Tuchlin's modus operandi to that of a hunter stealthily following a wild animal, to chase it and bring it down. Tuchlin himself used the term 'hunting', which chimes with the theme of stalking I raised earlier. As most of us will agree, this type of offender often gets as much of a thrill out of hunting his prey as the actual attack itself. Up until now, Tuchlin had been psychologically unable to bring himself to cross the threshold and commit a deadly assault. But it was now a case of 'needs must'.

> '[He would arm himself with] a hammer wrapped in a cloth. Later, Tuchlin explained that he bandaged the hammer so it would not chill his stomach when he put it in his trousers, simply for comfort.'
>
> Andrzej Gawrys: Lead Investigator
> Special Group Scorpion

Tuchlin seems to have thought about everything, it seems to me. Fancy that, I would never have thought about tucking a hammer into my Y-fronts, the head freezing my bellybutton, and nor would any of my male readers, I'm sure.

The police would later establish that on 9 November 1979, Tuchlin stalked and killed eighteen-year-old 'Irena H.' with a hammer blow to the head by the river Radunia, near the village of Niesępowo, some 15 kilometres west of the regional capital, Gdańsk. He did not rape her because his 'need to watch' was dominant, so he had no need for sexual intercourse; instead, he would masturbate over the body as she lay dying or postmortem. I used the term 'shyness' earlier. Maybe he had taken his voyeurism to another level this time. Now he could get up close and personal to a young woman as she lay helpless on the ground. It's a sickening thought, is it not?

After he was finished, Tuchlin fled the scene but lost his hammer in the river, where it was soon found by investigators. Police learned that local folk hunted water rats in the area using hammers wrapped in cloth to avoid damaging the fur, so initially they wrongly concluded that it could not be the murder weapon they were looking for. However, upon closer examination they found the letters 'ZNTK' ('Rail Rolling Stock Repair Workshops) stamped into the metal. The police immediately applied to the company for the names of all those individuals who had been issued with their tools; they duly received a list and interrogated all those known to have taken a hammer from the company's tool store: all had solid alibis, none was called Tuchlin. It seems highly likely that the store either failed to record Tuchlin's name, or that he had, quite simply, stolen the hammer while he was driving for the company.

Trophy-taking

Professor David Holmes observes: 'Tuchlin did not get off on normal sex. He had a paraphilia for masturbating over naked or stationary females, so this was his primary target.' For him to see a woman, to smell a women, was extremely important to him. Paweł later told his examining psychiatrists that he had put his fingers to Irena's vagina and did not wash his hands for two weeks so he could smell and delight in the scent – but why?

We true-crime aficionados know all too well that many sex serial killers will not leave a crime scene without taking something away with them. That might be a body part, like a bone, eyeball, fingernails or hair. Perhaps an item of jewellery, as did Joel Rifkin and Kenneth Bianchi. Gruesomely, Edward 'Ed' Gein, aka the 'Butcher of Plainfield', created lampshades, corsets and other décor out of his victims' flesh. James Desmond Lloyd, the 'Rotherham Shoe Rapist', collected at least 126 pairs of high heel shoes from those he attacked. I simply dare not imagine him tottering around Rotherham Market looking for some fishnet stockings in six-inch stilettos.

Necrophile Jerome Henry 'Jerry' Brudos (aka the 'Lust Killer' and the 'Shoe Fetish Slayer') started out on his singular path at the age of five, by playing with a pair stiletto-heeled shoes he found at a local junkyard. Quite how this footwear found its way into what we Brits call a 'scrapyard' beats the hell out of me. In the back seat of an old Ford Cortina, maybe…

Jerry Brudos also had a fetish for women's underwear,

which he stole from his neighbours. Australia's Ivan Robert Marko Milat (the 'Backpack Killer'), kept the sleeping bags belonging to his murdered prey. John Sweeny (aka the 'Scalp Hunter' and the 'Canal Murderer') was eventually convicted of two homicides because evidence of his visceral hatred of women was found in the form of a hoard of more than three hundred violent, lurid paintings and poems found at his home. One, entitled the 'Scalp Hunter', depicted a female victim with a bloody axe. These were souvenirs of Sweeny's crimes depicted in disgusting artwork and crude verse.

Intriguingly, the FBI distinguishes between 'souvenirs' and 'trophies' in this context. This may seem a bit like splitting hairs, but please bear with me. According to *The A to Z Encyclopedia of Serial Killers* (1996), by Harold Schecter and David Everitt: 'A "souvenir" is an item used to fuel a fantasy, while a "trophy" is taken as proof of the killer's skill. However, the end goal is the same. It allows the killers to feel powerful and relive their crimes as a fantasy, making it a "fetish" object.'

Nicole Mott agrees with Schecter and Everitt. In a contribution to the *Encyclopedia of Murders and Violent Crime* (2003), she observes that the 'trophy' is used to preserve the memory of the victims, which the killer can evoke in [post crime] sexual acts. Mott also notes that trophy-taking acts as a 'signature' and this can become part of a killer's preferred murder ritual.

Jeffrey Lionel Dahmer kept skulls, body parts and Polaroid photos of his victims. He admitted taking sexual pleasure in keeping the bodies of his victims in his home, as did the gay British serial killer Dennis Nilsen. My book *Inside the Mind of Jeffrey Dahmer: The Cannibal Killer* (2022) goes very deep inside of the head of one of history's worst serial murderers. But here's the thing. As disgusting as this will sound, to my knowledge never in the annals of all of criminal history has there been a serial killer who has physically taken away from his crime scenes an 'olfactory trophy' of such an intimate nature. I also think that there was more going on in Tuchlin's psychopathology than may appear at first blush, because his first kill might tell us a lot more about him than he could have known about himself.

The grip of homicidal violence

'When the fox hears the rabbit scream he comes a-runnin', but not to help.'

Thomas Harris: *The Silence of the Lambs* (1988)

On 1 February 1980, thirty-year-old 'Anastasja E.' was murdered in Gdańsk.

On 29 April 1980, thirty-five-year-old 'Alicja M.' was beaten to death at Skowarcz, Gdańsk County.

On 17 September 1980, twenty-one-year-old 'Cecylia G.' was bludgeoned to death near the town of Czarna Woda.

These murders, and that in 1979, had been committed two on a Friday, the following two on a Tuesday and a Wednesday. The crime scenes were often many miles apart. For an offender profiler, the dates and the locations would, even by today's improved methods of finding a potential 'centre of gravity' (the murderer's home base, maybe), have been all but impossible. However, these homicides did present several common clues:

1. That the killer was using a vehicle but seemed to limit his travels to the Pomeranian Voivoideship, seems most apparent .
2. He had a female gender victimology – the ages: eighteen to thirty-five years.
3. The killer was *possibly* a sexual inadequate, because his paramount compulsions revolved around masturbation, not penetration.
4. The choice of a blunt object – a hammer – might well have indicated that the offender was working class, and that this 'tool' felt comfortable in his hands.

Not much to go on there at all, and hindsight is a great thing, so of course it is impertinent of me to suggest what approaches the authorities might have taken back then. However, at each of those crime scenes, and later at autopsies, was there any other evidence to indicate a more 'intimate' kill? There was nothing – like the dog that 'did nothing in the night-time' – nothing visible and yet it was actually sitting in plain sight. I suggest – and I may be wrong –that it sat with (3) above. Furthermore, this killer moved upon his innocent victims after following them; he effectively sought out suitable prey and stalked them. There might have been a short chase, with the terrified woman running for her life before the hammer came down. Then, when she was unconscious and possibly dying, Tuchlin did what his warped psychopathology dictated: lifted up the victim's undergarments, touched her most intimate parts, masturbated over the inert form, left her dumped like so much garbage, then fled the scene as fast as he could, like the cowardly monster he was. I cannot speak for my readers, but if one of those young women had been *my* daughter, I would have gladly slipped a noose around his scrawny neck and hung him myself.

On 19 November 1980, twenty-two-year-old 'Izabela S.' was murdered at Malbor. a town in northern Poland, within the historical region of Pomerelia., noted for its thirteenth-century castle.

Later that same year, on 12 December, thirty-year-old 'Wanda K.' was murdered at Gdańsk. Tuchlin did not kill again until 14 November 1981, when he struck down nineteen-year-old 'Halina G.' in Gdańsk.

The hunt for 'Scorpion'

'Who knows what evil lurks in the hearts of men? The Shadow knows.'

Catchphrase from *The Shadow*, a popular American
radio programme that ran from
1930 to 1954

It seemed that this serial killer was like a ghost in the shadows. Despite all their best efforts, the authorities could not track him down. But we have to frame these events in their historical context. At the time, Poland was in the profound grip of social and political change. There was martial law. Police were focused on finding and capturing dissidents. These circumstances gave Tuchlin the opportunity to hunt with impunity, and he left little evidence.

'[Tuchlin] would gratify himself primarily, but his behaviour following this was actually kind of post-sex, not post-killing. He just rifled through the gear as if it was an opportunity at a jumble sale taking what he fancied, keeping things that he liked.'

Psychologist David Holmes

In September 1980, after killing twenty-one-year-old 'Cecylia G.', Tuchlin had satisfied his sexual desires, then searched her bag, taking souvenirs, as had become his habit. He truly was a homicidal magpie of sorts. Tuchlin had also found some food in Cecylia's bag, and sat down calmly to eat it while she was dying. He didn't feel any guilt or remorse. Tired after the attack, he simply had a snack. He was totally indifferent, unattached to any emotions; not once did he react to the death, carnage and suffering that he had inflicted on others. It is almost as if Tuchlin had a sort of split mind, or dual personality. Superficially, he appeared to be a good husband and a father; his wife and neighbours had no idea that he was capable of such wicked crimes.

For a fascinating parallel example, the reader might wish to look up the case of double killer, multiple rapist and Royal Canadian Air Force colonel Russell Williams. His full video-taped interrogation can be found online. Married to a devoted wife, he was a cross-dressing stalker, rapist, killer and trophy-taker by night. Yet hours later, he would be on parade, ordering the men and women of his command about. On one occasion, he ferried Her Majesty Queen Elizabeth II around in one of his planes as if nothing sinister had ever taken place in his life. After each attack, back at his home, he would cross-dress in his victims' lingerie, bras, high-heeled shoes and parade himself in front of mirror. You can find those photos online too.

At this point in Tuchlin's narrative, there is some variation in the dates to consider. Police say that in December 1982, Tuchlin went to a restaurant, where he drank a shot of vodka. He was walking around Skarszewy looking for a woman to attack and satisfy his sexual desires. Later that night, his eyes settled upon factory girl 'Bożena S', aged twenty-three (some say twenty-four). It was only after her terrible murder came to light that the senior officers in charge of the cases involving Tuchlin's previous victims acknowledged that a serial killer was on the loose. As Andrzej Gawrys, Special Group Scorpion's leading investigator, puts it: 'We had warned our superiors earlier [that a serial murderer was at large], but somehow this information got lost down the line. If our group had been formed earlier, several women would have been spared lots of suffering.' There is some truth in that statement. However it was not, I'm afraid to say, great detective work that caught Tuchlin. He caught himself.

Special Group Scorpion was inaugurated on 6 January 1983. Initially it consisted of eleven officers and was based in the Provincial Headquarters at the Investigation Building in Gdańsk. There had been long gaps in the hammer attacks since his first attempted murder in 1975, so after the murder of 'Bożena S.', police assumed that her killer would lie low for a while. Sadly, this proved not to be the case. Just eleven days after Special Group Scorpion was formed, Paweł Tuchlin went hunting again; this time in Gdańsk (not as some sources have it, in Narkowy, which is fifty-one kilometres south of the regional capital). His target was seamstress nineteen-year-old 'Jolanta K.'. Andrzej Gawrys is adamant that Tuchlin went out and killed Jolanta two weeks after his group was formed, which means that her murder would have taken place in mid-January – *not* 6 May, as other sources have it. It's all a bit messy if you ask me, but I am doing the best I can here.

This recent hammer attack bore all of the hallmarks of the previous kills. Tuchlin brought Bozena down with blows to the head, he removed her panties, pleasured himself and stole a ring from her finger, but the timing of this attack showed that he was changing his approach. His cooling-down periods between assaults were becoming shorter – another common trait with many serial killers who become very complacent, and thus vulnerable to making grave mistakes. Like all of his evil breed, Tuchlin had become addicted to committing sexually motivated homicide. He was now a murder addict. He simply couldn't stop himself.

Professor Ian Robertson, former director at Trinity College of Neuroscience, is one of the world's leading authorities in his field. I was particularly taken by the comments he made during an appearance on a BBC TV documentary about the sociopath Vladimir Putin. I have covered similar ground in previous writings, especially concerning the serial killer Michael Bruce Ross. However, what Professor Robertson says about Putin could be applied to Tuchlin and most sexually motivated serial murderers. He describes in a few lines what I would take a heck of a lot longer to say:

The human brain has a single reward network that gets switched on whenever we get paid a compliment, whenever we have *sex*, whenever we take cocaine and whenever we have *power* and *great success*.

What happens is you get a surge of intense pleasure and satisfaction from the stimulus, but as you repeat that at high level the brain needs more and more to achieve the same effects – it's an *insatiable appetite* [author's italics].

Was not Tuchlin getting the *feel-good* or reward stimulus almost from the start of his stalking and voyeurism? Of course he was.

Did he feel he had *power* and could *achieve great success* when he brought his vulnerable victims down?

Did his *brain need more and more* from this sexual stimulus? Was he now in the grip of an *insatiable appetite* to kill?

I think that we can agree on all of those points. For we all know that any type of extreme addiction can bring one's downfall. So many compulsive gamblers have lost their shirts *big time*. In playing the serial homicide game of chance, Tuchlin risked his own neck and the odds are always stacked in a bookies' favour. In this case, the 'house' was run by the police. Despite being a tad slow off the starting blocks, lead investigator Andrzej Gawrys and his team now hit the ground running.

Miraculously, his next victim, Ewa B., survived Tuchlin's attack and went for help. She was able to give the investigators valuable information about her attacker. Using her testimony and other reports, the team developed sketches of what the killer might look like, but these sketches varied because some of what this victim recalled was interpreted in different ways and no other witness saw the perpetrator clearly. True, there were a set of common themes: thin; a long rather sad face; sallow complexion; high cheekbones… but that didn't tell the police much, admittedly. Still, they did a have a few things going for them. The nature of the offender's attacks and the boot print impressions found at some of the crime scenes suggested that the killer was quite a young man, very active, quite strong and of medium height. He had left behind a small hill of evidence, yet it would turn out that Tuchlin was hiding in plain sight.

In his later statements to police, he said that he had followed this surviving victim, caught up and propositioned her. She refused his advances and ran off, but he chased her for some three hundred metres, then struck her down. He ran back to collect her bag then returned, hoping to beat her to death. Hitting her fourteen or fifteen times with a 1.5-kilogram hammer, he then took off her underwear, fingered her then brought himself off to orgasm. Such was the nature of this beast. The terribly beaten woman was found the next morning by the owner of the land. Miraculously, she had clung onto life. Now the local communities went into absolute panic: a homicidal sex maniac was running amok. Where he might strike next?

Then in spring 1983, Tuchlin made a rookie's mistake – one that would lead police right to his door.

The Scorpion is caught

'You have been trapped in the inescapable net of ruin by your own want of sense.'

Aeschylus: ancient Greek playwright

On 20 February 1983, Tuchlin committed a bizarre crime. Using a stolen van, he thieved four piglets from a local farm. While driving the vehicle the following day, he saw the opportunity to attack another woman, but again changed tactics. For the first time he used the vehicle to initiate an attack, running her down. He put the unconscious woman into the back of the van and drove her to a secluded spot. When he'd finished assaulting her, he rushed to drive away but the van got stuck in the mud. He was forced to leave it there and escape on foot.

When police searched the abandoned van they found something unusual in the back – pig faeces. They linked the van to the four stolen piglets – the tyre tracks at the location where the piglets were stolen and the place where the van was found, were identical. Now, the Scorpion had left two very significant clues for the investigators: the perpetrator was unlikely to be from the city, he'd probably have a rural location – after all, white-collar workers do not steal pigs. Police also knew that the man they were hunting could hotwire a vehicle.

Tuchlin was now acting foolishly – he even gave the piglets, along with some of his murder trophies such as jewellery he had stolen, to Mrs Tuchlin No. 2, who kept them at their farm. But it was another theft that would lead to his capture.

Tuchlin now needed a cooker to make swill for the little piggies in his sty. His next-door neighbour had just such a steamer, so brazenly he stole it and took it back to his own farm. How plumb-dumb stupid an act that was. If he had asked to borrow the cooker on the promise of several packs of bacon, I'm sure that his neighbour would have been delighted to help out, adding: 'O tak, Paweł. Kilka paczek boczku byłoby mile widziane', which I'm almost sure translates as: 'Oh yes, Paweł. A few packs of belly pork would be most welcome!'

The end was nigh, because his neighbour reported Tuchlin to the police for the theft. Soon the cops were investigating. They filed a report, which came to the attention of a support worker at Special Group Scorpion and she made a vital connection, joining the dots between the stolen piglets, the abandoned van containing pig excrement and the half-hitched pigswill steamer. Soon, detectives discovered that Paweł Tuchlin had a criminal record for theft and that his face matched certain aspects of the surviving witness's sketches.

On 31 May 1983 we came to a farm in three cars with the intention of arresting Paweł Tuchlin. We entered through his gate and the moment he saw us he thought that it was about those stolen piglets. Paweł changed his clothes and got his ID. He calmly accepted the handcuffs and was led to one of the cars. We were there 15 minutes. It was as banal as could be.'

Andrzej Gawrys: Lead Investigator
Special Group Scorpion

Tuchlin was initially arrested for the theft of the piglets and of a swill cooker, but when police searched his farm, they found a hammer stained with human blood – that of his last victim. They also uncovered the original number plate he'd removed from the stolen van: GDM 1418, and they found rings and wristwatches stolen from his earlier victims. At the police station, Andrzej Gawrys questioned his prime murder suspect, his first query being – naturally enough: 'How did these rings and watches end up in your house?' The thirty-seven-year-old Tuchlin lowered his head and took a couple of deep breaths, then step by step he confessed to everything. Today, even the police admit it was Tuchlin's careless mistakes that led them to him. It was Tuchlin's magpie behaviour that helped them to catch him. How clod-hoppingly unimaginative is that?

Over the next three months, a team of experts in various fields examined Tuchlin, delving into his history to determine if he was mentally incompetent to stand trial. 'All of his crimes were analysed. It's not about what his crimes say about his actions, but what the actions say about the offender,' observed lead forensic psychiatrist Jerzy Pobocha.

To help the authorities develop evidence, Tuchlin was taken from the former Nazi prison at Szczecin to some of the crime scenes, where he reconstructed his brutal assaults. He mimed them using a rubber hammer on a young policewoman, who acted out the role of the victim. Several times the female officer was so scared of him that she spontaneously crumpled her face, even though it was a reconstruction and he was in handcuffs. Tuchlin even demonstrated his sexual perversions on a mannequin lying on the ground and seemed to enjoy the experience, even joking with the officers. Kneeling down, he gleefully stated: 'Mr prosecutor, I could demonstrate better, if instead of the mannequin I had that police lady.'

During one of the reconstructions, a journalist approached the Scorpion to ask what he would do if he were to be released. Tuchlin raised his head; with a little grin, and slowly drawling his words, he replied: 'I would hunt... if I had the opportunity I would kill again!'

Even in prison Tuchlin could not restrain his perverse sexual desires, making vaginas out of bread so that he could become sexual aroused. Even safely under lock and key, his needs drove him to fashion substitutes for what he had done in reality; he even used bristles to make them more life-like. Bizarrely, he fell in love with his psychiatrist and gave her one of his bread vaginas; she had a breakdown. Nevertheless, the psychological investigation concluded that Tuchlin was sane.

Initially, he admitted ten murders and all of the attempted kills. However, at the hearing he recanted his testimony, claiming that the police had extracted a forced confession from him. On 6 August 1985, the regional court in Gdańsk sentenced him to death for nine homicides and eleven attempted murders. The supreme court upheld the sentence and the state council decided not to grant leniency. Tuchlin was hanged at the detention centre at 12 Kurkowa Street on 25 May 1987. After his death, he was for some reason unknown to me, decapitated and his head then placed in a jar of formalin, which subsequently went missing; the rest of his earthly remains were buried in Łostowicki cemetery in Gdańsk. According to Marek Maj, who had been part of Tuchlin's counsel, gravediggers urinated in the coffin before the lid was screwed down. (For the record, the last execution in Poland took place on at 5:10 p.m. on 21 April 1988, when twenty-eight-year-old rapist and murderer Andrzej Czabański was hanged in Kraków's Montelupich Prison.)

State of mind: a 'lust murderer'

'Many eat that on earth that they digest in hell.'
Thomas Brooks: seventeenth-century English
nonconformist Puritan preacher

There are two issues that have not been discussed very widely – if at all – in any of the literature on Tuchlin. The first is his need to 'smell' and 'taste' the vaginal area of his victims to gain sexual pleasure. It seems highly likely that he suffered from 'olfactophilia' or 'osmolaginia': a paraphilia for, or sexual arousal by, smells and odours emanating from the body, especially the sexual areas. Sigmund Freud employed the term 'osphresiolagnia' to describe odour-derived pleasure.

The origins of both words explain their meanings. 'Olfactophilia' – from the Latin *olfacto*, to smell (hence 'olfactory', pertaining to the sense of smell), and Greek *philia*, 'love'. 'Osmolagnia' – from the Greek *osme*, 'smell', and *lagneia*, 'lust'.

Much of it comes down to pheromones. In common with many animals, we humans can subconsciously make use of body odour to identify whether a potential mate will pass on favourable traits to their offspring, and this may provide significant clues about the genetic quality, health and reproductive successes of a potential mate. I very much doubt that Tuchlin had a clue as to why he found this practice so sexually rewarding. However, a 2018 German study, in which researchers measured 'odour thresholds' with sniffing sticks, showed that those with a stronger sense of smell have more orgasms, more intensely carnal come to that. It pays to have a big nose, perhaps?

Tuchlin was a 'lust murderer', an individual who searches for sexual satisfaction by killing someone. The term is synonymous with the word 'erotophonophilia', denoting sexual arousal, or gratification, contingent on the death of a human being. The term 'lust killing' was first used by Richard Freiherr von Krafft-Ebing, a German psychiatrist recognised in his time as an authority on deviant sexual behaviour .

Aside from the evisceration and dismemberment some-times associated with lust murder, related behaviour may include activities such as removing clothing from the body, posing the body in different positions (as in the case of Pedro Alonso López), the insertion of objects into bodily orifices, cannibalism and necrophilia. All of which stem from violent fantasies that the emerging killer struggles to control.

For my part, I think that one has to be very careful which sexually motivated serial murderers fall into this category, although admittedly the reader might think that I am splitting hairs here. For example, a study of the early twentieth-century killer Peter Kürten proves beyond any doubt that he was a lust murderer, while his homicidal contemporary, Friedrich Heinrich 'Fritz' Haarmann, was not. It is true to say Haarmann carried out sexual assaults on many of his victims, but principally his motive was one of financial gain. He metamorphosed into becoming a con artist and petty thief, serving several prison terms for offences such as larceny and embezzlement. It is known that all of his victims were dismembered before their bodies were discarded. Haarmann typically kept his victims' possessions, mostly their clothing and items such as watches and jewellery, for himself and his lover Hans Grans. These they would sell on the black market, or would give to acquaintances as gifts. There were rumours, after he'd been arrested, that he ate the flesh of his victims, or sold it on the black market. There is no evidence to support this putative cannibalism; however, the jury is still out on the matter of whether or not he sold the flesh of his prey as either pork or horse meat.

Tuchlin began to metamorphose into a killer during his early voyeuristic days. We know that he physically wanted a young woman but he'd been shunned for years because of the smell of urine on his clothes. He wanted discourse, he wanted physical touch, but could not engage with anyone because deep down in his psyche he felt a squalor, a vulgarity about himself. To compensate, he secretly watched as women sunbathed or made love with guys in quiet wooded places. Thereafter, his fantasies evolved into wanting to control his preferred female type without fear of rejection, and of course, sexual assault can be used as a means of control.

Although this is not unusual with his killer breed, we see in Tuchlin solid evidence that he was selective: once he had spotted his ideal prey, he stalked them before bringing them down. However, as with all lust killers – we can include Ted Bundy here, too – repetitive cyclic fantasies are a key component and can never be fulfilled. The reader might bear this in mind when studying any sexually motivated serial killers, which is why I quoted Professor Ian Robertson's observations above.

The second issue I want to raise here is this: why didn't Paweł Tuchlin sexually penetrate his victims? I think that perhaps having grown used to masturbating during his time spent as a stalker and voyeur, he would have continued masturbating with heightened excitement when he had an obligingly still woman's body at his disposal. This is difficult for me to explain, but I am sure that stalking gave him a tremendous surge of sexual anticipation; that he was in effect controlling his intended victim from afar – which is not at all unusual with serial sex offenders. That he didn't actually penetrate his victims *is* quite unusual, although US serial lust killer Harvey 'The Hammer' Carignan never once had penetrative sex with any of his many victims either. He did, however, use his hammer handle to rape his prey after he had forced them to commit fellatio on him.

Finally, the idea for the initial hammer blow to render his victims unconscious came from Tuchlin's childhood days, when he watched pigs being killed on local farms. To us that will indubitably seem a very cruel method of dispatching the animals, but back then it was common practice. He would have become accustomed to how effective it was, and it would have caused him no distress at all when he hammered the heads of his innocent victims.

So was Tuchlin sad, bad, mad, insane or evil? Well, a reader may think that the psychiatrists and the hangman have answered that question for us.

William Chester Minor:
sanity *v.* madness.

*'a1548 Hall Chron., Hen. IV. (1550) 32b, Duryng
whiche sickenes as Auctors write he caused his crowne to be
set on the pillowe at his beddes heade.'*

CITATION FROM HALL'S *CHRONICLE* OF 1548,
SUBMITTED TO THE *OXFORD ENGLISH DICTIONARY* BY
WILLIAM CHESTER MINOR ON A QUOTATION SLIP FOR
THE ENTRY ON THE WORD 'SET'

Get your head around that, if you will. But no compendium
of the legions of the *allegedly* criminally insane would be
satisfactory without a chapter dedicated to the man we are
about to meet, whose depth and width of reading led him to
define and identify usages of specific words, many of which
could have multiple meanings.

First, the background to the dictionary that has come to be
promoted as the 'definitive record of the English language'. In
1857, a committee of worthies of the Philological Society met

to discuss compiling a dictionary, and in January 1858 they launched a plan to create a fully comprehensive dictionary, which proved to be a herculean task involving hundreds of volunteers. The first volume of the first edition of *A New English Dictionary on Historical Principles* was published in 1888, covering A to B. The dictionary reached the end of Z in 1928. Then came supplements and in 1933, the 13-volume (10 volumes plus three supplementary volumes) *Oxford English Dictionary* was published, to which supplements were added, until the 20-volume second edition was published in 1989. And supplements continue to be added today, while an online edition has been created, regularly revised.

We have come a long way since those early days, but the value of the work of the original volunteers cannot be dismissed – and one of the most fruitful contributors was one W.C. Minor, whose thorough and dedicated work was invaluable to the early editors of the *OED*.

William Chester Minor was a remarkable man. Born in 1834, he trained in medicine at Yale University, funding his course with odd part-time work, including assisting with the 1864 revision of *Webster's Dictionary*, and it seems likely that this is when his interest in philology grew. He eventually became a surgeon with the Union Army during the American Civil War. He was also a killer, schizophrenic to the nth degree, and a sexual obsessive who, in his final years, took a knife to his own penis and sliced a good part of it off. *Ouch!*

In later years, he became an inmate of Broadmoor Criminal Lunatic Asylum, frequently haunted by hallucinations, plagued by paranoid delusions and tortured by twisted sexual fantasies. He was also a highly intelligent man capable of immense focused concentration, with the ability find examples of particular words and to understand and explain the various usages of the words, which made him a key contributor to this comprehensive resource for scholars and academic researchers.

The mad surgeon

If after reading this chapter you come to the conclusion that I need to be certified, then you might be correct. But if you presumed that the insane William Chester Minor was evil, you would be wrong.

Yours truly could write a *War and Peace*-length book about doctors, surgeons, nurses, carers, psychiatrists, psychologists et al., who have gone as nutty as fruit cakes, as mad as hatters – many of whom so evil they have committed serial homicide, while others have topped themselves. Specific knowledge about life and death and easy access to, for instance, toxic substances make it easier for those with medical training to get away with murder. Fortunately the idea of a Hippocratic oath in some form still exists and reminds doctors that they are trained to save lives ... We should not dwell on recent cases, so few and far between, but might consider a few historical ones, and then just those who actually *intended* to kill for some personal motive, and who became serial killers ...

Dr Thomas Neill Cream, the 'Lambeth Poisoner', for instance, who practised in Canada, the US and the UK during the second half of the nineteenth, giving illegal abortions, profiting from the distress of young women who had got themselves 'in trouble' and then giving fatal doses of strychnine to those who became an inconvenience to him.

In France, in the first half of the twentieth century, Marcel André Henri Félix Petiot, known as 'Doctor Satan', stole, embezzled and killed –with injections of cyanide – for financial gain.

More recently, in the UK, there is Dr John Bodkins Adams, suspected of defrauding his patients, a suspiciously great number of whom he treated with large doses of barbiturates ostensibly for pain – and then received inheritances from. He was tried for one murder – of a woman who had since been cremated – and was acquitted. Didn't someone once say 'the law is an ass'?

Last on my list, and thought to be the UK's most prolific serial killer, Dr Harold Shipman. He practised as a GP from 1974 to 1998, during which an estimated 250 of his elderly women patients died, even those who appeared in excellent health, from overdoses of painkillers such as morphine. He was convicted on fifteen counts of murder and one of forgery (of a patient's will – in his favour, of course). He committed suicide in his cell in 2004.

These were serial killers and their intention was to kill and they were not insane (though a question mark hung over Petiot when he was young). So, yes, they were evil.

The American physician, Dr Walter Jackson Freeman II, active during the twentieth century, is slightly different: his aim was to save or improve lives through treating mentally ill patients with psychosurgery. Lobotomy was being hailed as the new miracle treatment for psychiatric ailments of all kinds and Freeman embraced this rather dubious treatment for mental illness with great enthusiasm. In spite of never having been trained as a surgeon, he performed thousands of frontal lobotomies during the 1940s and 50s, using his 'transorbital' system, often administering only electric shocks as anaesthetic as he probed inside the brain with the ice-pick like instrument he invented, the 'orbitoclast', which was inserted under the upper eyelid so that it entered the brain just above the eyeball. I am sure you, my readers, must be squirming with discomfort – which would be a very bad idea if you did so with one of those instruments sitting on your brain.

A notable lack of success did nothing to dampen Freeman's zeal and he continued to lobotomise psychiatric patients in his quest for glory until he was banned from practising surgery in 1967. It is thought some 490 patients died at his hands, many more were reduced to dribbling wrecks. Famously, one of these unfortunate patients was a young woman suffering some intellectual disability and, as she grew older, subject to seizures and violent rages. Her father decided she needed a lobotomy and sent her to Freeman – with predictably disastrous results. She became incoherent and incontinent, forgot how to walk and was deemed to have the mental age of two. Her name was Rosemary and her brother Jack was to be president of the United States.

Yet Freeman was not an evil man: his aim was to improve lives (achieving fame and fortune in the process); he did not set out to kill; neither was he insane – unless his obsessive faith in the practice of lobotomy counts as insanity. In which case he was as mad as a box of March hares.

'So, Christopher' I hear you say. 'Enough already. We need to understand why this chapter-headed "William Chester Minor" – a man whom you seem to rate as being a first-rate candidate for a starring role in *One Flew Over the Cuckoo's Nest*, who was also a former US Army brevet captain surgeon, and one of the literary elite who worked as a lexicographical researcher for the *Oxford English Dictionary* while a patient at the Broadmoor Hospital for the Criminally Insane, and who chopped off much of his own penis while therein – deserves a place in this book?'

Well, to get the ball rolling, let's begin with a small titbit of his early narrative.

The Bible-thumpers

'The fact that there's a Highway to Hell and only a Stairway to Heaven says a lot about anticipated traffic numbers.'

Darynda Jones: US author

Baby William came into this world – in Ceylon (now Sri Lanka), to be precise – on 22 June 1834, to Eastman Strong Minor, a printer by trade, and his first wife Lucy, *née* Bailey. They had tied the knot on 27 August 1833 in Boston, Massachusetts.

Pre-colonisation and settlement, in the 1630s a certain Thomas Hooker and some of Eastman Minor's forebears had journeyed through the wilderness on their way to founding what would become Hartford. Very much like any pioneers, their primary motivation was not a desire for new land, nor a desire for a new state; they saw themselves as God's people, and initially as a congregation set up their first church on the banks of the Connecticut River, where they began Bible-thumping.

Shortly after their marriage, Mr and Mrs Eastman Minor arrived as Congregational Church missionaries in the Crown Colony of Ceylon (today Sri Lanka) to preach the good book. While there, Eastman Minor remarried, his first wife having, we must suppose, shrugged off this mortal coil. Further children were born, including Thomas Minor, in 1844, who was to follow his brother into medical school, and later to become the mayor of Seattle. I might add that spreading the word about God must have been an uphill struggle, because there was an abundance of religions, faiths and other pious bodies competing for Our Lord's Grace in Ceylon at that time.

When he was fourteen, William was sent back back to the the USA to live with relatives in New Haven and attend the Russell Military Academy. Founded in 1834, it was a military training college prep school that fitted students to apply for entrance to nearby Yale or West Point universities. They were also taught book-keeping skills, all of which suited William, for when he subsequently enrolled at Yale School of Medicine, he supported himself with secondary jobs, such as being an instructor back at the Russell Academy and also assistant on the 1864 revision of *Webster's Dictionary* under the supervision of lexicographer Noah Thomas Porter III.

According to the authoritative *Yale Medicine Magazine*, dated winter 2009:

After graduating from Yale – his handwritten M.D. thesis concerned muscular contraction – Minor performed autopsies on soldiers at New Haven's wartime Knight Hospital. A small book with his detailed and eloquent reports is still available at the Medical Historical Library along with his thesis. *Post Mortem Examinations Made at Knight U. S. A. General Hospital,* reveals haunting glimpses of Minor's time. Most of his autopsy subjects that year had previously fallen ill in the field with now-unusual lung ailments, including typhus, typhoid pneumonia, pleurisy and 'phthisis', or tuberculosis; but others had succumbed to the more familiar 'alcoholismus acutus' or even to choking. Minor also published an article in an 1863 issue of *Yale's American Journal of Science and the Arts* regarding the ability of certain worms to regenerate after being cut apart. Years later his erudition and exactitude would serve him well in Broadmoor [Hospital for the Criminally Insane].

We shouldn't completely bypass Noah Porter during our road trip into Minor's state of mind. As well as being a lexicographer, congregational minister, academic, philosopher and author, Porter was also an outspoken anti-slavery activist. To add to his rejoicingly glittering curriculum vitae, 'Porter Mountain' of the Adirondack Mountains, New York State, is named after him – he being the first person to scale its 4,059-foot peak in 1875, *at the age of sixty-four*! What a fine man Porter was, don't you think? He was buried in the Grove Street Cemetery, New Haven, and he's still there, I think.

Minor graduated in 1863 with a medical degree and a specialisation in comparative anatomy to become a brevet surgeon captain in the Union Army. As my astute readers will already know – especially all those who attend CrimeCon every year – the term 'comparative anatomy' describes the analysis of structural differences and likenesses between different species. Thus, we see the foundations of this young man's narrative as it slowly gathers substance year by year.

Musket fire, black powder and red-hot balls

'John Brown's body lies a-mouldering in the grave...
His soul is marching on!'

Union Army marching song about the
abolitionist John Brown

In terms of marching ahead in life, William Chester Minor had not put a foot wrong so far. It is claimed that he served at the remarkably short Battle of the Wilderness during the American Civil War on 5–7 May 1864, which came about when General Ulysses S. Grant, with 118,700 Union troops, came up against General Robert E. Lee, with 66,140 soldiers of the Confederate Army, at Spotsylvania, Orange County, Virginia. In reality, this turned out to be a most disagreeable affair, one where many, many surgeons would be overworked and many gravediggers kept busy too. The Union Army suffered 2,246 killed, 12,037 wounded, with 3,383 captured or missing in action (a total of 17,666 casualties – though an officer claimed that he had seen a general reducing these numbers in his report). The Confederate Army suffered 1,477 killed, 7,866 wounded, with 1,690 captured or missing in action (a total of 11,033).

I said it was a 'disagreeable affair' because there were no winners or losers, with both sides coming out pretty much quits in this mother of battles without wits. One rather thinks that this bloody fiasco might have been the first example of

'MAD', or mutually assured destruction. As the last day, 7 May, was mostly spent manoeuvring, I have to conclude that in barely over *two days* nearly as many as 4,000 (allowing for some creative underestimates) men were killed, some 19,900 wounded and at least 5,000, unaccounted for. In just forty-eight hours. That's what I would call a military clusterfuck if ever there was one.

Lieutenant-Colonel Horace Porter, a member of General Grant's staff, later wrote in his diary:

> Forest fires raged, ammunition trains exploded; the dead were roasted in the conflagration; the wounded, roused by its hot breath, dragged themselves along, with their torn and mangled limbs, in the mad energy of despair, to escape the ravages of the flames; and every bush seemed hung with shreds of blood-stained clothing...

That must have been a real shit-storm if you ask me, and it would have added a twist to this chapter if Surgeon Minor had been in the thick of it and perhaps suffered from some sort of post-traumatic stress disorder, one that might partly mitigate his later all-consuming mental collapse. But there is still room for conjecture here.

In his excellent book, Simon Winchester has it that Minor was sent into action at the Battle of the Wilderness, and that the experience haunted him. This is endorsed by Terry Trainor in his book *Bedlam: St Mary of Bethlehem* (2012). Although Minor may have served in this battle, sources in Wikipedia add, 'it is unlikely that Minor was present... as his military records place him at Knight USA Hospital in New Haven at that time and do not show him arriving at 2 Division Hospital at Alexandria Hospital until May 17,' – which would have been a week and a bit after the smoke had cleared, with both armies having left the battlefield with severely scorched tails between their legs. Whether or not Minor was present at that particular battle, he would nevertheless have probably been present during other battles and was certainly witness to the horrors inflicted upon the soldiers, having had to treat men who had been terribly wounded, some mutilated beyond recognition.

I almost forgot to say that it was also rumoured that Surgeon Minor had to brand a deserting Union soldier on the face with 'D' for 'deserter', but once again there is room for doubt here. Terry Trainor writes: 'At Minor's trial, years later, his defence suggested that the horrors of war had caused his illness [paranoid schizophrenia]. Particularly, he had witnessed an execution, and had been required to brand an Irish deserter from the Union cause with a letter "D".' While this theory will have to remain conjecture, it does paint a powerful picture of a traumatised individual, something that Minor certainly became.

At the end of the Civil War, Minor remained in the army and apparently rose through the ranks without any signs of insane or untoward behaviour. He moved to Governor's Island, New York City, which was then a garrison, and where he treated cholera patients. And it is at this point in Minor's narrative that sex enters his story, although, as Terry Trainor points out: 'It seems unlikely that Minor had not already been consumed by sexual thoughts before this point.'

Indeed, it could be said that he may have suffered from a hypersexuality disorder or sexual addiction – an excessive preoccupation with sexual fantasies, urges or behaviours that is difficult to control. Let's keep it simple and say that William had an overactive sex drive. This led to him spending much time in New York's red-light districts, which resulted in his contracting venereal disease.

Getting laid in New York

'In the realm of evil thoughts none induces to sin as much as do thoughts that concern the pleasure of flesh.'
Thomas Aquinas: thirteenth-century
Italian Dominican friar and priest, philosopher,
theologian and saint

Not being an ardent reader of the best-selling monthly top-shelf magazine *Seven Deadly Sins to Enjoy*, Friar Aquinas would have said that, wouldn't he? However, although this may seem like an unedifying subject to handle, it's necessary in order to place William Minor's middle narrative into perspective. That's essential to aid us in our search to find out why he went mad.

Circa this time, New York City was awash with 'hookers' – so called because these women fished for clients and hooked some. According to the *New York Post*: 'Anywhere from 3,000 to 10,000 prostitutes worked in a community of whorehouses, on street corners and even on the balconies or in exquisite theatres, where they thought nothing of propositioning men in front of their wives.' This could only have happened in New York, right?

There was no safety in numbers for the sex workers, though, and it was not unusual for a prostitute to be killed; in 1836 a young woman calling herself Helen Jewett was brutally murdered with an axe or hatchet in the brothel where she worked. The murder, and subsequent arrest of one of her clients, his trial and acquittal were quite a *cause célèbre*. Despite the shock-horror of this bloody slaying, however, it did nothing at all to deter prostitution, but seemed merely to encourage many more different ways of giving the seven deadly sins full rein. Sex workers serviced clients in their offices. Many staked out territories such as saloons or docks, with the *New York Post* reminding us: 'One enterprising fifteen-year-old became the prize hooker for men who worked on a particular coal barge.'

In any case, this is the vice-ridden world that William Minor entered, already becoming mentally unstitched.

Back in the nineteenth century, sex workers were thought to have a high risk of contracting syphilis (more familiarly, the pox) not as might be expected due to their increased chance of being exposed to infection, but because of their inherent immorality. As was the case in many major cities, in New York if the disease was a direct result of promiscuous intercourse, prostitutes were nothing less than a festering sore on society. As Anna Faherty writes in a 20 July 2017 article for the Wellcome Collection website:

Like plague-infected rats of cholera-swamped sewers, women who made their living selling sex were a problem that had to be monitored and improved.

Anna doesn't mince her words, does she? Nor did William Acton, who, much earlier, penned the following in *Prostitution, Considered in its Moral, Social, and Sanitary Aspects* (1857):

> The prostitute is a woman with half the woman gone, and that half containing all that elevates her nature, leaving her a mere instrument of impurity... a social pest, carrying contamination and foulness to every quarter to which she has access.

No quibble there, either. To dig deeper, try Stanley Renner's article 'William Acton, The Truth about Prostitution, and Hardy's Not-So-Ruined Maid', which appeared in the Spring 1992 issue of the journal *Victorian Poetry* (it's downloadable via libraries or schools).

And why am I dedicating so much time to this point? Simply to gauge whether it's a possible seed for Minor's madness. A least likely seed in my view is any post-Civil War post-traumatic stress disorder (PTSD) because he may never have heard a cannon fired in anger, seen the whites of a Confederate militiaman's eyes, come up close and personal with the pointed end of a bayonet an inch from his handsome nose, even less likely noted a distant puff of black smoke followed in short order by a lead ball whizzing past his ear. Yes, 'tis true he did some surgery on lots of wounded soldiers and amputations at the 2 Division Hospital, but this didn't seem to have affected his libido when he later arrived in New York. Indeed, by all accounts he had a problem keeping his pecker neatly tucked up inside his braced-up britches.

All this seediness led me to a 2 February 1901 piece in *The Journal of the American Medical Association.* Titled: 'Mental Symptoms of Cerebral Syphilis', the author – James H. McBride, M.D. of Los Angeles – starts out on a high note with: 'Syphilis may be the cause, either immediate or remote, of every form of disease of the nervous system, from neurasthenic conditions to coarse brain disease and insanity.' Could Dr McBride have been on to something here? Syphilis has for centuries been associated with a variety of mental conditions if not treated successfully. Today, it can be cured quickly with antibiotics, but in the nineteenth century it was another matter, exacerbated by the stigma attached to sexually transferred diseases. In its later stages, the bacteria reach and affect the nervous system and brain, which may become inflamed; this in turn may lead to a variety of mental disturbances from mild mood changes to hallucinations, even to psychosis. As we shall see, over the years Minor display such symptoms. They did nothing to quell his hypersexuality, which remained with him almost until his dying day. That he came from a religious background probably added feelings of guilt ,which in turn could have aggravated his growing paranoia. William Chester Minor was a man with many demons.

By 1867, Minor's loose behaviour had been brought to the attention of his superiors. Trainor writes: 'Such behaviour might be considered normal for a soldier, even tacitly encouraged, but there must have been something about Minor's behaviour that was not normal. Bearing in mind his subsequent history, the possibility that Minor was engaging in either homosexual or bisexual acts might be one possible conclusion.' Whatever the case, the upshot was that he was hastily transferred about as far away from the nocturnal temptations of the flesh to be found in New York as one can be – to Florida's panhandle, to be precise, approximately 1,150 miles south.

Pascua Florida

Pascua Florida is the Spanish term for Easter (also simply *Pascua*), which falls during the flowering season, and the state of Florida is so named because it was Easter 1513 when the flourishing peninsula was discovered by an expedition led by Spanish explorer and conquistador Juan Ponce de León. And it is there we travel to next as we follow William Chester Minor's mounting madness.

It's clear that this forced move to Florida did little to diminish his overwhelming sexual predilections; furthermore, his fellow officers, not unlike his comrades in New York, mocked him and talked behind his back, or so he believed. Just like his army kit and leather portmanteau, the rumours went with him and, if he had felt persecuted up north he would find no relief down south. Minor's delusions worsened and his behaviour became more and more erratic, with him at one point challenging a fellow officer to a duel.

In September 1868, army doctors diagnosed Minor as suffering from monomania. In The term monomania (from Greek *monos*, 'one', and *mania*: 'madness' or 'frenzy') was coined by a French psychiatrist, Jean-Étienne Dominique Esquirol, to denote, as explained by author Jan E. Goldstein in her 2002 book *Console and Classify: The French Psychiatric*

Profession during the Nineteenth Century, a condition 'characterised by the presence of an expansive fixed-idea in which the mind was diseased and deranged in some facets but otherwise normal in others' – which boils down to an extreme enthusiasm or zeal for a single subject or idea, often manifested as a rigid, irrational idea; in Minor's case, it was sex, but partnered with paranoid delusions. Minor's mental condition had now become so major that he was admitted into a lunatic asylum, as psychiatric hospitals were then called, in south-east Washington, DC, where for the next eighteen months he showed no signs of improvement.

Opened in 1855 as the Government Hospital for the Insane (and known as St Elizabeth's Hospital today), it housed over 8,000 patients at its peak; there are approximately 450 graves of the Civil War veterans and an unknown number of civilians on the West campus. To be honest with you, no one really knows how many graves *are* on site; as many as 125,000 individuals were treated here, although no one really knows the exact number of patients as their records weren't maintained accurately... *tch tch*! Author Kelly Patricia O'Meara reckons thousands are buried in unmarked graves, and that the on-site incinerator also needs to answer a few questions, the first of which being: 'How many bodies went into you?' Well-known patients have included would-be presidential assassins Richard Lawrence, who shot at Andrew Jackson, and John Warnock Hinkley Jr, who shot at and failed to kill Ronald Reagan, as well as the assassin of James Garfield, Charles J. Guiteau, who was housed here until his execution by hanging. The actress Mary Fuller was given a bed here along with the influential poet, Ezra

Weston Loomis Pound and James Edward Swann Jr, aka 'the Shotgun Stalker'. Of all these figures it is Guiteau who most interests me, so let's take a break from William Chester Minor and meet Charles Julius Guiteau, who was born on 8 September1841 and hanged on 30 June 1882.

While being led to his execution Guiteau was said to have continued to smile and wave at spectators and reporters. He notoriously danced his way to the gallows and shook hands with his executioner. On the scaffold he recited a poem called 'I am going to the Lordy', which he'd written while behind bars. He had originally requested an orchestra to play as he sang his poem, but this request was denied as the New York Philharmonic was having the day off, or so he was told by the priest who was anxious to get home and give the Ten Commandments another read.

Charles's body was buried in the jail yard. Intriguingly, at autopsy it was discovered that he had 'phimosis', which is an inability to retract the foreskin, and which at the time was thought to have caused the insanity that led him to assassinate President Garfield. That said, and as is par for the course in these matters, there are always conflicting opinions. The autopsy also revealed that Charlie's brain's dura mater was abnormally thick, suggesting that he may have had neurosyphilis, a disease that causes mental instability, leading to the suggestion that he could have contracted syphilis from a prostitute, though other commentators have even disagreed with that.

Sadly, despite his poem about going to 'the Lordy', Guiteau was not destined to rest in peace. Strands of the hanging rope were soon on sale as souvenirs to a morbid public, and rumours began to swirl about that jail guards planned to exhume the corpse to meet the demands of this burgeoning new market – selling cuts from his shirt and underpants, one suspects. To avoid scandal, it was decided to dig him up again and pack him off to what is now known as the National Museum of Health and Medicine; his skeleton was bleached and his brain and enlarged spleen were preserved in formaldehyde to be displayed for the edification of medical students and the general public. If by happenstance you ever find yourself in Philadelphia, pop into the Mütter Museum on 19 S. 22nd Street, where you can see what's left of Mr Guiteau. The museum is quite close to the First Unitarian Church and the Rogues Gallery, which one website lauds as a 'sunlit-free corner taproom with a simple menu of craft beers & chef-prepared pub grub'; after visiting a portion of Charlie's brain in a jar and *if* you have the stomach for it, you could enjoy some goolies *en croute* here too.

But let's preserve that thought for now, as we return to William Minor, who despite his obviously uncurable mental illness, was released from the asylum in 1871. Although he had been discharged from the army, he was in receipt of a handsome pension, which he could add to from his well-heeled family's funds. Now financially on a sound footing, at the end of that year he travelled to London.

So let's leave the 'Land of the Free' and the stirring music of 'The Star-Spangled Banner' and repair forthwith to London – to Southwark, to be precise.

Horsemonger Lane Gaol Monger

.1,1 A dealer, trader, trafficker. From the 16th c. onwards, chiefly, one who carries on a petty or disreputable 'traffic' …

The Oxford English Dictionary

As you might easily divine, the name 'Horsemonger Lane' derives from its having been a street where people traded horses; with the suggestion that you should really check the horse over carefully, teeth and all, before handing over your money. If you ever find yourself in Harper Road, Southwark, take a wander through Newington Gardens, which occupies part of the site of an old prison, Horsemonger Lane Gaol, which was closed down after almost a century in 1878.

Designed by eighteenth-century surveyor George Gwilt the Elder, this was at one time the largest prison in the country. And it is here that we next come across William Chester Minor. Although I cannot say for sure that the park is haunted, the chances are that it *could be*; that if you walked through Newington Gardens in the dead of night, perhaps with a scudding moon to light your way, you *might* see the shadowy apparition of Lieutenant Thomas Beauclerk, who committed suicide in the gaol during the night of 27–28 November 1832. He was committed to the prison to await trial on a charge of sodomy, and is buried close by, although exactly where no one seems to know.

Of some further grim interest, Horsemonger Lane Gaol remained Surrey's main prison and place of execution up until its closure. It had four wings – one for debtors and the other

140

NURSE GUILTY BUT INSANE

Murder of Woman

A verdict of guilty but insane was returned at Somerset Assizes at Wells yesterday against Noreen O'Connor (46), a former nurse, who was charged with murdering Friederika Alwine Maria Buls (77), an invalid with whom she shared a cottage at Loxton, Somerset. Miss Buls, known as Maria Buls, was found dead on September 1 in a bedroom.

Mr Justice Byrne directed that Miss O'Connor, who he said was apparently "extremely fond of this old woman" and looked after her while under no obligation to do so, should be kept in custody as a Broadmoor patient until the Queen's pleasure is known.

Both women were at one time employed by the late Mr Frank Tiarks, a former director of the Bank of England. In 1952 Mr Tiarks died, and since then Miss O'Connor, who apparently benefited under his will, had been living with Miss Buls.

Mr G. D. Roberts, Q.C., prosecuting, said that on September 1 Mr Peter Tiarks, son of the late Mr Tiarks, received a telephone call from Miss O'Connor who said : " Come over at once. Something terrible has happened. Marie is in the power of some evil." When Mr Tiarks arrived at the house, she said : " Marie had an evil look in her eye. The evil was so strong that I plucked them out. . . . It is not Marie who is dead, it is the evil that is in her." It was stated that Miss Buls's body had been found lying on the floor, fully clothed, with terrible injuries to her face.

Dr Thomas Christie, principal medical officer at Holloway Prison, London, stated that in his opinion Miss O'Connor was suffering from some disease of the mind. From talks he had had with Miss O'Connor he formed the impression that as she approached the top of the stairs she felt there was something evil up there that she knew would harm Marie. She did what she did to protect Marie. " In my opinion this delusional trend set up a defect of reason which was so severe that she was incapable of knowing that what she was doing was wrong."

The Judge said that while in custody Miss O'Connor was at first docile, and then became violent and had to be placed in a padded cell.

Below: In 1901, in what is now Iran, a French expedition discovered the stele bearing the Babylonian Code of Hammurabi, which dates from 1755–1750 BC. The ancient code contains the first recorded usage of the defence of insanity. *(Louvre Museum, Paris)*

Left: The *Guardian* of 19 October 1954 reports the court's verdict of guilty but insane on Noreen O'Connor for the murder of Marie Buls, 'because of the evil in her eyes'. *(© The Guardian)*

A view of the church of St Andrew in Loxton, Somerset. Noreen O'Connor was buried in the churchyard, following her death in a mental institution in 1983, aged seventy-six. She was by all accounts a model patient. *(© Derek Harper)*

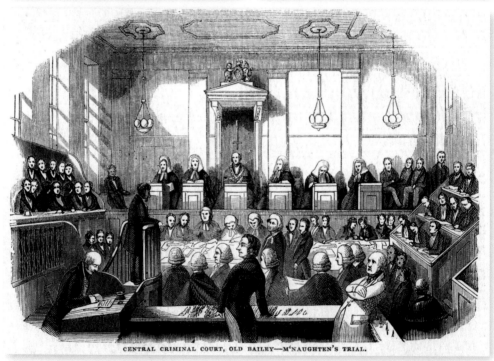

CENTRAL CRIMINAL COURT, OLD BAILEY—M'NAUGHTEN'S TRIAL.

Above left: A Victorian hatter at work. The use of mercury nitrate in the process meant that many hatters 'developed a number of disorders, mental as well as physical', the origin of the phrase 'as mad as a hatter'. *(© Chronicle/Alamy)*

Above right: One of Sir John Tenniel's drawings of the Hatter for his illustrations in Lewis Carroll's *Alice in Wonderland*; the book itself never uses the term 'Mad Hatter'. *(© agefotostock/Alamy)*

Below: The trial of Daniel M'Naghten at the Old Bailey, 2–3 March 1843, at the end of which the judge advised the jury that the defendant be found guilty of murder on the grounds of insanity, thereby giving rise to the so-called 'M'Naghten rules'. *(© Chronicle/Alamy)*

Daniel M'Naghten, a Scottish wood-turner and Chartist sympathiser, c. 1856, by which date he was confined in Bethlem Hospital – also known as Bedlam – where he died in 1865, aged fifty-two.

(© Alamy)

Sir Robert Peel, Bt, Prime Minister of the United Kingdom, 1841–6 and founder of the Metropolitan Police Force, leading to the nickname 'peeler' for a policeman. In trying to assassinate Peel in January 1843, M'Naghten mistakenly shot his private secretary, Edward Drummond, who died from his wound.

(© Alamy)

Left: The 'Monster of the Andes': Columbian-born Pedro Alonso López in police custody in Ambato, Ecuador, 8 June 1980. He confessed to raping and murdering more than 300 young girls in Peru, Columbia and Ecuador.

(© AP/Alamy)

Right: Pawel Tuchlin, nicknamed 'Scorpion', on trial in Gdánsk, Poland, 6 August 1985. A cold-blooded sexual psychopath, Tuchlin was sentenced to death for nine homicides and eleven attempted murders, all of women.

(© PAP/Stefan Kraszewski/Alamy)

Left: The grim exterior of Kurkowa City Prison, Gdánsk, where on 25 May 1987 Tuchlin was hanged. After his exeution he was decapitated; allegedly, gravediggers urinated in his coffin before burying it.

(© Artur Andrzej/Creative Commons)

Left: William Chester Minor, MD, an American surgeon committed to Broadmoor for murder in 1872, after he had been found not guilty by reason of insanity. Although he suffered with his mental health, he became a major contributor of citations for the *Oxford English Dictionary*, although it was not finally published in full volume form until 1928.

Right: An illustration from the *Strand Magazine* of the Lion Brewery, Lambeth, near where, on 17 February 1872, a delusional Minor shot and killed George Merrett, an employee of the brewery.

Below: An engraving from the *Illustrated London News* of 24 August 1867, showing Broadmoor 'Asylum for Criminal Lunatics', to which Minor was committed after his trial in 1872.

Above: *In the Madhouse*, an engraving from William Hogarth's series of paintings *The Rake's Progress*. This version dates from 1765, and depicts the interior of the Bethlem Hospital – it is not difficult to see how the word 'bedlam' derives from the hospital's name.

Below: A coloured engraving by John Pass of the New Bethlem Hospital, St George's Fields, Lambeth, dating from 1814. Daniel M'Naghten, among others, was confined in Bedlam for twenty-one years before being transferred to Broadmoor. *(Creative Commons)*

Above: Julio Mora on Death Row in Florida. In April 1997 he was convicted of two counts of murder and one of attempted murder, and sentenced to be executed by lethal injection, despite his attempts to plead insanity. He cheated the executioner, however, for he died in prison of natural causes in 2016, aged eighty-nine. *(El Pais)*

Below: Thomas Dee Huskey, aka 'the Zoo Man', presently in prison for four rapes, although the attempt to convict him of four murders was declared a mistrial. His defence argued that he suffered from multiple personality disorder.

Above left: Ronald True, looking every inch the lounge lizard, in a photograph he had printed as a postcard. Although he had served as a pilot in the Royal Flying Corps during World War I, he was soon discharged, although that did not prevent him from falsely claiming to have flown in combat. *(© Mirrorpix/Alamy)*

Above right: Olive Young (real name Gertrude Yates), murdered by Ronald True on 6 March 1922. Although married, she made a good living as a high-class 'working girl'. *(© Mirrorpix/Alamy)*

Below: Ronald True at West London Police Court, where he was charged with the murder of Olive Young aka Gertrude Yates. Originally sentenced at the Old Bailey to hang, he was reprieved on the grounds of insanity, and sent to Broadmoor, where he died from a heart attack in 1951, aged fifty-nine. *(© Mirrorpix/Alamy)*

three for criminals – and could hold about 300 prisoners. The gallows – where some 131 people, four of them women, were hanged between 1800 and 1877, stood on the flat roof of the prison's gatehouse so that executions could be watched by all and sundry, the idea being that they would act as a deterrent to crime. Some hope – the crowds came for the spectacle and pickpockets had a field day. Charles Dickens was appalled when he attended one execution, writing to *The Times*: 'I believe that a sight so inconceivably awful as the wickedness and levity of the immense crowd collected at that execution this morning could be imagined by no man and could be presented in no heathen land under the sun.'

Yep, now I think about it, I bet you the park is haunted after all. On a related note, I think that the reader might well enjoy a great online article titled 'The Horrible History of Horsemonger Lane Gaol'. It's a cracker, and after reading it you might truly believe Newington Gardens is very busy during the dark hours and that you might bump into a few ghosts, or feel the hairs on the nape of your neck bristle as a lonely owl gives you another hoot from a tree. The connection with Minor? He was on remand here for a short time.

And why did he decide to leave America and travel to Europe in 1871? It seems that his family and friends encouraged him to travel in the hope that a change in surroundings would afford him some rest, which would help his mental condition. First, though, he went to 'the Smoke'. London had become a global political, financial and trading capital. The city grew wealthy as Britain's holdings expanded, and where there are lots of men with money there is also prostitution. Nineteenth-century London was also a place of poverty, where millions lived in overcrowded and unsanitary slums. And the place stank to high heaven. For centuries the Thames had been used as a dumping ground for waste, and as the population grew, so did this distasteful problem. In what would become known as the 'Great Stink' of the summer of 1858, raw sewerage flowed directly into the Thames, from which most residents drew their drinking water – which was then recycled back into the river ad infinitum.

One would have thought that being a medical person, Minor would have been aware that at that time London was one of the filthiest cities on the planet, so he didn't go there to improve his physical health. Absolutely not! He stopped off in London because in the Victorian age, the number of prostitutes there was staggeringly high. According to reports from the city's police, approximately 8,600 sex workers were known to them, and it has been suggested that the true number during this time was closer to 80,000. William Chester Minor would have been in his element.

Upon his arrival, it appears that Minor first booked into Radley's Hotel in the West End. Named after hotelier James Radley, whose first hotel was built in 1826 in Liverpool, this was a place for the 'posh', and future guests included world leaders such as Franklin D. Roosevelt and Winston Churchill. This would have been a short stay until Minor got the lie of the land, because in 1872 he took up lodgings at 41 Tenison Street in Lambeth (today Tenison Way). Back then, when the budding Jack the Ripper might have been your next-door neighbour, Tenison Street was lined with three-storey terraced houses that had basements and featured cast-iron balconies on the first floors. There was a pub on the corner where one could watch horses and carts and some other mongers, including sex-mongers, plying their trade.

At the risk of sounding a bit like Victor Meldrew from the late great TV sitcom *One Foot in the Grave*, may I suggest that when schoolchildren are on coach trips to London, their teachers or tour guides should point out that back in the nineteenth century the capital was a shithole; that the water people drank back then contained around 60 per cent faeces and other toxic substances too numerous, and too disgusting, to mention in this chapter. Instead, we ferry the kiddies around, fleetingly pointing out Buckingham Palace or Tower Bridge.

Talking of pubs and bars – which, to many British men these days have become second homes – Minor took a liking to the Lion Brewery. According to old maps, the place was very close to the Thames; its courtyard backing onto Belvedere Road, all part and parcel of the Lambeth Waterworks. And guess from whence the brewery drew its water? Yep, congratulations, you win a gold star! Talking of the Thames reminds me that 'Thames' is Old English *Temese*, from Latin *Tamesis* (51 BCE), from British *Tamesa*, an ancient Celtic river name most probably meaning 'dark one'.

It has crossed my mind, that for a man whose noble profession dictated that he save lives, if not like his parents who strived to save souls, Surgeon Minor could have found a better place to help his mental condition; let's say in Scarborough or Eastbourne or Ryde on the Isle of Wight.. But no. Gulping in foul air, supping ale watered down by the polluted Thames and surrounded by brothels, while also suffering from escalating paranoid delusions, Minor once again took up the dissolute life.

The golden rule

'Only two things are infinite, the universe and human stupidity, and I'm not sure about the former.'

Albert Einstein: German-born
theoretical physicist

As my readers across the world will know, if one plans to kill someone, it would be more than advisable – a golden rule, for the most obvious reasons – to try to accomplish this task and *not* get caught... But did William Chester Minor abide by this rule? He did not. He did not plan to kill anyone, but his paranoia was such that it led him to commit murder. He then allowed himself to be caught.

Extremist members of the Fenian society, he believed, had followed him across the Transatlantic and were trying to break into his rooms. So, when in the early hours of 17 February 1872, Minor saw a man hurrying along in the shadows, it was quite clear to him that this was one of his persecutors. Armed with a revolver, Minor chased after the man firing several times before fatally shooting him, then, when he reached the man, he pulled a knife out of his clothing – some reports say it was a Bowie knife – and stabbed the now prone figure. A nearby police constable hurried towards them, and, he later reported, when he shone his lantern on the fatally injured man's face, Minor remarked, 'Why, that is not the man I wanted.' The victim was George Merrett and he had been on his way to his job as stoker at the aforementioned

Lion Brewery. He had a family to support: six children and wife Eliza, who was in the processe of adding another kid to their brood. The constable arrested Minor and carted him off to the police station, from where he was later remanded to Horsemonger Lane Gaol.

The year 1872 is a notable date in the context of executions in the British Isles, because up until then the 'short drop' type of hanging was still practised; it had effectively remained in place since the Saxons had introduced it in the fifth century. In Minor's case, one might imagine the justices would have seen little reason not to sentence to death anyone who had shot dead a hardworking, devoted husband who had several children. But he would prove an exception.

For the record, the last short-drop hanging took place in Britain on 3 April 1877. John Henry Johnson was found guilty of the murder of Amos Waite and sentenced to hang. When he plunged through the trap at Armley Jail, Leeds, however, the rope broke. He fell to his knees and had to be recovered from the pit and hanged again, ten minutes later. *The Yorkshire Post* reported that Johnson 'struggled for four minutes'. I might add here that the hangman, Thomas Askern, was a bit of a botcher, for evidence of which go to executedtoday.com and search for the date 28 December 2012.

So why was Minor *not* hanged? This comes down to politics once again. Standing quietly in court was a quiet, educated man, from a religious American family, its roots dating back to the Pilgrim Fathers, a military surgeon attached to the Union Army, one who was a brevet captain to boot and someone who'd probably saved many lives during and after the Civil War. To execute such an individual – and an American citizen at that – did not seem wise... Added to which, he was by now exhibiting signs of being completely mad: several witnesses, including his half-brother, testified that he had on numerous occasions shown signs of persecution delusion, convinced that he was being poisoned or drugged in the night by people who wanted to kill him – indeed the London police had already received letters from him in which he made wild claims. In one such letter sent Scotland Yard and produced as evidence, Minor had written:

Sir, I was narcotised last night into a stupor from about two in the morning until after one this afternoon. I suspect this was some attempt to take my life in ways that would not be apparent – either in some such way, or by attempting to give it the colour of a suicide. My life may be taken any night … will you assist in the matter. I shall be glad to do so. I trust your agents are not to be bought over, as American police have been by money.

The most satisfying way out of this conundrum was to declare him insane. The slur on the American police must have been a deciding factor. He would be given a bed in Broadmoor Asylum in Berkshire. This would serve the law's purpose very nicely, it being a place that had been built specifically for the criminally insane. Here, Minor could still enjoy his military pension; and as he wasn't considered a danger to staff or other patients, he would be given the most comfortable of quarters. He could buy and read as many books as he required. And some time later, he would cut off most of his penis here. After all of which, he would be freed to return to from whence he came: the US of A.

But off we go now to Broadmoor. En route, our driver will tell you some of its history.

Broadmoor

Any book about madness in its myriad forms would be remiss in not mentioning Broadmoor Hospital. Completed in 1863, this psychiatric institution stood in a secured 21-hectare area on about 120 hectares of Berkshire moorland. It was designed by Sir Joshua Jebb, KCB, a royal engineer and the British surveyor-general of convict prisons. He liked moving about, did Sir Joshua, for he had participated in the Battle of Plattsburg on Lake Champlain during the war of 1812 and had also surveyed a route between Ottawa River and Kingston, where Lake Ontario flows into Saint Lawrence River. Among his many other notable achievements, this distinguished-looking man was involved in designing prisons and related buildings, including Pentonville Prison in London, Woking Convict Invalid Prison and Mountjoy Prison in Belfast. He was certainly the go-to-guy when it came to building a secure mental asylum.

Sir Joshua's written works include *Modern Prisons: their Construction and Ventilation* (1844), with plates, and the somewhat longwinded tome entitled *Manual for the Militia, of Fighting made Easy: a Practical Treatise on Strengthening and Defending Military Posts in reference to the Duties of a Force engaged in Disputing the Advance of an Enemy* (1853). Then there was *A Practical Treatise on the Duties to be Performed... at a Siege*, third edition (1860), and finally his *Reports and Observations on the Discipline and Management of Convict Prisons* (1863). So, when someone cooked up the idea to build a place to house the criminally insane, it was Sir Joshua's bell they rang first. He had all the experience, right? He knew how to keep people inside a building, keep other people out of a building, micromanage anyone within and fight off anyone trying to enter the building from without.

Straying a little from Sir Joshua's usual construction works, the original design for Broadmoor was more for a contemporary medical building than a prison *per se*. The prevailing Victorian attitude was one of strict moral rectitude. Furthermore the approach to mental health was one of locking people away so as to be neither seen nor heard – often ever again.

As we noted earlier, one of the earliest British asylums was 'Bethlem' in Beckenham, London. This place dates back to 1247, when it was a priory, but in 1330 opened as a hospital. 'In every society there are those tortured by their own mind – individuals born mentally ill or afflicted by mental illness after suffering a grave misfortune,' as Steven Casale observed in Huffpost in March 2016. 'But there was once an insane asylum so notorious that its very name entered the English language as words for "chaos", "mayhem" and "confusion".' Casale is, of course, referring to Bethlem Royal Hospital, aka 'Bedlam', and the more one studies the histories of these places, the more fascinating the whole subject of madness becomes. Its reputation has seen this famous institution inspire a number of horror books, films and TV series, most notably *Bedlam*, a 1946 B-movie starring Boris Karloff as 'Master George Sims' and Anna Lee as 'Nel Bowen'.

Bethlem was Europe's oldest centre devoted solely to the treatment of the mentally deranged. The place was designed and built by the Italian bishop Goffredo de Perfetti, and for some godforsaken reason he built it directly atop a sewer that frequently overflowed. (Drat, not the Thames again.) Originally serving as a sanctuary for the insane, it also helped to raise money for the Crusades *via* alms collections. It was not uncommon for monks and other religious figures to take in the indigent, who were often mentally ill; but one smells a rat here – well it was built over a sewer, after all – because slippery Goffredo siphoned off alms intended to help those with loose screws to financially back the Crusaders in their own series of religious wars, which were initiated, supported and sometimes directed by the Latin Church in the Middle Ages. And the name 'Bedlam'? Well, that came about from the locals who ranted and raved, muttered and moaned that it was 'bedlam *out* there and *in* there', probably on account of the racket these insane people made.

Those people who suffered from mental illnesses were generally either already confined in an asylum or com-passionately cared for by their families at home; however, it appears too that those unfortunates who were too far gone, so to speak (the 'Unwashed Unmanageable', as it were), were kicked out onto the streets and started begging, stealing and sleeping rough. This social dilemma provoked a debate in Parliament and a search for a solution that would not only ease the problem but also mollify the overcrowding in already crammed places of refuge.

And it is at this juncture we find the genesis for Broadmoor:

As the nineteenth century wore on, the local asylums became extremely reluctant to take criminal lunatics at all; they were unwelcome in the prisons as well because they disturbed other prisoners.

Dr Harvey Gordon: Consultant psychiatrist at Broadmoor, author of *Broadmoor: An Inside Story* (2011)

Broadmoor's buildings were built south facing to take in vast areas of what was then moorland, all designed to give the 'patients' nice views, which it was thought would help with their rehabilitation.

The asylum started off with three main erections to house the men (on which subject, the staff reportedly put something like bromide in the tea in mental hospitals to decrease male libido); however, the first completed construction on site was a smaller building providing beds. In later works, another two blocks were added to accommodate more men, and the convicts from Reading Gaol were gainfully employed with the construction of these buildings.

It almost goes without saying that a 10-foot wall around the place was a necessary requirement, with add-ons including outer buildings of red brick and an impressive gate. The windows all had bars, of course. The main gate had two imposing towers with an Edward John Dent clock between them. And who better than Dent to make this timepiece for, in 1814, his talents had been recognised when he was given the honour of making the first Standard Astronomical Clock for the Admiralty. In 1871, Dent made the Standard Clock at the Royal Observatory, Greenwich; and in a timely fashion he also made the Observatory's Secondary Standard Clock, which initiated the Greenwich Time Signal – aka the six 'pips' heard daily, on the hour, by the BBC, first broadcast in 1924. Without doubt, Edward Dent made exceedingly good clocks.

The Surgeon of Crowthorne

Considered a low-risk patient on his arrival at Broadmoor, Minor was allowed two rooms to himself, as well as a number of other privileges, including essentials provided through the good auspices of the US consulate. Once ensconced there, Minor had plenty of time on his hands and was able to buy whatever books he wanted, and it is believed that it is through his correspondence with a London bookseller, that he learned about the need for volunteers to help contribute to what was to become the *Oxford English Dictionary*. The *Yale Medicine Magazine* (winter 2009 issue), however, gives a slightly different account: 'In the early 1880s – perhaps nine or ten years into his incarceration – Minor came across a pamphlet that would change his life. It had probably been placed in one of the many books brought to him by his victim's widow.' And if that last bit stops you in your tracks, you should know that Minor had been sending Eliza Merrett his military pension, which at first she had refused. He had even paid one of the hospital's staff to take money to her, but she slammed the door in his face. But his persistence paid off and eventually they became good friends and it is believed that she would sometimes collect the books he'd ordered and bring them to him.

Whichever version is immaterial – the pamphlet in question was an appeal in 1879 for contributors to *A New English Dictionary on Historical Principles*, as the *OED* was then titled. The Philological Society, whose brainchild the dictionary was, had only that year persuaded Oxford University Press to publish it; also in that year, they appointed as editor James Augustus Henry Murray.

Born into a poor family in the village of Denholm in Roxburghshire on the Scotland/England border, James Murray had to leave school at the age of fourteen because his family could not afford to continue his education. He was, however, a voracious learner and continued his education during his spare time. When he was seventeen, he became a teacher at the local grammar school, and three years later headmaster of another school. He avidly pursued a life of scholarship, having a particular interest in languages and in philology. In 1863 he and his wife moved to London (for her health!), and he soon joined the Philological Society; by 1869 he was on its board. Knighted in 1908, Murray remained editor of the *OED* until his death in 1915.

James Murray followed his predecessor's idea of 'quotation slips', but improved the system considerably. He would send out the slips – on which contributors would be expected to write their findings – with a request that they should report 'as many quotations as you can for ordinary words' and for words that were 'rare, obsolete, old-fashioned, new, peculiar or used in a peculiar way'.

Minor was quick to put himself forward, welcoming the task with eagerness. He was happy to spend hours raking through the books in his library – which during the ten years or so that he'd been incarcerated had become very large and was still growing – and many more books that he ordered, some of them brought to him by Elizabeth Merrett, and that were sent to him– and identifying lines and passages containing specific words. He would mail vast numbers of quotations (a sample heads this chapter) to the editor, each accompanied by a lucid outline of the words' usage and examples of their early appearances in written works in the English language. The research suited Minor well and even seemed to serve as therapy – at least during the day, for at night he continued to be tormented by paranoia and vivid hallucinations. He worked for Murray with great success for some twenty years, for which he deserves our unreserved admiration. Indeed, in 1899, Murray paid a fulsome compliment to Minor's contributions, stating: 'We could easily illustrate the last four centuries from his quotations alone.'

After many years of correspondence, Murray, who had learned of Minor's idiosyncratic history, was invited, in January 1891, to lunch by the Superintendent of Broadmoor, David Nicolson, who also invited Minor. The occasion seems to have been a success and Murray and Minor remained friends for many years.

Terminal decline

Schizophrenia is sometimes described as a type of psychosis. It is a serious mental disorder in which people interpret reality abnormally, and it may result in a combination of hallucinations, delusions, disjointed thought processes and behaviour that impairs daily functioning. Schizophrenia can be disabling and many sufferers require lifelong treatment. The exact cause is unknown, but most mental health professionals believe that this condition is caused by a combination of genetic and environmental factors. It is also thought that some people are more vulnerable to developing the condition, and that it can be triggered by certain situations, such a stressful event or drug abuse.

While researching this chapter I came across the excellent CBC documentary *NCR: Not Criminally Responsible* (2013), produced by the National Film Board of Canada. In 1999, Sean Clifton stabbed a stranger, Julie Bouvier, outside a Walmart in Cornwall, Ontario. Clifton was found not criminally responsible for knifing his victim six times (although thankfully she survived) and he spent many years in the Brockville Psychiatric Hospital, Elizabeth Township, overlooking the banks of the St Lawrence River. I specifically mention this documentary because it is perhaps the most moving, in-depth, fly-on-the-wall TV doc of its type one could wish for, a bit of a tear-jerker too. And while watching it, I found myself comparing how Clifton's schizophrenic symptoms likely matched with those suffered by William Chester Minor. Actually, when Clifton was a very young lad he spent hours with a dictionary by his bedside, struggling to attach even a flyspeck of meaning to the words. Later, as he was being considered for parole, he learned basic PC skills; his first ever typed letter, printed from his word processor, he fearfully sent to his victim, Julie Bouvier. I won't say any more because I do not want to spoil your enjoyment of the documentary, but a large box of tissues at the ready, please.

As for William Chester Minor, after many years of

relative stability the turn of the century saw his mental state decline alarmingly. By 1902, when he was sixty-eight, he was regularly plagued with the delusion that he was being spirited away from his rooms at night to far-off lands and made to sexually assault children, and – as he explained to the authorities at Broadmoor – 'forced to fornicate with between fifty and one hundred women "from Reading to Land's End"'.

'Despite the therapeutic effects of his work on the dictionary,' Trainor notes in *Bedlam: St Mary of Bethlehem*, 'Minor's condition deteriorated over the years. The delusions and frustrations never left him.' Trainor had read some of the notes that Minor made, and speculates that 'sometimes he probably internalised them, and that when it all got too much he would suddenly explode, making an accusatory outburst to the attendants or the Super.' When his nightly sexual hallucinations finally became intolerable, Minor committed another alarmingly violent and destructive act – this time upon himself. Trainor: 'Eventually he took matters into his own hands, and on the morning of 3rd December 1902 he tied a tourniquet around the base of his penis and sliced off the offending organ.' When questioned about why he had so grievously injured himself, he bluntly replied: 'In the interests of morality.' If that was his aim, it was unsuccessful. Trainor relates, 'In his last letter to Dr Brayn, shortly before his discharge, Minor was complaining still of "these nightly sensual uses of my body that I experience and struggle against".'

Minor's story had reached the ears of James Murray and his wife, who were now vigorously campaigning for his release from Broadmoor and, in 1910, on the orders of the then home secretary, thirty-five-year-old Winston Churchill, Minor was deported back to America. On 15 April 1910, he was escorted to the Tilbury Docks, where he was handed over to his half-brother and put aboard a steamer for the journey across the Atlantic and to the St Elizabeth's Hospital in Washington, DC, where he had been confined forty-two years earlier.

It was there that he finally received the firmest diagnosis of dementia praecox, an early term for schizophrenia. A year before his death from pneumonia he was transferred, still delusional, to the Retreat for the Elderly Insane in Hartford, Connecticut, where he was nearer to his family. Minor died on 26 March 1920 aged eighty-five and was buried alongside members of his family in New Haven's Evergreen Cemetery in March 1920; where his headstone may be viewed. Yale University, in reporting his death at the time, noted solely that during his stay in England 'he was found to be mentally deranged... and [in Broadmoor] he remained... gradually recovering his mental balance [which he didn't], and devoting his time to scholarly pursuits.' Though Minor's sanity was never restored, and tragedy haunted him to the end, we might say he found a kind of redemption in the outstanding contributions he made to the *Oxford English Dictionary*. Proving that being clinically insane needn't stop you from being one of the most learned people on the planet – which should give us all hope, don't you think?

From the Code of Hammurabi: the insanity defence from its earliest days

'God ordered me to kill prostitutes because they were killing men with that disease; I only had sex with them just to find out who had AIDS or not.'

US SERIAL KILLER ARTHUR JOHN SHAWCROSS:
LETTER TO THE AUTHOR

The first recorded usage of the insanity defence can be found in Hammurabi's Code, which stated that those who were seen as unable to distinguish between good and evil were considered to be insane. By extension, if the accused were not able to distinguish between good and evil, they were found guilty of the crime but were in another sense considered not guilty – a view echoed in the much later M'Naghten rule (see p. 70).

Reportedly proclaimed by the Babylonian King Hammurabi, who reigned from around 1792 to 1750 BCE, the Hammurabi Code of Laws is a collection of 282 rules that were developed during his reign. These established standards for commercial interactions and set fines and punishments to meet the requirements of justice. The code was carved onto a 4-ton, finger-shaped, 7-foot 5-inch tall black diorite stele (pillar) that was looted by invaders and finally discovered in 1901in what is now Iran. Which raises the question: how does one make off with a 4-ton pillar? It was in three large pieces when found, but a one-ton lump of stone would have been hard enough for a pillager to filch.

During the days of the Roman Empire, the government found obviously unhinged citizens to be 'non-compos mentis', meaning 'without control of the mind' and so they were seen as not guilty of their criminal actions. One might imagine that *not* being nailed to a cross, thrown from a cliff into a river, buried alive or being sewn into a heavy sack with a rooster, a snake, a monkey and a dog, would have come as some relief even to a gibbering cretin who been caught committing a capital crime. Murdering a person of equal standing was considered worthy of just a few lashes and some stone-breaking, but if one were pot-less, pinch a grain of rice from a dignitary and oh boy, were you in deep shit!

A number of significant variations on the theme of insanity law arose over the centuries before the emergence of M'Naghten. An early example being the 'good and evil' test. May I direct you to the Bible and Exodus 21: 12–14:

He who strikes a man so that he dies shall surely be put
    to death.
However, if he did not lie in wait, but God delivered

him into his hand, then I will appoint for you a place where he may flee.

But if a man acts with premeditation against his neighbour, to kill him by treachery, you shall take him from My altar, that he may die.

New King James Version

For my part, I am rather taken by Proverbs 26: 18–19. It's a bit more to the point, I think:

Like a madman who throws firebrands, arrows and death,
Is the man who deceives his neighbour,
And says, 'I was only joking!'

Exodus is full of great and cruel punishments. Aside from the Ten Commandments, it tells you what to do with idols and altars, how to handle Hebrew servants (if you have any), and issues surrounding personal injuries, the protection of property, social responsibility and laws of justice and mercy.

Let's fast-forward to another major step in the concept of insanity defence: the emergence of the 'wild beast test'. In the fourteenth century, King Edward II – who seems to have been slightly more civilised than many of his contemporaries (which is not saying much) – upheld the assertion in 1256 of Judge Henry de Bracton that an insane person was not morally responsible because he was 'not far removed from brute beasts'. Under English Common law, Edward II declared, a person was deemed insane if their mental capabilities were no greater than a 'wild beast's' Meaning any wild animal from a squirrel to his pet lion (that presumably did not understand such commands as 'sit' or 'fetch'). The first recorded instance of the use of the 'wild beast test' is thought to be the 1724 British case of *Rex v. Edward Arnold*, in which Lord Chief Justice Robert Tracy leaned towards ruling the defendant to be acquitted by reason of insanity because Arnold did not know what he was doing, and was doing no more than a 'wild beast'. The deluded Arnold had shot and wounded one Lord Onslow, convinced that his lordship was controlling and torturing him. With imps, no less. The jury didn't buy into it. After the trial, a certain Sir Mathew Hale recalled Chief Justice Tracy's words to the jury:

> This is the evidence on both sides. Now, I have laid before you; and you must consider of it; and the shooting of my Lord Onslow, which is the fact for which this prisoner is indicted, is proved beyond all contradiction; but whether this shooting was malicious, that depends upon the sanity of the man.
>
> That he shot, and that wilfully is proved; but whether maliciously, that is the thing; that *is* the question; whether this man hath the use of his reason and his senses? *If* he was under the visitation of God and could not distinguish between good and evil, and did not know what he did, though he committed the greatest offence, yet he could not be guilty of any offence against any law whatsoever; for guilt arises from the mind, and the wicked will and intention of the man. If a man be deprived of his reason, and consequently of his intention, he cannot be guilty;

and if that be the case, though he had actually killed my Lord Onslow, he is exempt from punishment; punishment is intended for example and to deter other persons from wicked designs; but the punishment of a madman, a person that hath no design, can have no example. This is one side.

On the other side, we must be very cautious; it is not every frantic and idle humour of a man that will exempt him from justice, and the punishment of the law. When a man is guilty of a great offence, it must be very plain and clear, before a man is allowed such an exemption; therefore, it is not every kind of frantic humour or something unaccountable in a man's actions that points him out to be such a madman as is to be exempted from punishment; it must be a man that is totally deprived of his understanding and memory, and doth not know what he is doing, no more than an infant, than a brute, or a wild beast, such a one is never the object of punishment; therefore, I must leave it to your consideration... whether he was doing good or evil, and understood what he did; and it is to be observed, [the defence] admit he was a lunatic, and not an idiot. A man that is an idiot, that is born so, never recovers, but a lunatic may, and hath his intervals; and they admit he was a lunatic.

You are to consider what he was that day, when he committed this act. There you have many great circumstances about the powder and the shot, his going backward and forward, and if you believe he was sensible, and had the use of his reason and understood what he did, then he is not within the exemptions of the law, but is as subject to punishment as any other person.

This was quite the most remarkably fair set of legal instructions that could be given to any trial jury; however the defendant failed the 'insanity test'. Edward Arnold was found to be sane and was sentenced to hang... but afterwards reprieved at the request of Lord Onslow, the very gentleman he'd tried to kill. In my book that makes his lordship a very fine fellow indeed.

A traitor is everyone who does not agree with me... Once vigorous measures appear to be the only means left of bringing the Americans to a due submission to the mother country, the colonies will submit.

King George III, sounding a bit like the present-day Donald Trump

The pivotal case in the history of insanity defence occurred in London during the reign of King George III, aka 'Farmer George', who himself was pretty much permanently deranged during his later years. He suffered from 'acute mania' which was possibly a symptom of the genetic disease porphyria. Treatment for mental illness was primitive by modern standards, and the king's doctors treated His Highness by forcibly restraining him until he was calm, or applying caustic poultices to draw out 'evil humours' – and there isn't anything humorous about that treatment, I can assure the reader!

On 15 May 1800, James Hadfield (sometimes written as 'Hatfield') discharged a horse pistol at the King as he entered the royal box at the Theatre Royal in Drury Lane, London – and by heck, just as the national anthem had started and His Majesty was standing to attention. Yet the-would-be assassin missed his target. As the black powder smoke cleared away – along with most of the people in the stalls down below, probably – Hadfield said to the King: 'God bless your royal highness. I like you very well. You are a good fellow.' But this quick thinking didn't prevent him for being tried for high treason, during which time three doctors gave their opinions as to his state of mind: Hadfield was as mad as a hatter, so his plea was insanity.

Aside from the fact that Hadfield was patently not a decent shot, the case itself was somewhat pedestrian, with the defendant maintaining that he had acted alone. That wasn't entirely true. The idea for the assassination attempt had been instigated by Bannister Trulock (sometimes spelt 'Truelock'), a shoemaker whom Hadfield knew. And here, I'd like to quote from Sophia Gal's enlightening blog post 'James Hadfield, The French Revolution and the Redefinition of Insanity' which you can find on the Bethlem Museum of the Mind website:

Trulock was a 'millenarian', who believed that he was a 'true descendant of God', that 'the Virgin Mary was a bloody whore, that Jesus Christ was a thief, and that God Almighty was a blackguard', and that he would destroy the world within three days. When questioned in Hadfield's trial, he brazenly admitted, 'I told [Hadfield] he might be a very great man… by becoming my Son.'

The jury ultimately concluded that Hadfield was not guilty. This displeased the House of Commons. Thus, the Criminal Lunatics Act of 1800 was passed on July 28th that year. This act meant that if a court found an individual unfit to plead, he would be confined 'at His Majesty's Pleasure'… The bill was introduced [by the attorney-general, Sir John Freeman-Mitford, later first Baron Redesdale], on the grounds that insane people who are acquitted continue to commit crimes, and these people are usually unfortunates with few friends or family to look after them.

Changing tack for a moment or two, as is often the case when some form of conspiratorial mental disillusionment sets in, it is worth noting, Gal writes, that 'Hadfield's co-defendant, Bannister Trulock, was one of many "British Jacobins" who supported the French Revolution and its ideals. Their beliefs included opposition of taxes, greater access to education for the poor, and opposition to the monarchy'– and not much has changed, since today the rich get richer and the poor keep getting poorer. 'Such groups were forced underground through political suppression, and their leaders would be tried for treason.'

'Sympathisers of the French Revolution had an affinity for apocalyptic symbolism and anticipation of a religious millennium as well a political one,' Gal continues, referencing Richard Moran's 1985 article for *Law & Society Review* 'The

Origin of Insanity as a Special Verdict: The Trial for Treason of James Hadfield (1800)', 'As such, self-styled prophets (among them Trulock himself) emerged in the 1790s. They saw the struggles as a prelude to the end of the world and the second coming of Christ.'

Hadfield's case was not the first assassination attempt on the 'Farmer King'. In 1786, George III was attacked by a certain Margaret Nicholson. Ten years later a stone had been half-heartedly thrown at him by one John Frith. Both assailants were judged to be stark-raving bonkers. Nevertheless, the king rightly feared for his life.

Along with Trulock, Hadfield was detained in Bethlem Royal Hospital ('Bedlam') in Southwark. While confined here, Trulock murdered another inmate, Benjamin Swain, by punching him. The death was determined to be accidental. In *Sketches in Bedlam*, published in 1823 under the pen name 'A Constant Observer' (possibly one of the hospital's attendants, James Smyth), the writer says of Hadfield that 'his impatience of confinement sours his temper, in spite of all the indulgences allowed him.' He is described as 'ever grumbling and discontented without cause, and finds fault with every thing'. More positively, he made 'handsome straw baskets', which he then sold to visitors.

One of Hadfield's visitors was Flore Celestine Thérèse Henriette Tristán y Moscoso, better known as 'Flora Tristan', the French-Peruvian grandmother of the artist Paul Gaugin. A socialist activist, writer and proto-feminist, her publications include *Peregrinations of a Pariah* (1838), *Promenades in London* (1840) and *The Workers' Union* (1843). Flora reported that Hadfield owned two dogs, three cats, some birds and a squirrel called 'Jack'. He wrote and illustrated epitaphs for each of these pets after they died. Bless him.

And at this point I am obliged to digress once again, so please forgive me. Flora Tristan's account of visiting Hadfield highlights another aspect of life in Bethlem. Its name has been blackened more than once over the years, so by way of redressing the balance let's consider the following.

'Pawprints in the Hospital'

In an undated article bearing the above title, written for the Society for the Social History of Medicine by Isobel Toy of the University of Birmingham, the writer refers to George Augustus Sala. A journalist who wrote both for the *Daily Mail* and the *Illustrated London News,* Sala paid a visit to Bethlem in 1860.

'Whilst there,' Toy writes, '[Sala] noted the obvious presence of animals on the wards and, following his visit, documented their ability to uplift patients and soothe the minds of the "unhappy persons who dwell [there]". In particular, he commented on the use of bird song to transport patients' minds to "green fields"... [and] sparkling streams.' However, she reminds us that beneficial effect of the presence of animals on mentally troubled individuals was nothing new. Some sixty years earlier, the same approach had been adopted at a Quaker-run asylum near York called 'The Retreat', founded in 1792 by philanthropist William Tuke, a tea merchant and his family. 'William knew nothing about mental health when he started this unique organisation, but he cared about people; he cared about equality and he wanted to share hope,' notes The Retreat's official website.

According to Bethlem's records, on 27 July 1802, Hadfield escaped. He was caught five days later and sent to Newgate Prison for fourteen years. On 25 March 1821, a Dr John Monro reported that Hadfield was now sane, and keenly wished to be removed from Bethlem. On Christmas Day, 1826, Dr Monro again reported that Hadfield was sane, adding 'but of weak capacity'. Our 'Birdman of Bedlam' died in 1841. Bannister Trulock had passed away in Bethlem on 2 November 1830

NB: a fascinating account entitled 'The Monro dynasty and their treatment of madness in London', can be found online (see *Neurosciences and History* 2015; 3(30: 116-124), and I would recommend it to anyone interested in the treatment of madness in the eighteenth century, which had changed little over hundreds of years. One of the most powerful influences over the management of the insane in London, the Monro dynasty (1728–1882) comprised five generations of physicians, four of whom practised at Bethlem.

But what of those 'origins of the insanity defence' referred to in the heading for this chapter, one of the main foundations for this book? Lawyers and shrinks have been abusing Lord Chief Justice Robert Tracy's most honourable instructions to Hadfield's jury right up until this very day, and will continue to do so ad infinitum. In 1840, the standard for insanity was further clarified in the case of *R. v. Edward Oxford*. The defendant was found to be suffering from the effect of a 'diseased mind', and was 'quite unaware of the nature, character and consequences of the act he was committing'. This ruling redefined insanity, and set the stage for the major rules on insanity that were soon to follow. And again, it revolved around the attempted assassination of a British monarch.

The Edward Oxford trial for High Treason was held on 9–11 July 1840 at the Central Criminal Court, more familiarly known as the Old Bailey, before Lord Chief Justice Denman, sitting with fellow judges Baron Alderson and John Patteson. The charge? High treason, no less. On 10 June 1840, as Queen Victoria, then pregnant with her first child, and her husband Prince Albert were driving up Constitution Hill in an open carriage, she was fired at twice by an unemployed Londoner, eighteen-year-old Edward Oxford. He missed, and the couple continued their journey. No bullets were found, and neither were any bullet holes, and it is very likely that there was only powder in the two guns that Oxford was carrying. He made no attempt to escape, and indeed seemed to be at pains to draw attention to himself.

At his trial a number of witnesses, including neighbours and medical men, attested to Oxford's weak mental state/ A picture emerges of a troubled and troublesome child, given to fits of manic laughter or bursting into tears: 'a very peculiar boy,' said one acquaintance, while doctors remarked that he seemed of 'deficient understanding' ... 'an occasional appearance of acuteness, but a total inability to reason' ... 'imbecility' ... 'decidedly of unsound mind' ... The verdict was 'Not Guilty being insane. To be detained at Her Majesty's pleasure.'

In short, Edward Oxford was found 'not guilty by reason of insanity', and sent to Bethlem Hospital. There from being what would now be termed a 'disturbed youth', Oxford became an apparently sane, educated and talented individual who had taught himself multiple languages, learned how to knit and also to play the violin, and who could draw, paint and play chess. His case notes read: 'With regard to his crime he now laments the act which probably originated in a feeling of excessive vanity and a desire to become notorious if he could not be celebrated.' In 1864, he was transferred to the newly opened Broadmoor Hospital. He was now in his early forties and began to petition for release. Eventually, and on condition that he never returned to the United Kingdom, he departed for Australia, where, under his new name of John Freeman, reportedly made a success of his life. His case is interesting because he was not truly insane but appeared so as he was a very disturbed young man at the time of the shooting. That the guns were not loaded must have played in his favour, too.

So how do we get from back then to now? Well ... three years after Oxford's trial came that of Daniel M'Naghten, which in turn led to the formulation of the M'Naghten rules (see pp 55—70) in which the defendant in a criminal case is assumed sane unless it can be shown otherwise, in an effort to clarify the degree of responsibility an accused individual might have had for their actions. As the discipline of psychology established itself, and the complexity of the human mind and of mental conditions were recognised, so did assessing a person's mental capacity and its relationship to a crime they might have carried out become more complicated.

Under different jurisdictions worldwide the concept of insanity as a defence differs to some extent, as does the definition of insanity in legal cases, which is scarcely surprising given how complicated it is. In most countries, it is up to the defendant to prove that they are insane, which might inspire a few to try to produce Oscar-winning performances.

Broadly speaking, the insanity defence, in some countries known as the 'mental disorder defence', is an affirmative defence by way of 'excuse' in a criminal trial, arguing that a defendant is not responsible for their actions because of a psychiatric illness, or an episode of psychiatric illness at the time they committed the criminal act in question; also to be taken into consideration is the question of the defendant's mental condition and whether they are actually fit to stand trial at all. These days in the UK, Ireland and the US, use of the insanity defence is rare. Mitigating factors – including intoxication – are more commonly taken into account,

There are also, in English law, mitigating factors known as 'partial defences to murder' – these may be the defence of 'loss of control', or the defence of 'diminished responsibility' (aka 'diminished capacity').

Under 'loss of control', where the accused person *is* responsible, but the responsibility is lessened due to a temporary mental state, may fall self-defence or defence of another (if, for example, a thug punches your toddler in the face) or provocation, for instance,

an argument between two people becomes more and more heated, with each provoking the other, and in a fit of rage A kills B: his defence would be that he was provoked beyond endurance.

Under 'diminished responsibility', mitigating factors might include a psychotic episode brought on by medication or some other trigger. Alcoholic intoxication is usually an exception unless *involuntary*, which could be hard to prove.

By way of an example of provocation combined with intoxication, a little personal story. Not so long ago I was invited to lunch in Brighton by a very senior former Scottish judge.. Quite a remarkable man, he related a murder trial that he had 'refereed'. The facts were as follows: a man and his wife invited a male friend around for drinks. Both men became drunk, things got out of hand and the guest began making sexually explicit remarks and suggestions to the wife. When he was ordered to leave, he refused. A knife was produced and during the struggle the guest was stabbed through the heart. The prosecution had charged the defendant with murder; the defence was one of provocation. Over luncheon, my friend and host explained to me that as far as he was privately concerned, the defendant was guilty. The jury retired and just ten minutes later they returned with a unanimous verdict of not guilty, which stunned the court *and* the judge. The defendant rose to his feet and shouted: 'Well, how else is a Scotsman supposed to get rid of an unwelcome guest who won't leave his house?' A cheer went up, leaving the irate judge to storm off to his chambers.

Dr Julio Mora: a tale with a remarkable twist

'Bravo! Bravo, Judge!'

DR JULIO MORA, AS JUDGE PAUL L. BACKMAN FINISHED
READING OUT THE TWENTY-EIGHT-PAGE ORDER IN WHICH HE
EXPLAINED WHY THE PRISONER SHOULD BE EXECUTED
BY LETHAL INJECTION

I first came across this fascinating case many years ago. Dr Julio Mora died from natural causes some years ago, but at the time he came to my attention he was aged seventy-two and was then the oldest man on Florida's death row. Questions about his mental health had surrounded Mora's trial from the very beginning. In brief, this man's bizarre case is as follows.

On 30 April 1997, Mora was convicted of two counts of first-degree murder. The victims were his former boss, fifty-four-year-old Clarence Rudolph, and attorney Karen Starr Marx, aged thirty, who at the time was four months pregnant with her first child. Mora was also found guilty of attempted first-degree murder for shooting Ruldolph's attorney, Maurice Hall.

Broward County Court papers reveal that three years earlier, on 27 May 1994, Mora had been the plaintiff in a $10-million employment suit, which he then made into a sexual harassment suit against his former employer, the American Association of Retired Persons (AARP). In this litigation, Clarence Rudolph, who was project director for AARP, was represented by Maurice Hall, while Karen Marx acted for AARP. Mora acted on his own behalf. Also present was court reporter Patricia Charelton – later Grant – and the deposition was held at Coastal Reporting Court Reporting Agency located on the sixth floor of the Cumberland Building in Broward County, Florida.

So far so good, but suddenly things went south.

Prior to the deposition, Hall had arranged the seating in the room so that Rudolph and Mora were physically separated as much as possible. When Mora turned up, he objected to this set-up, yet despite his protests nothing was changed and the deposition began at around 10 a.m. As those being deposed spoke with foreign accents, the court reporter Patricia Grant used a tape recorder as well as her stenography machine.

Some thirty minutes into the deposition, Mora suddenly announced that he had one more question. This surprised Patricia, even more so when she looked up and saw him standing with a 9-millimetre automatic pistol in his hand. The tape of this deposition reveals that she shouted, 'No, no, no, Dr Mora, no!' One bullet fatally struck Rudolph, another round hit Hall and another hit Marx, then Mora let off another volley of shots. As the terrified Patricia Grant fled the room, she turned and saw Mora lean over the table and shoot Marx again. Although he'd been shot, Maurice Hall had hidden until he saw a chance to make a bolt for the nearest door. A bullet struck the door frame as he left the room, with Mora in hot pursuit. A scuffle ensued before Hall wrestled the now jammed handgun away from his assailant, then Brett Tannenbaum, owner of Coastal Reporting, restrained the out-of-control Mora until the police arrived.

For the firearms aficionado, the tape used by Patricia Grant reveals that ten shots were discharged within forty-eight seconds. Shots one through nine occurred in the first seventeen seconds, with the final round being fired thirty-one seconds later. After the initial barrage of shots, Marx can be heard crying out, 'Help me, help me, help me,' before the final shot. Paramedics took the unconscious Karen Marx to Broward General Medical Center, where she died on the operating table about two hours later.

The medical examiner, Dr Nelson, determined at autopsy that the pregnant Marx received four gunshot wounds, one of which went through her uterus, while Rudolph also had four gunshot wounds, including one to the back of the head. 'One of the bullets may have caused two of the wounds,' Nelson reported, meaning an entry and exit wound as the round had been fired at point-blank range. For his part, Maurice Hall later testified that he received two gunshot wounds: one to his abdomen and one to his shoulder. None of this would have happened if Coastal Reporting Court

Reporting Agency had not allowed the defendant to stroll in with a loaded gun in his pocket, of course.

Let's back up a tad here. Thus far we have learned quite a bit about the M'Naghten rule, its various variants, and what constitutes a valid insanity defence or not. In this case, we know that Mora, a plaintiff in a lawsuit, entered the deposition room perhaps not the happiest person in the world and tooled up with an automatic pistol. Suddenly, he rose to his feet and started shooting at innocent and vulnerable people. Under Florida statute this type of mass shooting qualifies for the death penalty, and to my mind rightly so. So what could *possibly* be his defence? In a nutshell, it rested on his reported 'persecutory delusional disorder', which led Mora to believe that his victims, particularly Rudolph, were out to kill him.

Ah, so it was all provocation, was it?

Mounds of defence psychiatric testimony

Three mental health experts testified that dating back to the mid-1970s Mora had had suffered more than the odd mid-life crisis. He was once evicted from an apartment because he had wired his front doorknob to the electricity supply. Inside another apartment, he had built a makeshift hut to keep out laser beams, which he imagined were being sent by his wife.

Yes, yes, I get it that many of us have our own matrimonial differences from time to time; oft-times with the missus cutting up one's clothes or repainting one's Porsche in many colours. The first question I would have asked in this case would have been: 'Where did the disgruntled Mrs Mora get a laser from? Walmart?'

The evening before the 1994 deposition, Dr Mora had squirted foam sealer into his home's electrical sockets, judiciously placed fans to keep the air circulating and installed a giant exhaust fan in the front window. Then he rigged up an oxygen tent above his bed. He did this, he said, because Rudolph and his associates were regularly pumping toxic gas into his apartment at night; he added that he'd had to take several pills that morning.

But this wasn't the end of it by a long chalk.

'A man who is his own lawyer has a fool for a client' is an English proverb meaning that if a person who has not studied law is trying to defend himself in court then he's a fool. The proverb is said to have first appeared in print in Henry Kett's book *The Flowers of Wit*, published in 1814. However, like all things, there is a dispute over this. Prominent legal writer Bryan A. Garner states that a variant of this saying has been traced back to 1809 in Philadelphia: 'He who is always his own counsellor will often have a fool for his client.'

Perhaps the most famous example in this context was Theodore 'Ted' Robert Bundy who, during his trial for the Chi Omega murders and assaults in June 1979, and despite enjoying the assistance of five court-appointed defence attorneys, demanded that he handle most of his own defence. From the beginning, he sabotaged his attorneys' efforts out of spite, distrust and grandiose delusion. He even fired several of them who were trying to save him from 'Ole Sparky'. The egotistical narcissist Bundy *could* have accepted a plea-bargain arrangement whereby he would have received a life sentence. Instead, he refused the deal and was executed in Florida's electric chair on 24 January 1989.

Prior to Mora's trial in 1997, the court conducted a mental competency hearing, after which the trial court found him competent and able to fully understand the nature of the proceedings. Jury selection began on 7 April, with the trial itself starting three days later. Very much like the Bundy trial, from the outset there was disagreement between Mora and his guilt phase counsel, Dennis Colleran, over strategy – among other things, his counsel wished to contact Mora's siblings in Spain, which the defendant was firmly against. Mora wanted primarily to pursue a self-defence theory, a ploy doomed from the get-go. Wisely, Colleran advised they opt for an insanity defence citing the Florida Statue 775.027, which is all but the same as the M'Naghten rule. Mora finally agreed with his attorney, and a queue of witnesses gave evidence describing Mora for many years having lived quite the most abnormal existence. Apparently he had constantly filed police reports alleging that people were attempting to kill him, usually by piping gas into his apartment.

Testifying in his own defence, Mora described an incident where another of Rudolph's associates by the name of Wong Chung shot out one of his tyres the day before the shootings. Law enforcement did in fact find a shredded tyre in the boot of his car, but there was no evidence to suggest that it had been shot at.

Enough already? Um, no!

Mora further testified that his actions were in self-defence, because during the deposition, a masked gunman, whom he believed was Wong Chung, opened the conference-room door and pointed a pistol equipped with a silencer at him. At that, Mora said, he threw his briefcase at Chung's head.

According to him, Rudolph threw himself down to the floor to snatch his (Mora's) gun, and Marx seemed to be reaching to take a gun from her bag. He said that at that moment a memory from 1936 came to him of watching two brown-shirted Nazi soldiers kill two emaciated Jewish boys.

Notwithstanding this, and despite another mental competency hearing on 20 March 1997, the jury found Mora guilty of first-degree murder. He was sentenced to death on 21 October 1998.

The competency hearings

During the first competency hearing conducted on 20 March 1997, the court had accepted testimony from Dr Patsy Ceros-Livingston, Dr Trudy Block-Garfield, Dr John Spencer and Dr Thomas H. Macaluso. As might be expected, differences of opinion between them began to emerge.

For the defence, Dr Ceros-Livingston from Fort Lauderdale opined that Mora suffered from paranoid schizophrenia and was not competent to stand trial. She testified that the defendant had a delusional belief system which influenced how he viewed events. She also noted that he had previously been in court, charged with mostly minor or unproven offences.

For the State, Dr Trudy Block-Garfield claimed that Mora was very manipulative, but she also concluded that he was competent.

Dr Spencer claimed that Mora met all the competency criteria and therefore was fit to stand trial, adding that he had the ability to understand humour.

Dr Thomas Macaluso, however, indicated that while

Mora satisfied many of the competency factors, he was not competent because he could not testify relevantly or disclose important facts to his attorneys.

The reader will appreciate that in this case, and there are thousands of similar ones every year, forensic psychiatric opinion is all over the shop. As for it being a real forensic science, it is about as far away as you and me and the 'Man on the Moon', which is most certainly not made of cheese!

The appeal

At his appeal hearing, aside from some trivial arguments put up by Mora at trial – one being that he was not allowed to give a final statement – he fell back on arguing that he had been entitled to an involuntary intoxication jury instruction, and he knew enough to cite a number of cases from the Fourth District recognising an involuntary intoxication defence. This argument came too late in the day, however, and fell apart at the seams.

In a nutshell, involuntary intoxication was not in his case seen as defence for murder. During his trial Mora had testified that Rudolph had gassed him in his apartment the night before the shooting, and claimed that this had happened on earlier nights too. Unlike the previous alleged gassings however, according to Mora, the gas that Rudolph used this final night was different – this time, he said, it was chlorofluorocarbon, or CFC – a refrigerant. He claimed that the gas caused him to pass out but that the gassing ceased about 2:30 a.m. At 3:30 a.m., he said, he went to the bathroom, vomited and took a cold shower. He got dressed, he said between 4 and 4:30 a.m., adding that Rudolph called him several times on the phone and threatened him. No telephonic records could be found to support this claim.

To further try to wheedle his way out of this fine mess he had gotten himself into, Mora claimed that at some unspecified time in the morning he took several drugs – Percodan, Darvocet and Tylenol 3, all for pain, to which he added for good measure the muscle relaxants Inderal and Flexeril. There was no evidence in any medical records that he was prescribed these drugs, or that he was allowed to mix any alleged prescriptions. It is more than likely that if he had taken all of this medication, he would have been lucky to even be able to stand up, yet he armed himself with a pistol and then called a taxi at 9 a.m., to visit the sheriff's department and then to the deposition chambers because he felt 'like zombie' and 'was totally drugged'. Those who met Mora that morning claimed that he was able to successfully conduct himself, and that he was not in any way acting abnormally. The taxi driver had testified that Mora was 'a perfect gentleman', was not nervous and engaged him in a conversation. Ana Benitez, a community service aide stationed at the sheriff's office, gave evidence that Mora came in early that morning and had asked for the location of the records department and the bathroom. Surviving victim Maurice Hall testified that initially Mora had what he described as an 'appropriate demeanour' during the deposition, and although Mora was not skilled as a lawyer, the man's performance was consistent with other *pro se* ('for oneself, on one's own behalf') litigants Hall had seen. The court stenographer Patricia Grant said that Mora was able to conduct the deposition, and that it had not in itself been unusual. Her tape recording reveals that Mora was able to articulate questions, and the first police officer on the scene, Officer Hoelbrandt, had told the court that Mora was calm and told him to 'be fair'. Therefore, in this instance, there was no evidence suggesting that Mora was under the influence of any gases or drugs at the time of the shootings – yet another reason why the involuntary intoxication defence would not fly.

Bullshit *almost* baffled some brains

'This man should be in a mental institution.'
Officer Hoelbrandt after the trial

Although some of Mora's mitigation *did* find favour with the court, the jury were persuaded that Mora was sane. That he was given a fair trial and a fair appeal is not in question. Indeed, the trial court bent over backwards to accommodate his every whim, despite his occasional ramblings when he went way off beam. The reader will see some similarities with the M'Naghten case above; perhaps similarities such as suffering under a delusional impression that people were trying to hurt him did carry some weight during the jury's deliberations; likewise that Mora was a good employee. That he had had a difficult childhood carried little to no weight. Neither did the fact that he had long-standing emotional problems, had previously committed minor criminal offences, and a history of mental illness in his family, carry any weight. He had vehemently argued that his counsel was 'ineffective', which was patently untrue. So finally, it was firmly established that Mora had fully understood the criminality of his actions; he understood the trial proceedings, was able to instruct his lawyers and was mentally capable of conforming to the requirements of the law. He was ruled guilty.

The twist? Rewind to 1984 and the trial of one Mario Zamora who had been charged with the attempted murder of his wife Sylvia the year before. They were in the process of getting divorced and were engaged in a custody battle over their thirteen-year-old daughter. They were reportedly in the laundry room of their Miami apartment when their arguing became increasingly heated and then escalated into a physical struggle. In the course of this, Zamora, who had a loaded gun in his pocket, pulled it out and shot his wife twice.

Fortunately, she survived (and presumably got custody of their daughter). At his trial for attempted murder, Zamora undertook to represent himself, pleading self-defence. He presented himself and his case well, and, as there was little evidence to prove or disprove that he had acted in self-defence, he was acquitted.

Some time after that little episode, Mario Zamora changed his name – to Dr Julio Mora (the title to add weight, perhaps).

Julio Mora was seventy-two years old at the time of the appeal, and there were further appeals, but the sentence was upheld. It can often take decades of legal wranglings before an execution is slated, and it was so with Mora. In 2016, still on death row, he died of natural causes. He was eighty-nine.

Thomas Dee Huskey:
aka the 'Zoo Man'

'After [a rape-strangulation murder] I throwed off down and left her lying there.'

THE ANGRY VOICE OF THOMAS HUSKEY SCREAMING
OUT AT TRIAL, KNOXVILLE, TENNESSEE, 1999

Having looked up all of the notable people who have lived in Knoxville, Tennessee, I can tell you that architects, painters and a few photographers get a good showing. There are a lot of tycoons – some as bent as paper clips – there is former mayor George Dempster, the stolid inventor of the uniquely named 'Dempster-Dumpster'. We find Rex David 'Call me Hamburger Dave' Thomas, restaurant owner/ founder of Wendy's and whose wife was called Lorraine; his mother's name was Molly – so who was Wendy? Only 'Call me Hamburger Dave' knows. Others listed are some writers James Agee and Cormac McCarthy, the renowned film director Quentin Tarantino, and the lovely actress/

singer Polly Bergen, who was born there in 1930. And there are many more. Yet, Thomas Huskey signally fails to get a mention.

In Thomas Huskey, we find a man who kills four prostitutes, commits countless brutal rapes yet serves no prison time for any of the homicides. And get this: even after being caught red-handed at an intended murder scene with his hands around a naked young girl's neck, then bang to rights with the jewellery of one of his victims, and the rope he used to bind his other victims discovered in his mom and pop's trailer-park home, where he lived, he still gets away with barefaced murder. He presented a raft of multiple personalities, confusing even the most experienced homicide police, who admittedly acted like modern day Keystone Cops by bungling their search warrants and blowing his Miranda Rights (standard police cautions) out of the window, while believing that they were interviewing someone who *was* Thomas Huskey yet *wasn't* at the same time. But it will be for you, dear reader, to sort the wheat from the chaff, and for you to decide whether the 'Zoo Man' is sad, bad, mad, insane or pure distilled evil – or – was the Tennessee criminal justice system itself as mad as a field full of March hares? And get this: a detective, also named 'Huskey', who interviewed his namesake at length, ended up confusing everyone because the court started to think that defendant Huskey had been interviewing himself. You could not make this up if you tried.

The first thing to consider when taking a peek into the grey matter residing between Huskey's ears is his defence for committing multiple rapes and murder most foul. He tried to use the M'Naghten rule, or Tennessee's equivalent of same, as his defence. I am sure my astute readers will already be au fait with '210 Tennessee Code Title 39 – Criminal Offenses Chapter 11 – General Provisions Part 5 General Defenses 39-11-510 – Insanity'. If this has slipped your mind, however, it runs as follows:

(a) It is an affirmative defense to prosecution that, at the time of the commission of the acts constituting the offense, the defendant, as a result of a severe mental disease or defect, was unable to appreciate the nature or wrongfulness of the defendant's acts. Mental disease or defect does not otherwise constitute a defense. The defendant has the burden of proving the defense of insanity by clear and convincing evidence.

As used in this section, mental disease or defect does not include any abnormality manifested only by repeated criminal or otherwise antisocial conduct.

(b) No expert witness may testify as to whether the defendant was or was not insane as set forth in subsection (a). Such ultimate issue is a matter for the trier of fact alone.

In short, here we have a defendant who was attempting to knit a dissociative personality disorder, tagged into a multiple personality disorder, woven into a variation of the M'Naghten rule. And what a yarn it all turned out to be.

'Dissociative personality disorder?' I hear you ask. Allow me to explain.

Dissociative personality disorder

There are four types of dissociative disorders:

- dissociative amnesia – referring to the loss of memories, such as facts, information and experiences. Though forgetting your identity is a common plot device in movies and on TV, that is not generally the case in real-life amnesia (also called 'amnestic syndrome'). Sufferers usually know who they are, but they might well have forgotten much that they have known or that has happened to them..
- dissociative fugue – a type of amnesia that is caused by extreme psychological trauma instead of physical trauma, illness, or other medical condition. It is a very rare condition but can have severe impacts.
- depersonalisation disorder – marked by periods of feeling disconnected from one's body and thoughts. This disorder is sometimes described as feeling like one is observing oneself from outside one's body or like being in a dream.
- dissociative identity disorder – a rare psychological condition in which two or more personalities with distinct memories and behaviour patterns *apparently* exist in one individual [author's italics]. This might also be described as a 'multiple personality disorder', to keep it simple.

I enjoy simplicity, don't you? But I can almost visualise smug Huskey now. There he is, reading some books on psychiatry – at a stretch, perhaps including my book containing a chapter on Kenneth Bianchi's alleged multiple personality persona – and he's thinking: 'Way to go, bro'. Let's give 'em some of this M'Naghten rule playbook. That Berry-Dee guy has given me some hints and tips here. Yep, I'll forget who I am, where I've been. I won't even recognise myself in a mirror. I will invent some bullshit fugue stuff and extreme psychological drama, then say that one of my personalities done the murders behind my back. Um, what shall I call him... yes, "Kyle" will do. That will really screw up the shrinks and give 'em summit to unpack.'

Levity aside, we'll find much to interest us in the UK's NHS's takeaway on personality disorders, inter alia: a person who thinks, feels, behaves or relates to others very differently from the average person. And trust me, as we scramble through Huskey's grim narrative you'll realise pretty quickly that he certainly *was* 'different'. But was he a person with a borderline personality disorder (one of the most common types), who tends to exhibit disturbed ways of thinking, impulsive behaviour and problems controlling his emotions? Previously he'd had intense but unstable relationships (well, many of us do, that's a given). He was always worrying about people abandoning him (bless him, but so fucking what?). Someone with an antisocial personality disorder will typically get easily frustrated and have difficulty controlling their anger. Such individuals may blame other people for problems in their life, become aggressive and violent – even homicidally so – and upset others at the drop of their Mad Hatter's

Wellington beaver-felt top hats. But still, can't the reader scent extreme narcissism coming into play here? Doesn't it smack of the transference of blame onto others – an issue discussed elsewhere in this book? And alongside this alleged personality disorder we might just find some other mental-health problems, such as depression and substance abuse, adding up – just maybe – to a psychopathological powder keg waiting explode.

And here's another thing to consider: would a person with such a debilitating personality disorder make for a confident elephant keeper (Huskey's former job), work that requires confidence and swift decision making? That's a silly question isn't it? Therefore, the next question we must ask ourselves is, would Thomas Huskey be mentally contained enough to handle a pissed-off Dumbo; one that can reach a shoulder height of around 13 feet 10 inches with a body mass of up to 10.4 tons? Moreover, these animals can shift their bulk at speeds up to 25 miles per hour – which is moving about a thousand times faster than queues at any UK international airport.

I said 'pissed-off' for a very good reason. Let me tell you point-blank, one doesn't want to venture within a mile of any bull elephant when it is in 'musth'. Trust me on this one. Musth, you see, is a normal periodic condition in bull elephants, characterised by highly aggressive behaviour and a *ballistically* large rise in reproductive hormones, temporal drainage (from the temporal glands in the temple area), and dribbling of urine. This typically lasts between two or three months. Testosterone levels in such a male elephant can be on average sixty times greater than in the same elephant at other times. When one these mega-horny Elephantidae loses its temper and goes crazy… Well, there are many videos on YouTube where one can be seen wiping out half a village, overturning buses and trampling people to death. They can also lose the plot when in captivity, too.

'Elephants in musth…what the heck has this got to do with the defence and prosecution of Thomas Huskey?' you might wonder. To be brief, the so-called experts completely overlooked the very vital point I have been making in the last two paragraphs. Not even the consulting forensic psychiatrists in this case could see the wood for the trees. In truth, Huskey's saneness was hiding in plain sight! Surely it did not warrant a small tribe of shrinks, hours upon hours of psychiatric legal debate to rummage around in the '210 Tennessee Code Title 39 – Criminal Offenses Chapter 11 – General Provisions Part 5 General Defenses 39-11-510 – Insanity', and vast amounts taxpayers' money on appeals, to conclude that an elephant handler has, by the very nature of this work, to be extremely fast on his feet, able to accelerate from standstill to top speed in microseconds, lucid, compos mentis, mentally the full wicket. Most certainly not certifiable.

But things will get a lot more farcical as we move on.

The killings in brief

'The law isn't justice. It's a very imperfect mechanism. If you press exactly the right button and are also lucky, justice may also turn up in the answer.'

Raymond Chandler, American-British novelist
and screenwriter: *The Long Goodbye* (1953)

That the oldest profession in the world is certainly *not* the safest is evidenced by the fact that hundreds of 'working girls' across the world are murdered by their clients – consider, among so many others, the victims of Peter Sutcliffe and Steve Wright, most of them sex workers, and those who were not were in the wrong place at the wrong time – their killers did not care. Tragically, the Huskey case is no exception. He was known to the local sex workers, who called him 'Zoo Man' because he would take them to a spot close to his place of work, the zoo. As he became notorious for his rough and violent behaviour, sex workers in the know started avoiding him, and Huskey resorted to giving them no choice in the matter.

The case began in February 1992 when a sex worker came to the Knoxville police with a story that led cops to a man caught in the act with a young woman who'd been stripped naked. That man was none other than Thomas Huskey.

> She told me she'd been abducted inside the city limits, taken to a spot in the county and raped, then tied up and robbed. She lied to begin with because she didn't want to admit she was a prostitute. She took me and showed me where it happened.
>
> Tom Pressley: Knox County Sheriff's officer

The woman, who seemed mostly anxious to retrieve her belongings, led Officer Pressley to a secluded patch of woods off Cahaba Lane in East Knox County, not far from the zoo. 'Me and the guy got to a dead end,' she explained as they walked along the insalubrious path. The spot, locally named the 'City Mattress' was, and no doubt still is, littered with the detritus associated with late-night liaisons: stained mattresses; empty beer bottles, torn underwear and used condoms – and it does come to a dead end; all making it patently obvious to Mr and Mrs Normal People walking their dogs that it is a haunt favoured by sex workers and their clients.

Suddenly, sounding somewhat startled, she cried out, 'There's his car!' Pressley recalls, 'As I went up on there, she saw her stuff. We went into the woods, and she said, "There he is now." He had this other little girl naked on her knees.' Pressley took out his sidearm; advancing tactically (as seen in the movies), he arrested Huskey, cuffing him behind his back. Knox County Sheriff's Office investigator Stewart took up the case. But after the woman explained that she was a sex worker, and had gone with Huskey willingly, and as the girl caught in the sex act refusing to make a complaint, the police had no option other than to set Huskey free.

As all of us true-crime buffs know, rape moving onto serial rape then passing over the dread threshold into homicide, then serial murder, can become a pathologically addictive process. I have interviewed many offenders in America who have followed that path, notably Michael Bruce Ross, who has since been executed. This sickening graduation also applies to Harvey the 'Hammer' Louis Carignan and fits precisely with the modi operandi of both Peter Sutcliffe and John Cannan in the UK, and to a different degree the voyeuristic Polish serial murderer, Paweł Tuchlin, whom we met earlier. Once in the spiralling grip of serial rape, there comes a dread moment when the offender crosses the Rubicon. He learns that if he allows a rape victim to go free, she might identify him. It's all about self-preservation. This incident with the sex worker in Cahaba Lane was the threshold over which serial rapist Huskey graduated into becoming a serial killer. 'Dead women tell no tales,' or at least this what all serial killers think. And oh boy, do they get that wrong!

Thomas Huskey had learned a hard lesson in Cahaba Lane. He would have come within a gnat's whisker of being convicted of rape – which can carry a life term in Tennessee – if the young naked girl had made a complaint. That was unlikely, because she too was a sex worker, but it had been a close call. Next time around, Huskey would kill with cold-blooded premeditation.

So it was that, in October of that year, a man walking through the wood came upon a body in a shallow grave. The body was identified as that of Patricia Rose Anderson, a sex worker. Over the next few days, police investigating the area came upon another three bodies. All four had been strangled to death and horribly disfigured. They were identified as Patricia Ann Johnson and Susan East Stone, both believed to have been prostitutes, and Darlene Smith.

Premeditation shows intent – murderous forethought – and there can be no affirmative defence when pleading guilty by reason of insanity (meaning that the accused lacked the ability to understand that they had committed a crime – to know right from wrong – or was unable to understand that their behaviour was not legal) when killing is followed by more killing. That sort of defence does not fly in pretty much every legal jurisdiction in any civilised society across the world.

Alas, as events would later prove, the self-invented multiple personalities that made up this disgusting Huskey blew enough psychiatric smoke into his multiple court hearings and appeals that it's a wonder that the jurors, shrinks and attorneys could make out the judge's bench. Indeed, so thick was the BS that his trial for the murder of the sex workers ended in a mistrial due in no small part to bungled police work. After several trials and many years, the homicide cases were dismissed on appeal. What a lash-up that was, to be sure!

Bhagavan 'Doc' Antle

Some of us will have watched the three-hour Netflix series *Tiger King*. Plentiful information about 'Doc' Antle's dreadful history of wild animal abuse and his money-laundering crimes can also be found online. During the investigation into Antle's activities, it was rumoured that a fellow worker of his who worked for the Kodak, Tennessee, big cat compound and travelled the fair circuit with him doing pay-to-watch sessions with tigers, was a criminal by the name of Thomas Huskey. This was also verified by eyewitness accounts from TN Network for Animals, who stated that Thomas Huskey, nicknamed the 'Zoo Man', was working for Antle and in charge of elephant care. There were reports that he had lost his job at the zoo because he had been abusing animals. In short, that's how some initial tittle-tattle that the 'Zoo Man' might have been a serial rapist, even the killer of four women, came to the cops' attention.

'I have never seen a situation so dismal that a policeman couldn't make it worse.'

Brendan Francis Aidan Behan: Irish poet, playwright, novelist and short-story writer

At first the police did everything by the book. They looked up Huskey's rap-sheet, to find that he had committed several offences in the past, and had more recently come to their attention when Officer Pressley had arrested him in Cahaba Lane in the company of a very young prostitute. But the cops needed probable cause to interview him as a possible rape and/or murder suspect. In this regard, they sort of came up trumps.

In the event, following Huskey's arrest, four women came forward to report that they had been brutally raped by him. Three were from the Magnolia Avenue area, noted for sex workers, and their stories were similar: they had assumed he was an ordinary client when he propositioned them, but he would then drive them to a secluded spot where he would tie them up with rope and rape force them to perform sex acts. The fourth told how she was walking to a friend's apartment one morning when a man whom she later identified as Huskey, had slowed his vehicle down alongside her, asked her for directions and then pulled her in through the vehicle window, and drove her to a secluded spot where he raped her. She noted that he was wearing a T-shirt with 'Doc' Antle's set-up's logo.

Bad to sublimely ridiculous

It fell to Knox County Sheriff's Detective Michael Upchurch to lead the investigation into the rapes and homicides that had occurred in the vicinity of Cahaba Lane. The dead bodies had been bound with orange rope, and his investigation had now led him to focus on Huskey as a suspect, so the officer checked for outstanding warrants against Mr Huskey. He found one for failure to appear in Knoxville Municipal Court on a charge of solicitation for prostitution. Now the cops had reasonable cause to arrest him at least for something, and in doing so get the chance to sniff around inside his trailer-park home. Along with detectives Darrell Johnson, Dan Stewart, Mike Freeman, Mike Grissom and Jerry Huskey, Upchurch went to Huskey's parents' place, where they saw his truck parked outside.

At 9:30 p.m., Detective Upchurch and Officer Jerry Huskey knocked on the door while the other cops stealthily went around back. Ma Huskey, answered the door and was curtly told that her son was to be taken into custody for failing to appear in court. She explained that her son and her husband were in their beds and then went to get Thomas, who duly came to ask what the officers wanted. Having explained about the outstanding warrant, Huskey breathed a sigh of relief – no mention of rape, least of all serial homicide – and he asked, 'Is it OK if I put my shoes on?' Detective Upchurch agreed, but on the condition that he and Detective Stewart would go with him; in doing so they would discreetly have a peek-about.

While the two officers were standing just inside the bedroom doorway, they saw a coil of orange hay-baling rope on the floor and recognised it instantly as the same type of rope used to bind the murder victims. (The same rope was later found at the zoo where Huskey worked.)

Like so many trailer-park residents, the Huskeys had no electricity, so it was dark inside the mobile home. As Thomas put on his socks and shoes, Upchurch illuminated a dresser with his flashlight. He saw a pair of women's earrings and a necklace on the top. Indeed, only the day before, one of the homicide victims' boyfriends had told Upchurch that his girl (Patricia Rose Anderson) had earrings in her purse. Trying to be canny, Upchurch did not mention the rope, earrings or the necklace to Huskey. The suspect refused to sign a 'Consent to Search' form, so he was taken to the Sevier County Jail, where he was booked in on the outstanding warrant. Other officers waited at the mobile home, then Huskey's father gave them permission to search his property, but this *would* require a search warrant. It was drafted by an assistant district attorney (ADA), who later acknowledged that he was not familiar with Rule 41 – Search and Seizure of the Tennessee Rules of Criminal Procedure. The ADA later explained the extent of his experience in these matters: 'I have undergone some training relating to search warrants… I have written a few of them, and I am familiar with probable cause.'

US search warrants have to be *very specific* as to what law enforcement is searching for. The ADA later managed to wheedle his way out of this problem by arguing that the police had made no mention of a search warrant specifically being issued for the suspect's bedroom, least of all for any items of jewellery. Nonetheless, with the warrant drafted, Upchurch told Officer Huskey to hotfoot it along to Bruce Baker, the Sevier County magistrate. Baker signed the warrant and three copies were made, but there was no mention at all in the warrant of searching Huskey's bedroom. *Only* the mobile home could be searched with his permission. For his part, Huskey had refused to sign any warrant that would allow police to search his own room. Little could the police or anyone else on our planet have realised back then that this would prove to be become monumental cock-up, one that would cause the case of sexual homicide x 4 against the 'Zoo Man' to finally collapse. No officer was reprimanded, not one of them given a slap on the wrist. It was later all put down to 'legal oversight'.

Nevertheless, now armed with their search warrant, the cops returned to the mobile home and Detective Stewart went into the suspect's bedroom – an unlawful act, not permitted by the warrant he held. He picked up the earrings to bag them. Detective Upchurch saw blonde hair entwined with the necklace (this hair was later proven to be microscopically identical in every way to that of Patricia Rose Anderson). It must have seemed to the investigators to be a slam-dunk case, with Huskey caught bang to rights. We might have forgiven the cops if they'd done high-fives for an hour then hit the local bar. Alas, this was not to be the end of it.

Had this warrant been issued with Huskey's permission to search his bedroom, then the rope and jewellery would have come under the 'in plain sight' rule. Huskey gave no such permission, so anything else found there was deemed in law not to have been seen at all.

And the orange rope? As the police were searching the place, Ma Huskey tried to edge it out of sight discreetly, with her toe. Oh, for a mother's love. She had also tried to sneak into her lad's bedroom with the excuse that she wanted to turn off his radio; she remarked that without going into the room it was not possible to see the chest of drawers that had been built into the wall; later she added: 'I only went in there to pick up Michael's laundry and change the lazy fucker's sheets.' Gosh, a mother's love is limitless.

Back at the police station, and with Huskey refusing to say anything (as was his legal right), the cops now needed to get possession of a capias, or warrant, ordering Huskey's arrest on the murder charges. One was issued by the Knoxville City County clerk... who it turned out was not authorised to do so, which meant that the warrant was not lawful – the second of the compounded legal errors that would later car-wreck the State's case.

Despite having an illegal arrest warrant, Lieutenant Johnson (Head of the Homicide Division), Knox County Sheriff's Department, Detective Upchurch and Tennessee Bureau of Investigation Agent Davenport went to the jail on 29 October 1992 to interview Huskey. But oops-a-daisy, they didn't bring with them the official waiver forms that required the man's signature. So, Huskey's Miranda Rights were read from a card. This was the law's third mistake.

We now know that Huskey not only handled elephants, he was involved with tigers too. C'mon guys, you've certainly got to have your wits about you in that kind of work, can we agree on that? Moreover, while meeting these investigators in jail, Huskey came up with a cunning plan. He told the cops that his name was not Huskey. He insisted that he was 'Kyle'. This threw a spanner into the works, and set the cops off on a wild-goose chase trying to find anyone who knew a man called 'Kyle' – which, unsurprisingly, they could not.

The next day, Lieutenant Johnson found the correct waiver form and returned to the jailhouse to interview 'Kyle'. At 5 p.m., the officer noted that the arrested man said: 'I do not want a lawyer at this time, and will not answer any more questions now.' This was a Tricky-Dicky move by Huskey. If his attorney had been present he would have had to instruct counsel using his real name and not that of an alter ego. Nonetheless, Agent Davenport responded with: 'If you don't have anything else to say, there's no point in us continuing to talk.' The investigators left the jail feeling a tad deflated, for at this point Huskey had the bit between his teeth. He would run the law ragged and he'd only just started.

Having given police time to think things over, on 10 November the manipulative 'Zoo Man' summoned a correctional officer and told him that he needed to talk to Lieutenant Johnson and Detective Upchurch. Eager to sort matters out, the investigators returned to the jail with yet another waiver form that they hoped would be signed this time. The statutory Miranda Rights warning was read and when asked to sign the waiver, Huskey signed it 'Phillip Dax'; he explained that 'Dax' was an Englishman, no less. 'Phillip Dax' didn't want an attorney present either.

'Well, here's another nice mess you've gotten me into!'
Oliver Hardy to Stan Laurel (famous catchphrase)

Lieutenant Johnson and his colleagues now found themselves talking to what appeared to be another one of Huskey's purported alter egos. As he noted in his report, Johnson said that in all the interviews he conducted he would start off chatting to Thomas Huskey but would end up talking to 'Kyle' or 'Phillip Dax'. Johnson added: 'My most extensive and detailed conversations were with "Kyle", who was the one who admitted involvements in the four murders and numerous rapes.' The detective recalled that when Huskey was either 'Kyle' or 'Dax', he would have to go through the rigmarole of advising each them individually of their rights; and every time, each alter ego acknowledged that they understood their rights and kept talking. It was fine mess indeed. And this very fine mess would get even worse when suddenly up popped 'Timothy', a new alter ego, this time a homosexual, who claimed to be protecting Huskey from 'Kyle'.

Please Christopher, enough *is* enough

'This case presents a somewhat tortuous procedural history,' opined judges Richard Baumgartner and Everett Williams in the case of the *State of Tennessee v. Thomas Dee Huskey* in the Court of Criminal Appeals of Tennessee (Assigned on Briefs December 13, 2011) No. 459829. No. E2001-00283-CCA-R3-CD – Filed October 10, 2012.

Drilling further down into this farce, we can be assured that the cock-up resumed momentum when the police later testified that Huskey had given detectives Upchurch and Stewart verbal permission to search his room… a claim that this Mad Hatter character strenuously denied. As it turned out, not only did their search warrant not give the police any legal right to search his bedroom, it was also in breach

202

of Article 1, section 7 of the Tennessee Constitution , which held that 'Evidence obtained in violation of [that law] should be excluded as evidence.

To further muddy the waters, the search warrant and copies of same were not signed by the executing detective, nor any peace officer. Can I say that more often than not the law can be a complete ass – yes, why not? And to quote Michel de Montaigne's *Essays* (1595): 'Is there anything so assured, resolved, disdainful, contemplative, solemn and serious as an ass?' Yes, almost assuredly, the US Constitution, as in the *Hughes v. State* case (1922) below, where the arrest (of a man who had murdered his travelling companion) was lawful but as supporting evidence had been collected in violation of the law, it could not be used in court):

The State, having through its executive representatives produced the evidence of a violation of the law by one of its citizens by means prohibited by the Constitution, cannot be permitted through its judicial tribunal to utilize the wrong thus committed against the citizen [in this case the 'Zoo Man'], to punish the citizen for his wrong; *for it was only by violating his constitutionally protected rights that his wrong has been discovered.* It is no answer to say that it matters not how a citizen's sins have been found out. Security from an unlawful search is the right guaranteed to the citizen, *even for the discovery of the citizen's sins.* This right we must protect, unless we may with impunity disregard our oath to support and enforce the Constitution. The experience of our forefathers with unlawful searches and seizures was deemed by the people who framed the Constitution sufficient to warrant the provision by which, in instances, even the guilty might escape detection and punishment [all italics are the author's].

The defence

'You can call me a goddamn son of a bitch, as long as you don't call me "Tommy".

'You can't get me an' Tommy mixed up. You can't get that goody-goody little son of a bitch mixed up with me.'

Thomas Huskey's alleged alter ego 'Kyle',

confessing on tape

The jurors must have gone wide-eyed when both State and defence attorneys started agreeing with each other. Having heard serial killer Huskey's confession angrily stating: 'After that [one of the strangulation murders] I throwed off down [sic] and left her lying there,' both sides of the legal aisle believed that it *was* Huskey's voice. So did the jury. They could hardly disagree, because the confessions to four murders were made at a police station and everything was video-recorded too. However, Huskey's attorneys, Gregory Isaacs and Herb Moncier, argued that the man on the tape was not Huskey *per se*: the words came from an alter ego that had taken control of their client's body; a completely different personality named 'Kyle'. Adding weight to their uphill struggle to mitigate Huskey's murders, the defence attorneys – possibly with tongues in cheeks – claimed: 'Even though "Kyle" confessed to murder on this tape, it is not proof that Mr Huskey, a soft-spoken and reserved man, committed any crime.' Oh, so now we're presented with a male version of seventh-century Saint Dymphna, the so-called 'Saint of Calmness', whose father was anything but, because he murdered her by chopping off her head when she was just sixteen (fifteen, some say).

As the reader will now realise, this defence was really an effort to test the bounds of reality. If the jury were to believe that BS, they must have realised that 'Kyle' didn't live in the Huskeys' trailer park home. His parents had never heard of 'Kyle', nor had anyone else for that matter, not even at the zoo where he'd been employed. So, it must have been 'Kyle' who'd stolen the earrings, the necklace and left the orange rope by the doorway? Yeah, right. In fact, the first time 'Kyle' entered this world was when his host was being interviewed by the cops.

To try and get a grip on the real world here, can one imagine a British jury, or any jury anywhere else, believing this claptrap? But in the US they buy into this legal garbage time and time again. God only knows what they put into the water in Sevier County. It's no wonder the jurors were to end up at odds with each other. The upshot: a mistrial because the jurors could not reach a unanimous verdict.

In a second trial, Huskey wriggled free again by successfully arguing that the police who raided his parents' home in Sevier County used an invalid search warrant; he was correct, of course. Thus, the property seized from his bedroom, and his arrest for homicide, were both illegal. Things truly went south for the State when it was revealed that it had failed to carry its burden to prove Huskey's right to remain silent was scrupulously honoured, had failed to read him his rights and badgered him into confessing over several days.

Having read through much of the trial papers, I do feel some sympathy with the homicide investigators. It is patently true they did start off by screwing up the search warrant; had failed to bring the proper consent forms from the outset; and by the time they did, they were faced with Huskey and three alter egos. They had to get each alter ego to sign a waiver and have their Miranda Warnings read over again and again.

To make matters more complicated for the officers, Huskey and each of his alter egos refused to have an attorney present during the interviews. Huskey knew if there were three other people living in his body, one lawyer could not solely represent him. That would have required a further three public attorneys.

Now really pushing their luck, the defence argued that Huskey, who claimed to experience fierce headaches and blackouts, suffered from a multiple personality disorder, often referred to as 'dissociative identity disorder'. This being so, the attorneys said that according to Tennessee law (and with a slightly modified M'Naghten rule in their back pockets) their client would 'not be responsible for criminal conduct, if at the time of the conduct, as a result of a mental disease or defect, he lacked substantial capacity to either appreciate the wrongfulness of his conduct or to conform his conduct to the requirements of the law'.

Huskey's lawyers posed the question, 'How could an uneducated man with a low IQ improvise so many characters with distinctive styles, histories and cultures and vocabularies?'

adding: 'Our client says that he did not remember killing anybody. He didn't even know about the murders, The tapes are simply evidence that Mr Huskey is mentally ill.'

To further support their claim, the defence showed the jurors psychiatric reports that described Huskey as '*possibly* schizophrenic' [author's italics]. They pointed to his 1984 divorce from a woman who noted his 'mood swings' and 'scary split personality'.

To add some psychiatric weight to the defence's case, into the witness box stepped Dr Robert Sadoff. One of the nation's leading forensic psychiatrists, he told the court that he had been with Huskey when 'Kyle' emerged. In the manner of someone trying to paint a monstrous Stephen King character in a horror movie, Dr Sadoff declared: 'It's the same body, but his facial expressions were different. He was angry, he *was* vicious, he *was* violent, both in speech and lunging and trying to get at us to hurt us.' Pausing for breath and to let his words sink into the jurors' minds, Dr Sadoff proceeded: 'Huskey used his left hand to write, but "Kyle" was right-handed.' To conclude, Sadoff claimed: 'If indeed "Kyle" did commit these acts, Thomas Huskey at the time of the commission of these acts would have lacked substantial capacity to appreciate the wrongfulness of the acts.' This was simply a defence of: 'Not me, Guv, it was my mate living inside me.'

To me, this seems to be the fundamental problem with these paid-for-hire forensic psychiatrists. Whether they are taken on by the defence or the prosecution, they have to come up with a psychiatric diagnosis (meaning simply an opinion) that fits with their employer's requirements – fits in with their briefs, so to speak. Had not Dr Sadoff truly figured out that never before in Huskey's miserable worthless life had any of these alter egos appeared? If not, then he might have handed back the deposit he had just banked and re-evaluated his career.

The prosecution

'The first step towards madness is to think oneself wise.'
Fernando de Rojas: Spanish writer and dramatist,
in *La Celestina: Or, the Tragi-Comedy of Calisto and*
Melibea (1499–1502)

Having had a lot of fun running rings around law enforcement in having his first trial abandoned because of a hung jury, there can be no doubt that Huskey thought himself a bit of a smart aleck. However, for the State, Dr Herbert Spiegel, a forensic psychiatrist in private practice, told the court:

Diagnosis of dissociative identity disorder is very rare. In cases of serial homicide where there is a cooling off period between the events during which time the offender resumes a normal life, using it as a legal defense is an embarrassment to the entire psychiatric profession.

Wow, now I feeling like popping the caps off the few remaining bottles off of the mega-strong, chilled Red Horse beer I brought back from Manila last trip around, then I'll erect a shrine to commemorate 'Saint Common Fucking Sense'. You see, Dr Spiegel didn't stop there. Boyo, did he lash out. Looking sternly at the jurors with the steely-eyed confidence of a man who *does* know the difference between his backside and his elbow, he explained in measured tones: 'The defendant is *not* a victim of the disorder, nor *did* a separate personality kill four women outside Knoxville. Rather, Huskey is simply a psychopath trying to pull off a sham.'

The trial judge leaned forward, his eyes glued to the shrink in the box. Huskey sat in his chair looking as dumb as a dumb person can look. His lawyers shifted uncomfortably as their efforts to prove their client insane started to evaporate like the Cheshire Cat.

Moving up a gear: '"Kyle" is a figment of his imagination,' Dr Spiegel insisted. 'Even the most unlikely people can be capable of a brilliant imagination and a stunning performance... I think [Huskey] has an incredible ability to manipulate people and giving a stunning performance... he is now, if anything, manipulating the *whole* state of Tennessee.' Of course, Dr Spiegel was pushing his professional credentials a bit too far, but as the defence team remained mute and did not object, this tongue-lashing scored mega points for the prosecution.

To show that the other personalities were just a hoax, the prosecution called a certain William Fletcher, a convicted rapist and jail mate of Huskey's. 'Fletcher. Prisoner W #111516-1' is presently serving his bird at the Cannon County Jail in Woodbury, Tennessee, and of course it goes without saying that such witnesses are not the most reliable at the best of times, many of them becoming jailhouse snitches and cooperating with police in return for a reduction in their sentences. Nonetheless, Fletcher declared, '[Huskey] told me he was going to play crazy and act like he had blackouts, because he knew they didn't give the electric chair to crazy people... he thought that would be the best thing to do.'

Indeed, that *was* a wise move because Tennessee's last execution took place in February 2002, after which the death penalty was abandoned for nine years from 2009. But the state is once more red hot on executions and they have put seven prisoners to death since reinstating the death penalty in 2018. Yet, we cannot even begin to hint that Tennessee is unfair. They offer two types of capital punishment. The first is lethal injection, or the 'Goodnight Juice' as I've called this pseudo-clinical procedure. The second is a fry-up in 'Ole Sparky' – previously called 'Ole Smokey'. Two of the seven criminals executed since 2018 opted for the 'Goodnight Juice'. The other five went for the 'fry-up' option after being informed by their lawyers about the horrifying effects of the relatively untested multi-drug execution cocktail. And they would be right there, as is confirmed in the Death Penalty Information Center's (DPIC) online article 'Court Documents Reveal Widespread Irregularities in Tennessee Executions'. You will need a strong stomach to digest it, with the following proviso: when one understands what these totally evil men had done, the utter depravity of their rapes and murders, there will be many who will say: 'They got their due comeuppances!'

And, I want to make a strong observation of my own here. If those who disagree place me in the stocks and pelt me with eggs and rotten fruit, so be it be. We have a saying in the UK: 'If you can't do the time don't do the crime,' and this extends to murder most foul. None of the last seven men executed in the 'Volunteer State' of Tennessee qualified by a long chalk for the M'Naghten rule defence – although several of them tried it on. They all knew what punishment they could expect if they committed first-degree murder: execution. Wikipedia's article 'Capital Punishment in Tennessee' provides a first-rate history and lists the aggravating factors that qualify in a killer being put to death. These stone-cold murderers are like all of the serial killers I have interviewed or corresponded with over decades – they are cowards at heart. They take human life as easily as one swats an annoying fly. In many instances, they torture, rape and cause terrible suffering to their innocent prey and exhibit no remorse. Any remorse they do show comes in the form of crocodile tears, a sudden phony turning to God having 'seen the light', yet still they whine and waste millions of dollars of taxpayers' money on years of appeals, fly-specking every legal decision as if they are the wronged parties and it's the system that is at fault.

Then I ask myself: 'Christopher, how would you feel if it were one of your children who had suffered at one of these monsters' hands?' I would be at the front of the queue to press the switch or start injecting lethal substances into the perpetrator's body and heart. Whether he suffered or not would matter little to me. Then, as he was strapped down, I would whisper in his ear: 'If you can't suck this up, you shouldn't have done the crime… God bless the United States of America.'

Deliberations about Huskey's state of mind went on for five days. These were the longest deliberations in the state's history, as the jurors circled around the same questions.

After the trial, juror Leslie Boone went public, stating: 'It's a very difficult decision, and people saw it in diametrically opposed ways.' Big words, are 'diametrically opposed', dear Leslie. But please be more specific, because this author hasn't a clue as to what you are referring to.

Juror Carolyn Vaugn asked herself: 'Could [Huskey] control "Kyle" coming out... I didn't think that they gave us enough evidence to make a good decision.' How about using some streetwise common savvy, Carolyn? The answer was staring you straight in the face.

The jurors finally sent a note to the judge indicating that they could not reach a unanimous decision. Five out of the twelve of them voted that Huskey was guilty and sane, while four deemed him not guilty by reason of insanity. Three jurors went down the rabbit hole into *Alice in Wonderland*, remaining undecided either way. Two frustrated jurors later told Primetime TV that they felt that the system itself was the problem. That they only had two choices: guilty or not guilty by reason of insanity. They said that they hadn't been given the option of recognising Huskey's illness while also holding him responsible for his crimes.

'He's guilty by reason of insanity,' declared a somewhat confused Carolyn Vaugn, 'which only changes what happens to him afterward. It don't say he didn't do it.' So eloquently put, Carolyn...!

The other juror, also a Carolyn – Trainor – agreed: 'I really do feel that if we'd had that third option of guilty but insane, I feel very definitely that many of the jurors would have gone with that.'

Perhaps not all of the jurors, 'Sweet Carolyn'. Besides, if

you had kept your ears open, you would have realised that that option *was* put to you anyway.

What the jurors *didn't* know

'A jury is composed of twelve men of average ignorance.'

Herbert Spencer

And Spencer, the nineteenth-century English philosopher, psychologist, biologist, anthropologist and sociologist, knew a thing or two about common sense. He pretty much invented 'savvy'. After all, he did come up with the expression 'survival of the fittest', which he coined in *Principles of Biology* (1864), after reading Charles Darwin's *On the Origin of Species* (1859).

A one-time sex-worker had told police that Huskey took her to the Knoxville Zoo, where he beat and raped her. She explained that when a mail truck happened to pull up, Huskey fled. She was in no doubt it was Huskey, and that he never mentioned anyone named 'Kyle'. The prosecution did not call her simply because she was a working prostitute, the suggestion being that she was 'a person not of good character and not totally possessed of common sense', and therefore might be shot to bits in the witness box.

'There's no other person in him,' another sex worker told the police. 'He's just a rotten, dirty, excuse my language "bastard". That's it!' Well, lady, what other type of person do you expect to meet as you drop your pants in some dark lane in the middle of the night – an Archangel Michael, patron saint for all in need of protection. A pope, perhaps?

More to the point, the jurors never heard that Huskey

213

had been previously tried for raping three other prostitutes: one more at the zoo, and the other on Cahaba Lane, where the bodies of four slain women were discovered. And during Huskey's previous rape trial, after which he was sentenced to sixty-four years in prison, there was never a mention of a multiple personality disorder.

'Knowing what I know now, I believe that he was guilty [of serial murder] and sane at the time he did it,' said juror Carolyn Trainor.

Hedging their bets, Huskey's lawyers said that they had wanted to introduce the client's multiple personality disorder in the rape trials, 'but the judge made it too difficult'.

Summary

'Diagnosis of dissociative identity disorder . . . *using it as a legal defense is an embarrassment to the entire psychiatric profession*' [author's italics].

Dr Herbert Spiegel

Hip, hip hurray, Dr Spiegel. I had to repeat his words here. Out of this entire sordid affair the late, much lamented Dr Spiegel seems to have been the only person who had his head screwed on right – aside from Mr Huskey, that is, who pretty much ran rings around everyone else including the state of Tennessee. In my book – this very book – which is *your* book now – as Doc Spiegel *is* undoubtedly sane, this makes Huskey sane too. Any sane person reading up on this case will understand – or should do soon – that Huskey was in full mental health, of sound mind, *mens sana*, and in no way a prime candidate for a bed in a funny farm.

To me, it beggars belief that Huskey's lawyers truly believed that their client was possessed by the most convenient and sudden emergence of four alter egos. Had this investigative shambles gone on much longer, there could have been coachloads of new alter egos arriving at the jail every week.

That the eminent psychiatrist Dr Sadoff was wheeled into the witness box to support this – one the most of obvious cock-and-bull mitigation scams in US criminal history – and to offer an opinion, and to *actually believe* that his opinion was sound, reminds me of a line in the short story 'Clovis on the Alleged Romance of Business' (1924) by Saki (aka H.H. Munro): 'A little inaccuracy sometimes saves tons of explanation.'

Perhaps a better way to sum up would be the comments made by Chief David Davenport, who later gave an interview for the TV documentary *Appalachian Unsolved*:

> It's like you go over here and there's another body... and you go over there and find skeletal remains. First time I interviewed him [Huskey] I thought he was 'Tom', and when we left and came back he was 'Kyle' who was an aristocrat, and he has the voice... uh... pretty good... a good actor. I thought it was all an act. I think the whole system got the bum.

District Attorney Randy Nicholls later claimed in an interview with *Appalachian Unsolved*: 'I had never any doubt. It was the first time I had been called upon to decide whether or not we [the State of Connecticut] are gonna to [execute] somebody. I misjudged it tremendously. And I will go to my grave believing that the last victim was driven from Cahaba Lane to Huskey's parents' mobile home where he lived, and I don't believe she'd been dead an hour [before police arrived].'

Craig Issacs, one of Huskey's defence attorneys, stated: 'I remember quite vividly a picture of Thomas and his father with an elephant that he shared with us. It was very moving.' Yes, Mr Issacs, there could not have been a dry eye in the house. Lucky for ya'll that Jumbo wasn't in musth or you would have been moved a damned sight faster.

I rest my case.

Angus Ronald True:
a fractured psyche

'I would shoot a man as soon as a mad dog, but I would not even say "damn" to a woman.'

ANGUS RONALD TRUE: ENGLISH MURDERER

The great Swiss psychologist, pipe-smoking Carl Gustav Jung, believed that every personality has a 'shadow' that is in direct conflict with the rational self. 'Recognition of the shadow is a reason for humility, for genuine fear of the abysmal depths in man,' Jung wrote, ominously adding: 'Those who ignore this other self, the shadow, do so at their peril. They would force this "other self" to take a dangerous course of its own.' Having now read about Thomas Dee Huskey, might we be so impertinent as to enquire: if Jung had accepted that the 'Zoo Man' had many shadows – four to be precise, but at his peril Huskey only ignored 'Kyle', with the other three shadows being of no consequence, what would have Jung made of that?

I see Jung's scenario as an individual fighting himself like a boxer in the ring, with moral compass being the referee. More simply put, he's describing a Dr Jekyll and Mr Hyde personality. Good *v*. Evil. A pinch of salt over one's shoulder. Hang garlic over one's bedpost at night in case the 'Shadow' calls to plunge one into 'the abysmal depths of man'. And if one finds someone really possessed by multiple shadows, one could reasonably diagnose that to be completely mentally ill or, or subject to a multiple personality disorder. Or a con artist.

In the 'Zoo Man's', case, if Jung's standard had been applied, might we flippantly ask: which one of Huskey's alter egos would have been prosecuted, sentenced to a natural life term for serial rape? Of the remaining alter egos, would they singularly, or as accomplices, have been charged with conspiracy to murder? And which prison would they have ended up in? I am being obtuse, of course I am. Nonetheless, the great Jung is proposing that only 'two opposing selves' must be accepted before true inner balance and peace of mind can be achieved – or, one might say, the gluing of a fractured psyche back together.

Reuniting all four alter egos would have been a bridge too far, methinks.

For those readers interested in this area, let me point you in the direction of an online paper by Sarah Wong Hui Min of University College London: 'Split minds, splitting hairs?: An interdisciplinary perspective on renaming schizophrenia'. And, I add a proviso here: schizophrenia and multiple personality disorder are unrelated. A schizophrenic does not have two different personalities; rather, they have false ideas or have lost touch with reality. This is, of course, where the defence psychiatrists botched up big time in the 'Zoo Man' case. In trying to cover all of the diagnostic bases, they ended up claiming that their client was not only schizophrenic but had a multiple personality disorder as well. A very strange psychiatric combo indeed, but as we have seen thus far in this book, trying to find two shrinks to agree with each other is like expecting Donald Trump to know the difference between fact and fiction.

To be fair, the idea that people with schizophrenia have more than one personality is a common enough misconception. Yet it is an issue that any aspiring psychiatrist should learn from day one at Shrink Junior School. There is, however, one mental condition that causes people to adopt different personalities. This phenomenon is known as 'dissociative identity disorder' (DID). A person with DID has two or more distinct identity states, sometimes known as 'alternate identities', or 'alters'. Neither condition has one definitive cause, but DID is associated with trauma, while schizophrenia is more often associated with the presence of certain genes. And here's the thing: psychiatrists are not entirely sure about this.

According to the Sidran Institute, most people with DID have a history of severe childhood trauma. An estimated ninety per cent of people with DID have a history of neglect or abuse. The condition can arise when a child dissociates as a defence mechanism to escape an intolerable reality. I have given many solid examples of the abusive childhood suffered by so many serial killers in my book *Talking with Psychopaths and Savages: Beyond Evil*. This is not to suggest any sort of mitigation for the dreadfulness of their crimes.

It would also be fair to say that millions of children are raised in dysfunctional homes, but they don't all develop a dissociative identity disorder, do they? For my part, I adopt a very cynical 'True Brit' stance. I have interviewed several serial killers who resorted to a defence of DID/MPD, Kenneth Bianchi being one of them. What intrigues me is that these alternate identities only ever appear when a criminal is about to go on trial, and their alters vanish just as quickly once the offender is behind bars, as did those of the 'Zoo Man' after he was caged for life. Since his incarceration none of 'em have been seen or heard from since… funny old world he lived in, would you not agree?

Let's move on and get to grips with the remarkable case of Ronald True. And I'd argue that it's remarkable for two reasons. The first is to do with the story of the chief protagonist, who had a febrile personality and whose life from the very start was often bizarre. It was an existence that propelled him towards inevitable catastrophe. The second reason concerns the question that lies at the heart of it all, and the plea of insanity – finding mitigation for an individual's acts in a case of brutal murder most foul.

Indeed, there was one basis and one basis alone from which Ronald True could be saved from the hangman's noose: a successful plea of insanity. As we shall learn during our road trip into this man's mind, all his life True was anything but true: he was a pathological liar preferring to conveniently forget, or blot out, his dismal record of failure. He was a fantasist who lived in Cloud Cuckoo Land, the place where elephants fly, lead balls bounce and fairies reign supreme. He passed himself off as a hero, impressing listeners with tales of derring-do in strange lands. But was he really insane? That is the question, as we travel back in time to Chorlton-upon-Medlock, the date being 16 June 1891, when Ronald True was born.

Formative years

'The lazy, worthless, and ignominious class who pursue their [sexual] self-gratification at the expense of the earnings of the industrious part of the community. The vicious mother thus relieving parish funds. It is a great offence against the sacrament of marriage with the putative father absolved of any responsibility for his illegitimate offspring.'

'Bastardy Clause', new Poor Law of 1834

Ronald was the son of William True – a 'journalistic artist', in his own words – and a precocious and beautiful sixteen-year-old girl. And from the very get-go we run into a problem. *Murder Casebook* Vol. 98, puts her down as 'Agnes', but later has her as 'Annabel True', for reasons that entirely befuddle your author as she did not marry the child's father. William and his young love interest did not splice the knot, for it seems that as soon as he learned that she was with child, he scarpered – probably in the interests of self-preservation and perhaps for the following reasons too.

Her family name was actually Angus, but to confuse us even more, initially the registrar put her down on baby Ronald's birth certificate as 'Agnes Bell'. Maybe the reason for this name-switch came from the fact that her father was a no-nonsense innkeeper in Banffshire, Scotland. Mr Angus would have been none too pleased that his young daughter had become pregnant out of wedlock. Later, however, and according to the aforementioned *Murder Casebook*, she changed her mind and asked to be put down as 'Annabel True'. Make of that what you will.

For the sake of simplicity, from here on in we shall call her 'Annabel'.

History tells us that the young Ronald never saw his natural father after infancy; he was indeed a 'bastard'. By the late nineteenth century, illegitimacy had been stigmatised in society for years and our cousins north of Hadrian's Wall took an even dimmer view of it than the English. All across the British Isles promiscuity was punished in the most efficient and least costly manner possible, added to which, the law at that time was uncompromising and singled out these 'fallen women' to 'face the humiliation of giving birth to an illegitimate child'.

Whether or not Mr and Mrs Angus were religious folk we will never know, but had they read the Holy Book they would have known that Deuteronomy 23:2 says (in the contemporary English Standard Version, anyway): 'No one born of a forbidden union may enter the assembly of the Lord. Even to the tenth generation, none of his descendants may enter the assembly of the Lord.' Psalm 27:10 (again, in the ESV) gives us the more enlightened: 'For my father and my mother have forsaken me, but the Lord will take me in.' This is one of the big issues with the Bible; it's jampacked with contrary ideas, advice and rules of engagement required if one wants to curry favour with the Lord.

But I have digressed. In a contemporary context, millions of kids born illegitimately do not metamorphose into insane killers, although if they experience severe stigmatisation it may serve to poison their formative years, as evidenced by the likes of serial killers Ted Bundy, Harvey the 'Hammer' Louis Carignan, Kenneth Bianchi and Fred West, among dozens of others murderers.

Annabel was sent away to have her child, who was born in Manchester on 17 June 1891. The idea might have been that she would return after a couple of years, a grieving widow with a child. It was a common enough occurrence and discretion was politely maintained. In the meantime, Mr Angus died and Mrs Angus went to run an hotel in Rothes, with the help of her daughters. Young Annabel, although by all accounts she doted on her baby, was not the most maternal type and relied on the help of her sister, Grace, to raise baby Ronald in the best way that she could. He was a sensitive child pretty much from the get-go. And he soon developed violent tendencies. Grace later recounted that she found four-year-old Ronald crying. 'I have been burying my rabbits,' he said, 'but I have left their heads up so that I can go and see them every day.' The rabbits had starved to death. He also mistreated his pony. Most commonly, children who abuse animals have either witnessed or experienced abuse themselves – be it psychological or physical – yet there is no evidence that Ronald had been at the wrong end of any of that; quite the contrary. Then, once he'd started school, he started to play truant. His excuses for missing school were strangely bizarre. One morning, he told his mother quite seriously that his dinner had been cooking since 6 a.m., and he would miss it if he left the house. Other pathetic excuses followed in short order.

After a few years Annabel travelled to London to work in an hotel there; it is assumed that she left her young son with her sister Grace. In 1899, she met and married a handsome young Army officer, Lieutenant Henry Lethbridge Alexander. Not long after, the couple travelled to India with Alexander's regiment. A year later, in 1900, Annabel travelled to London for minor surgery. She did not return to India – she had met another handsome young officer, Arthur French, and, scandalously, was living with him. This duly reached the ears of Lieutenant Alexander and he divorced her. In July 1902 Annabel and the Hon. Arthur Reginald French, heir to the fourth Baron de Freyne, were married. Whereupon Lord de Freyne, highly unamused, cut off his heir's allowance.

In the meantime, following Annabel's mother's death in 1899, Grace and Ronald had moved to London; French seems to have accepted Ronald and his money would have made for a more comfortable life, and paid for Ronald's education.

For some children the insecurity of such a lifestyle poses has little, even no effect on their psyche, but for Ronald having a beautiful, loving mother was not much good when she was not often about. A couple of years after her marriage to French, his aunt Grace told the thirteen-year-old Ronald that his mother was gravely ill, and was shocked when he replied: 'Oh, well, if she dies all her property will be mine, and I shall give you her two best rings straight away, and you can have anything else you like of her things.' With that statement now in mind, we can see, as plain as day, that the boy had developed a cruel, even a spiteful streak. And once this behaviour is embedded in a youngster's psyche at such an early age, it proves all but impossible to eradicate, for it becomes the bedrock for all that is to come.

Aged thirteen, Ronald was sent to Bedford Grammar School. Established as a writing school, and founded using endowments left by Sir William Harpur in the sixteenth century, its programme focused on education that would bring practical benefits to its students, who were initially boys – mainly the children of local businessmen. However, 'Over time, military and professional families from both Bedfordshire and further afield were also increasingly attracted to the school,' according to the school's website.

Ronald remained at Bedford Grammar School for five years. There are few records of his time there, although his reports were universally poor. During this period, his mother recovered from her illness, and then, in 1905, accompanied her husband to the United States. He was beginning to feel the effects of having lost his allowance from his father and hoped he would be able to make money. He almost immediately disappeared. A month later he was found to have enlisted in the US Army, and Annabel sailed back to England. French remained in the US Army until his father died in 1913, and he inherited the title. Annabel became Lady de Freyne. When World War I broke out, Lord de Freyne rejoined the British Army and was killed in action in France in 1915.

But, we must return to Ronald's unhappy career. Annabel knew that her son lacked the discipline and staying power to make good in almost any profession, so when he turned eighteen, she sent him out to New Zealand to learn farming. Quite why his family thought that this was a good bet remains a mystery. Ronald lasted a mere year there, He became homesick, so his parents brought the lad back home to try another self-improving agricultural experiment. They parked him on a farm in Yorkshire, and guess what? After a month the farmer told Ronald's mother that he could do nothing with him. They say that patience is a virtue and, by gosh, didn't Ronald's family do their best to straighten up this born loser of a son!

What follows might make you reach for a very stiff drink

Ronald True: the English fighter ace who allegedly equalled Germany's *true* World War I ace, the 'Red Baron'

'Fight on and fly to the last drop of blood and the last drop of fuel, to the last beat of the heart. Success flourishes only in perseverance – ceaseless, relentless perseverance. If I should come out of this war alive, I will have more luck than brains. I like to fly, not to kill.'

Manfred Albrecht, Freiherr von Richthofen, aka 'the Red Baron', who carried out 80 kills

I guess that you would not have expected a reference to the greatest German fighter ace of all time during our road trip into Ronald True's mind. Still, extraordinary though it sounds, this concocter of half-truths and whole lies actually did enlist in the elite Royal Flying Corps in 1915. But let's unpack a little more of his narrative before we take to the blue yonder. After their doomed attempt to get their lad onto a Yorkshire farm, his family sent Ronald off to the prairies of Argentina. The result was the same – abject failure. In 1913, we find True in Canada, where he had a brief and inglorious stint in the North-West Mounted Police. Quite why it was 'inglorious' the organisation failed to elaborate upon following my freedom-of-information request. It might have been due to the fact that they'd never heard of him.

This shiftless man's next port of call was Mexico and, for reasons unknown to us, the episode became another setting for one of True's yarns, one in which he was in dispute with an unnamed German over a mining deed. According to True, his adversary had threatened to kill him on sight, but he had shot the German dead having been warned by a 'Red Indian' – whose tribe slipped his mind when pressed further. True had then allegedly written out his mining claim in his victim's blood. It seems that True was engrossed, even then, by the sight and smell of blood, by the idea of emerging triumphant from an armed feud. To him, the German prospector was no more flesh, blood and sinew than the German aircraft pilots he would later falsely claim to have shot down during World War I.

By 1914 he was in Shanghai, but when he learned that war had broken out, he rushed home, determined to join the elite Royal Flying Corps (RFC), the forerunner of the RAF. Somewhat incredibly, he was successful in his application. Medical checks failed to reveal that the starry-eyed True had become addicted to morphine during his travels.

'White Lady'

'*Per Ardua ad Astra.*'

'Through adversity to the stars': RFC

(and RAF) motto

At the start of World War I, the flat green fields on the western edges of Gosport, southern England, became military airfields. In 1914, the Grange Airfield (more recently HMS *Sultan*, a Royal Navy shore base) became the home of the RFC. It was also the base for the 'Special School of Flying', where, despite his addiction to the 'White Lady' True managed to get his pilot's licence at the third attempt. Thrilled to bits, he had the brightly coloured insignia of wings specially made at three times the regular size, all worked in silks of rainbow colours, then was promptly banned from wearing them. Guy Dent, a pilot who trained with True at Gosport, remembered him for his feverish, hysterical laugh and utter incompetence in the air: 'He was always rushing about and laughing with a loud voice, and he seemed deficient in common sense. When I saw the case [after True had been charged with murder] I thought is this the same True... he was unstable six years ago.'

Only a few months later, by which time his stepfather had been killed in France during the Battle of Aubers, True crashed a single-seater Avro 504 on his first cross-country solo flight at Farnborough. The accident knocked him unconscious for two days; however, no sooner was he on his feet than he was in the air again – for a remarkably short time, I might add. Morphine and flight obviously don't mix.

Again as high as the proverbial kite, he suffered a second crash – this time in Gosport. This accident was far more serious, and as a result he suffered a nervous breakdown. With the RFC by now doubtless ruing the day that it had ever let True within a mile of anything that flew, he was discharged from the service seven weeks later as an invalid. Just a month thereafter, he would be briefly hospitalised following a collapse in the King's Theatre, in Albert Road, Portsmouth. He would later ascribe this period of hospitalisation to his having contracted syphilis; there is no evidence to suggest that this was true – tests were negative.

Incredibly, this was not the end of Ronald True's 'Biggles' adventures. Somehow – and only God and the Government Control Works in Somerset at Yeovil, Somerset, know how – he persuaded them to hire him as a test pilot early in 1917. Fortunately, as soon as he'd signed on the dotted line he was dismissed after staff discovered that, in all probability, True could not even fly a model aeroplane. Added to which, he was arrogant, behaved erratically and his work performance was abysmal. That said, even if he was already marked out in life as a dead-cert loser, we have to at least applaud True for his perseverance. Later that year he was in New York posing as a fighter ace. Indeed, he so impressed a young actress called Frances Roberts that she agreed to marry him, having fallen completely for his fairy-tale stories and roguish charm. And the US War Department fell for his bullshit too: they gave him a job as a test pilot!

Frances Young

Frances, bless her over-the-knee white cotton socks, was introduced to Ronald True by friends at the end of July 1917. A pretty-as-a-picture aspiring actress living with her mother in New York, she noticed that True had a bandaged cut under one eye and what he called a 'poisonous leg', which he passed off as 'war wounds'. He said that he was on leave from the trenches in France, over which he claimed to have shot down many German aircraft and, that he had once duelled with the 'Red Baron' himself. Frances was much moved by his heroism and upper-class-cut-glass British accent, although afterwards to her cost she found out this was mostly fabricated BS. On 5 November that year the couple married.

True then left New York to take a job as a test pilot with the US War Department in Houston, Texas. When that fell through – possibly in part because the Houston Riot (a mutiny and riot by 156 soldiers from the all-black 24th Infantry Regiment) was in full swing – he again travelled to Mexico, then Cuba, before bringing his wife to England. Six months later they were off to West Africa, where True's mother had got him a job as an assistant manager with the Taquah Mining Company in the Gold Coast (now Ghana). And no, we do not need a crystal ball to foresee what happened next. In May 1919, Frances gave birth to a son. Three months later, the couple were on their way home again, True having been sacked. They settled on the south coast at Portsmouth, where Frances endeavoured to combine looking after her difficult husband with raising her son while also secretly returning to her work as an actress to bring in much-needed money.

This dismissal from the Taquah Mining Company was the final straw. While his mother still doted on True, other family members were infuriated with him. They severed all contact with him thereafter, but under pressure from Annabel did continue to give him a modest allowance to support himself and his family. Much of this money was being squandered on True's morphine intake, which had increased to about thirty grains per day.

Exactly when True began taking the drug morphine (or morphia) is not known, but the doctor who discovered his addiction in 1916 believed that the habit dated back many years. Shanghai, with its seedy nightlife and readily available drugs, seems the most likely starting point to me.

He was persuaded by his wife and mother to sign into a Southsea nursing home to be treated for his addiction – Dr Henry Jeans, who treated True, found that the small doses of morphine used to dull pain had no effect on his patient, whose long-term use had given him an immunity to the drug. Worse were the mental ailments that accompanied his addiction, which included the first signs of possible 'split personality', now known as dissociative identity (or personality) disorder. He was given to alarming mood swings at times and at other times would sit for hours staring out at the sea or the sky and saying nothing. He would absent himself from the nursing home on occasion, becoming well-known as an eccentric in this seaside resort; often seen on the promenade in his bathchair with a hooter attached, waving a doll and blowing a squeaker. He was also convinced he was being shadowed by a doppelgänger who shared his name – but spelled 'Ronald Trew' – and who he claimed was his mortal enemy. If he were presented with a bill, he would declare angrily: 'It's not meant for me – it's for the other Ronald Trew.' On those occasions when True's absences took him as far as London, he would get by through stealing and passing forged cheques. When caught, he would insist the crime in question was not his doing – it was all down to 'the other Ronald Trew'.

Upon his discharge from the nursing home, after about six months, True, his wife and child moved to Portsmouth. In September 1921 he was convicted at the Portsmouth Police Court of procuring morphine from a pharmacist by means of forged prescriptions. He was fined – and no doubt his mother paid up.

Ronald followed a further stint at a nursing home by moving in with his aunt in Folkestone. To her, he claimed that three fortune tellers from across the globe had told him he was to be murdered at 'the hands of a woman', and that he intended to make the most of his remaining days. Soon after, towards the end of 1921, having learned that Frances had resumed her acting career just to make ends meet, he abandoned his wife and child and removed both as beneficiaries from his will – which can't have made much difference to them. Shortly thereafter, in True's upside-down narrative, he relocated to London, falsely claiming that a 'Mr Harris' had offered him a lucrative job. Thereafter, he supported himself using his weekly allowance and by committing various acts of petty theft and fraud,

The great pretender

By 7 January 1922, True was frequenting various West End bars and clubs, living affluently but still surviving upon his allowance, thievery and paying hotel and restaurant bills with forged cheques. When challenged, he informed those who interrogated him that it was Ronald Trew who did it.

But, never one to give up on possibly lucrative ventures, and although he had never held down a steady job, at the age of thirty True finally dreamed up a scheme that appealed to his tastes. He would form a 'Murderers' Club' – its members would be hired out to the public at a fee of one shilling for each murder; as True put it, 'a bob a nob'.

Bearing in mind the legal definition of the M'Naghten rule, I do not see this as evidence of insanity. I do see True as a crackpot posing as a man-about-town with an alleged glamorous past, certainly a morphia addict, a thief and a congenital liar. To possess that crock of chicanery, one has to have one's wits about oneself – even with a scheme as half-witted as True's proposed club.

We next find this rascal at the Art Deco-style Lyons Corner House in Leicester Square, London. There, one day early in February 1922, and passing himself off as Major True, a former World War I fighter ace, he confided his plans for a 'Murderers' Club' to a bisexual called James Armstrong, an acquaintance that he'd known for barely a week. Although, just days before, Armstrong (then an unemployed car salesman) had sold True an automatic pistol with 100 cartridges for £2, he assumed the idea was merely a harmless joke. True had spoken plausibly of piloting aircraft and Armstrong believed his story of flying valuable cargoes for a civil airline between England and France. Added to which, True claimed that he needed the gun on the pretext that he might have to make a forced landing in a dangerous area of France — ignoring the fact that the war had ended more than three years previously.

It's said that the easiest person to sell something to is another salesperson, for these folk live in a world where all that glitters is gold — after all, that is what they try to convince us in order to earn a quick buck or two. And, although most second-hand car dealers, like politicians, are totally honest to a fault, as I am sure my readers will agree (with tongues in cheeks), it would be fair to say that Mr Armstrong spotted a lucrative deal here. He'd team up with 'Major True' and would milk the alleged flying ace for all he could.

Armstrong found 'Major Meal Ticket True' a humorous companion, if rather odd. He was always smiling, with a slightly zany, glazed look in his eyes — a sign of morphine use. True stood out in a crowd. He was 6 feet 1 inch tall, and he never wore a hat, which was unusual at the time. To James Armstrong, True seemed to be some kind of well-heeled gent of means. One who spent his nights in expensive hotels such as the Grand in Northumberland Avenue, or the all-male Savoy Turkish Baths at 92 Jermyn Street where guests could pass a night on a private couch. Might this be a hint that True was bisexual?

> Very pleasant sensation. Completely sensuous, but very healthy. It is extraordinary to find one's resistance to anything [i.e. sex] gradually weakening.
>
> Composer (Edward) Benjamin Britten, after being introduced to the Savoy Turkish Baths by the writer Christopher Isherwood

The Savoy Turkish Baths opened in 1910. Today, 92 Jermyn Street is the UK's flagship store for Crockett & Jones shoes. Back in the early 1920s the baths was one of three similar establishments that were open all night, and were widely known to be much frequented by gays. Thereafter, True and Armstrong teamed up for what degenerated into a month-long debauch in public houses, tearooms, nightclubs and cabaret halls across London – with True paying *all* the bills from his parents' allowance and his criminal activities. Point of fact: when he had no money, he paid none of the bills at all. Once again, pulling all of the above threads together, I still see no signs of anything approaching madness in the legal sense. True seems more of an out-and-out scoundrel.

One evening around 8 February 1922, at Murray's Cabaret Club in the West End, True struck up a conversation with a Mrs Elizabeth Wilson, who was drinking alone. To set the scene, Soho was a part of London that during most of the twentieth century was known as a shabby den of iniquity and the heart of the sex industry, but, situated in Beak Street was Murray's Cabaret Club, a club that brought class to sleaze. Founded in 1913 as a cabaret club, it was a members-only venue, exclusive and expensive, where its patrons could wine and dine, listen to music, enjoy cabaret acts and tableaux, watch or try out the latest dances like the then risqué tango. Neither man was a member, but they managed to sneak in as 'guests'. (Many years later Murray's became famous as the nightclub where Christine Keeler met Stephen Ward, who would eventually introduce her to John Profumo and scandal.)

Immediately drawn to Mrs Wilson, True began to force his

attentions upon her. He confided to her that there was a man – 'the other Ronald Trew' – who was impersonating him, a story he had been telling and retelling people for years. He also told her he would like to meet her husband – so that he could shoot him. Unable to dance himself because of an old hip injury – allegedly caused by a duel with the dashing 'Red Baron' in the skies above France – he nonetheless forbade her to dance with other men. And if that streak of possessiveness wasn't enough, he told her that if she refused to meet him again 'there would be trouble'. He added, ominously, that because he was a highly decorated war hero he 'could get away with murder'.

Foretelling the future

Allegedly, the world's most consummate foretellers of good fortune are sports pundits, most of whom could not give you a genuine tip for the favourite in a one-horse race. But True was very convincing. Elizabeth Wilson became very nervous. She decided that he was quite mad. Rather than report his threat to the police who would probably not take her seriously, she felt, especially as they would see her as a woman of 'loose morals' for frequenting a cabaret club, she reluctantly agreed to see him once more, on condition that a third person was present. Armstrong was happy to step in, and until True's interest began to wane and he redirected the focus of his gaze, the three went on to meet up at Murray's on most nights.

One evening around this time True telephoned Elizabeth with the dramatic news that he had just been to his mother's house, where he'd found her lying on the floor battered almost to death. It goes without saying that this was a total lie. 'She is unlikely to survive,' he exclaimed. He added that she had been taken to hospital and was being operated upon by a surgeon called – Mr Wilson. The next day, Elizabeth asked him why there was no report of the attack in the newspapers. 'I am keeping it quiet for the time being. There is going to be a big case about it,' True replied, mysteriously. On another evening, True told Elizabeth flatly, 'I will murder someone one of these days. You watch the papers and see if I don't. I am perfectly certain I will get off – I want try it out.'

At first blush one might think that this was just a throw-away comment made with this man's usual braggadocio, but let's hold our horses here. Let's look at the line: 'I am perfectly certain I will get off – I want to try it out.' In saying this, True is anticipating a future event. But if we use the M'Naghten rule as our yardstick, those individuals who kill and are later judged to be clinically insane, genuinely insane people who commit murder, absolutely *do not* boast about trying to 'get away' with anything. Once more, I suggest that in making that statement to Elizabeth Wilson, True showed himself to be well up to speed in the sanity department.

Although he was certainly living in his own La-La Land, True was about to test his luck again. He was clumsily going to try to make a name for himself in the annals of British criminal history. Having failed to recruit any members to join his 'Murderer's Club', it appears that he was going to try to his hand at homicide himself, and keep all the proceeds of a his nefarious crime – he would kill for financial gain.

Elizabeth Wilson, however, was not worth killing for any sort of financial gain. She, like True, was almost on her uppers. The woman herself was by now convinced that True was truly a fully riveted nut-ball. Armstrong, on the other hand, still saw nothing but harmless eccentricity in his friend.

Much to Mrs Wilson's relief, True lost interest in her after meeting a very attractive twenty-five-year-old call girl calling herself Olive Young (her real name was Mrs Gertrude Yates). Olive, it appeared from her expensive clothes, gold jewellery and classy tastes, would make for a good 'mark' – a suitable target for the criminally minded True. So out of the window went Elizabeth. He had now set his beady eyes on Olive.

Gertrude Yates had been a shop girl. She drifted into prostitution, adopting the name Olive Young, and because of her intelligence and attractiveness she'd built up a 'business', one successful enough that she could be choosy about her clients. True paid his first visit to Olive's basement flat at 13a Finborough Road, Fulham, on Saturday, 18 February 1922. It was, and still is, a smart residence, so it seems that she was a popular lass amongst her clientele. The next day, Olive found that a £5 note was missing from her handbag. This was a considerable sum back then. She was also concerned about the fact that True carried a pistol, which he had proudly shown her, and by his hawkish interest in her diamond rings and diamond platinum watch. Understandably frightened, the young woman decided to avoid him in future and for almost two weeks she was successful, despite his frequent attempts to contact her. She made sure that each night no light was visible from her flat. She let him hammer on the door in vain. She would not even speak to him on the telephone. He simply was not her type.

So at this juncture during our road trip into True's mind, shall we take a tea break? I'd like to address my readers on the subject of something that most of them will probably already be familiar with. It is quite obvious to me that Olive, with her expensive tastes in attire and well-heeled men, was innately aware of that famous phrase 'clothes make the man'.

'Clothes make the man'...

... has its origins in the Greek expression 'the man is his clothing'. The phrase has a long history. In his *Adages* (1500) – a compendium of Latin and Greek proverbs – the Renaissance humanist Erasmus includes '"*Divitiae" vestis virim facit*', which translates as '"Ornamental" clothing makes the man.' The first recorded usages of the saying in English are from the fifteenth century: in *Peter Idley's Instructions to his Son* (1443), we find, 'Ffor clothing oft maketh man.' Take the character of Eliza Doolittle from George Bernard Shaw's play *Pygmalion* (1913). Eliza is turned into a different person by Professor Higgins, mainly through the way she is presented: everyone assumes that she is from the upper class because she dresses and speaks as though she is.

Almost everyone who knew Ronald True assumed that he was from the upper classes because he tried to dress well and spoke as though he was – and his mother was a baroness. But, he had a flaw. His shirt cuffs were frayed and had been roughly trimmed with scissors. His collar was likewise scruffy, his shoes were down-at-heel, his suit certainly didn't have the cut of a man who claimed to be former RFC ace.

I suggest that Olive smelt him out in almost a heartbeat. He was as fake as a Bangkok wristwatch with a bamboo spring. He was an oily, smug creep, one who couldn't resist showing her his pistol and eyeing up her expensive jewellery. He was casing the joint from the get-go!

OK, folks. Tea break over. On 28 February, True pawned a gold wristwatch which did not belong to him before he and Armstrong visited the Palais de Danse in Hammersmith, west London. Back then, the place occupied a large site at 242 Shepherd's Bush Road. The first club in the UK to be called Palais de Danse, this entertainment venue opened in 1919 and was considered the grandest and most opulent of such venues in all of Europe; it lasted until 2007, by which time it was known as the Hammersmith Palais. It was here that True recognised Robert Dare St Aubyn Sach, an American. The two men had previously met in the US in 1917, when Sach was employed, like True, as a test-pilot by the United States War Department, but a much better one. Sach remembered True as being an oddball but, like Armstrong, found him amusing company. As was his wont, True took the opportunity to ask the American to lend him a gold sovereign – circa £350 in today's money. Noticing that his pal was short on cash, it dawned on the sponging spiv Armstrong that the once-laden money tree was now dropping less fruit. Ronald True was indeed almost cleaned out – fresh out of valuables, either his own to sell or other people's to pawn – and even with his family's allowance he was living well beyond his means. Yet, he still survived through his talent for avoiding bills, gaining credit and using his silver-tongued spiel to get by.

Scotland Yard

Early on 2 March 1922, True checked into the Grand Hotel on Northumberland Avenue. He had stayed here before when previously flush with cash and had always settled his bill. Goodness gracious me, he was after all a war hero, a former flying ace with a dicky leg. Imagine him now, dear reader. Let's sit down at a nearby table and observe.

Look on as the tip-dependant, obsequious waiter, fawns over True as he tucks a white napkin into the top of his shirt. 'And, what is the Major's pleasure this morning – sausages or a fresh herring? Sir, it's *so nice* to be at your service once again.' But, oops-a-daisy. This time after breakfast, our cheeky Major True slips out without paying, and with the downright nerve of this professional confidence trickster, he hires himself a car and a chauffeur to be driven around in style for the next four days – without paying even a brass farthing. Behaviour most certainly *not* characteristic of someone who is psychologically unanchored.

That evening True dined with Armstrong, who lived near Hyde Park with his mother. Mrs Armstrong had met him before and was uneasy enough about him to warn her son to be careful, she felt that True was not quite 'right in his mind'. While he was at their home, True slipped her purse into his pocket. Among other things, he'd spotted that it contained a cheque for £7 (today it would have the purchasing power of £490). After dinner, the chauffeur he had hired picked him and Armstrong up and they drove to Olive Young's flat. True ordered the chauffeur, Luigi Mazzola, to stop and wait on the corner of nearby Fulham Road. Armstrong stayed in the car. True climbed out, to return shortly afterwards and announce, 'My friends are out.' Of course she was out, you dumb fuck. She was a 'working girl' and servicing a well-heeled client!

Now, True was still married to his American-born wife, Frances, and the reader will be wondering why I have not mentioned her as I recall the narrative of her husband's amoral life. In fact, she had been worried about his peculiar behaviour for a long time. His absenteeism from the marital home, his total indifference to their child and the lack of financial support had all had played heavily on this young woman's mind. At her wits' end, on the very same day, 2 March 1922, she visited Scotland Yard and appealed for help in tracing her missing spouse.

There is something about the name 'Scotland Yard' that is embedded in the DNA of us true-crime aficionados. It resonates in our minds as do Blackfriars Bridge, the Old Bailey, Tyburn and the hangings, the gallows long past with the 'short drop'; according to some sources, the crowds for public execution days far exceeded those of any present-day World Cup football match.

Frances explained to the police that her husband was given to delusions, fits of violence and melancholia. She said that he had been in and out of nursing homes for years. He was addicted to morphine and incapable of work, she explained. He posed as a war hero and daredevil pilot, while living off charity from his family. The police officer listened carefully as she revealed that True had left their Portsmouth home on a false pretext in late January that year, but had twice met her by arrangement in London. On the second occasion, in mid–February, he had been unusually hostile and had shown her a pistol. At this, the officer's ear pricked up, but as no criminal offence had been reported there was little else the police could do other than to recommend her to a former chief inspector, James Stockley, who now ran a private detective agency.

Frances hired him the following day and instructed him to trace her husband as quickly as possible. Stockley doubtless understood the urgency of finding a man who was allegedly deranged, short of money and armed, and his gumshoes began searching for Ronald True. Trivia note: detectives are often called 'gumshoes' because back in the day, their shoes and boots were made of gum rubber, as their soft soles allowed for a quiet step. To 'gumshoe' came to mean to sneak around quietly, but could mean anyone who needed to be stealthy, both thieves and thief–catchers alike.

The evil doppelgänger

Back to Ronald True, who on 3 March 1922 took David Sach, his wife Nancy and Armstrong to Hammersmith's Palais de Danse. During the floor show, True quietly told the couple about his feud with the man who was impersonating him. This man, he said, had run up bills of £5,000, which his mother had been obliged to settle; he added that he intended to shoot his alleged double. He even pointed out a man on the dance floor as 'the other Ronald Trew' – much to the Sachs' utter bewilderment, as the man looked nothing like their friend, being considerably shorter for a start.

As they drank, Ronald True added a new twist to the plot. He revealed that he had a second enemy whom he was also planning to kill. This man, he said, lived in a basement flat in Fulham, and had a revolver. The Sachs were now becoming more concerned by the minute as the garrulous True went on to announce that, on the following Sunday he intended to visit the flat and kill the man. 'Look out for it in the papers on Monday morning,' he said, while drawing a plan of the place on the back of a menu card. 'It will be one or the other of us.'

David Sach knew that True had always been eccentric; now he was beginning to wonder whether he was insane. He did not believe a word True said any more. In fact, True had drawn the plan of an *actual* property: and, unbeknownst to Sach, it was that of Olive Young's basement flat.

After the party broke up, True and Armstrong again drove to Finborough Road. Once more, True told Luigi Mazzola to park at the corner, then alighted and returned soon after, reporting that his 'friends were out' this time too. The reader surely must see the significance of True's second late-evening visit to Olive Young's home: he was planning to steal her valuable possessions. And she would have to be in her flat when he committed the theft – all terminating in a fatal outcome. He had to murder the woman because otherwise she would turn him in to the police.

Now events quickened apace.

On the following day, Saturday, 4 March 1922, True persuaded Mrs Sach to cash the cheque stolen from Armstrong's mother, which he had fraudulently endorsed to himself on the reverse side. True and the American couple then drove to Windsor for tea at the Castle Hotel. And as we are on our own road trip into True's mind, let's stop off here ourselves. I quote below from the hotel's website:

The Castle Hotel began life in 1528 as 'The Mermaid Inn' – humbly brewing beer and cider for the people of Windsor which, at the time, was a small town of just 1,000 people. During the 1700s, innkeeper Richard Martin was awarded the first of the hotel's Royal Warrants – to provide horses and carriages for the royal household. The hotel grew with the population of Windsor to become one of the grandest places to stay in the Royal Borough.

By the nineteenth century, the Castle Hotel Windsor had solidified this reputation as the connoisseur's choice of accommodation in the area. The hotel was so popular among the elite that the Duke of Wellington stepped in to dine after his victory over Napoleon at the Battle of Waterloo.

And having learned of this remarkable hotel during the research for this book, I plan one day to take afternoon tea there – as did Ronald True on 4 March 1922.

After sitting down, this devious rascal now revealed to the couple that a man at the next table was a third enemy of his and was mistreating a young lady called Olive who lived in Bedford. The name 'Olive' meant nothing to the Americans, who noticed that not a flicker of recognition, nor hint of tension, registered on the face of the other man, who was innocently sipping his Earl Grey a few feet away. When the man had left, True was called to the telephone – a ploy he must have devised beforehand. He returned to say that he had been speaking to Olive, and had reprimanded the man about his behaviour. What the couple could not have known was that in his confused way, True had been telling them about a serious danger to Olive Young. And that it was True himself who was the danger.

That evening, Mazzola drove True to Fulham again, arriving just after 11:30 p.m. As before, True returned after a few minutes away from the car, complaining that 'he was on urgent business and could not find the right people'. In fact, for the third night running he had seen that Olive was not at home; she was in the habit of leaving a light on in the entrance passage to deter burglars and switching it off when she returned.

On Sunday, 5 March, True and Armstrong were driven to Reading, where Armstrong had the use of a bungalow. True was near penniless but was keeping his hired car and driver until the last minute, although payment was now more than due.

After spending an idle day by the Thames, they returned to London that evening. The two men drove to Fulham once more. True left the car and saw that Olive was, at last, at home, but, instead of first knocking, he returned to the car, declared that his 'friends' were still out and drove Armstrong to his mother's house. Then, with Armstrong out of the car, he ordered Mazzola to drive back to Fulham and park right outside Olive's place. For once, Olive Young had relaxed her vigilance. Through the glass of the front door True saw a light in the hallway. He knocked, and Olive opened the door. In view of her efforts to dodge him, the girl must have been dismayed when she saw the tall figure of the 'Major' looming in the doorway. But in her profession she could not afford to create a 'scene' in such a quiet, respectable street.

A few minutes later, True returned to the car to tell his chauffeur that he would be staying at the flat overnight. Mazzola later told the court at True's trial: 'As I drove away I heard Big Ben chiming midnight.'

Murder most foul

'Do not wake Miss Young.'

Ronald True to Olive Young's maid

Olive Young was a striking young woman. At the trial she was somewhat bluntly painted as 'a member of the unfortunate class', but in fact, as mentioned above, she made a good income from her profession and had a lifestyle that many would have envied. By the time of her death at the age of twenty-five, she was living well from her selected clients or 'friends'. She wore expensive jewellery of diamonds, gold and silver, and had the healthy sum of £150 (equivalent to £10,500 in spending power today) in her Post Office Savings bank account.

The next morning, Monday, 6 March, Olive's maid, Emily Steel, arrived as usual at 9:15 a.m. She found both the mail and the *Daily Mirror* newspaper on the doorstep and let herself in using her pass key. She entered the kitchen and then the sitting room, where she found a man's blue coat and red-and-blue muffler on the table. The bedroom door was shut, but she noticed that the glass panel in the door was newly cracked.

In the kitchen, Emily cooked sausages for her own breakfast, and afterwards as she was tidying up the sitting room, a man came down the hall whom she recognised immediately as Ronald True. 'Do not wake Miss Young,' he said calmly. 'We were late last night. She is in a deep sleep. I will send the car round for her at twelve o'clock.'

Miss Steel helped True on with his overcoat, after which he generously tipped her half a crown. Miss Steel would later tell the trial court that she saw him hail a cab at about 9:45 a.m. Then she went on to explain that despite True telling her not to disturb Olive, she went straight to the bedroom door, discreetly knocked and upon hearing no reply walked in.

Olive appeared to be asleep under the bedclothes. Turning the bedding back, Miss Steel was alarmed to discover 'two pillows laid lengthways down the bed and covered with blood'. Under the eiderdown was a rolling pin. The drawers of the dressing table were partly open, the contents disturbed. Some jewellery, kept in a box in the cupboard, was missing together with about £8 in cash.

The maid then opened the bathroom door. The body of her mistress was sprawled across the floor, naked except for a pyjama jacket draped across one shoulder. Her head had been severely battered. There was a belt from a dressing gown around her neck and a towel had been stuffed down her throat. The police arrived within thirty minutes and Chief Inspector William Brown of Scotland Yard reached the flat at 11 a.m. In the bedroom he found a visiting card that read 'Mr Ronald True. 23 Audley Street' – an exclusive address in Mayfair, although it was for appearances only. True had never lived there. Then police found a note that had been written by Olive Young. It included yet another false address where True claimed he'd lived.

At postmortem examination, pathologist Dr William Lee noted that Olive Young had been clubbed on the head by five separate blows from a blunt instrument – the rolling pin found in her bed. He found that they had been delivered with 'considerable force to the back and front of her head, causing broad cuts and extensive bleeding, and any of those blows would have rendered this decedent unconscious.' The piece of rough towelling had been rammed down Olive's throat and the belt of the dressing gown was tied rightly around her neck. Dr Lee ascribed death to asphyxia – the inability to breathe – rather than to the blows to the head.

True was a stealthy killer. There was no sign that he'd fired his pistol – any gunshots would have been heard by the other residents in the building. The only evidence that even hinted at a struggle was the crack in the glass panel in the bedroom door, therefore it is likely that True attacked Olive Young while she was sipping an early morning cup of tea. A broken cup and saucer were found on the floor beside her bed.

Jung's observation that 'Those who ignore this other self, the shadow, *do so at their peril*. They would force this "other self" to take a dangerous course of its own' [author's italics] is borne out by True's remarkably bizarre behaviour following the murder. After leaving the flat, where he had unaccountably lingered for at least an hour after he killed Olive Young, and where he had advertised himself to the maid, True moved at a frenetic pace in a confused effort to throw off the police, who were almost immediately onto him. The result was a trail of further incriminating evidence that could point only to him as the heinous killer.

Ordering his taxi to stop at a post office in Fulham Road, True telephoned Mazzola and told him to collect Armstrong and meet him at the Strand Corner House, near Trafalgar Square, and not, as previously arranged, outside Olive Young's flat. True alighted at Horne Brothers, a men's tailoring shop in Coventry Street, Piccadilly, where he was a client. He showed the manager bloodstains on his grey trousers, explaining that he had had a flying accident that very morning, and he chose a brown suit off the peg, saying: 'It is not so bad for a reach-me-down.' He also bought a bowler hat (a 'disguise', because he was well known for never wearing a hat) along with a collar and tie. True actually showed the manager a lady's wristwatch and a string of pearls that he claimed to have bought in France. He then left and visited a barber shop in Wardour Street, Soho.

While at the barbers, True left the parcel containing his bloodstained suit, saying that he would collect it later. One might have thought that anyone in their right mind would have found a more secret location within the ten square miles of central London to dump a parcel, but not the bungling True. He then went to a pawnbroker a few doors away, where he redeemed a silver cigarette case and watch that he had pawned two days beforehand. He also asked the absurd price of £70 for the two rings he had stolen from Olive Young. The canny pawnbroker, Herbert Elliot, gave him £25 for other jewellery stolen from the flat, which True signed for in his own name.

Perhaps we can now imagine Ronald True at his next stop, the Lyons Corner House on the Strand, having just told Mazzola he wished that he had instructed him to wait the night before, because he had stayed only twenty minutes in the flat at Finborough Road. He has, he said, left almost immediately because, as he was to inform the police, a man and a woman were 'in the midst of a violent argument and blows'. He even gave a description of the man in his written statement: 'Aged 31. 6ft, 2in., dressed in a dark suit, light grey overcoat, and bowler hat'. His shadow, clearly.

The police found it fairly easy to pick up True's trail, despite the fraudulent Mayfair address on his visiting card. They made contact with James Stockley, the private detective hired by True's wife, who warned his former cop colleagues that True was armed, and should be considered highly dangerous.

Into cuffs, into custody

'Where are you taking me?'

Ronald True: to Chief Inspector Brown

True kept up his dizzy pace all afternoon; travelling with Armstrong and Mazzola for drinks in Hounslow, and Feltham in west London, and Croydon to the south-east, where he bought the *Star* evening paper. The front-page headline was about the murder of Olive Young. 'Nothing of interest,' True casually commented to Armstrong, who was either blind, deaf or dumb. The party then drove across to south-west London, where True bought and put on a shirt in Richmond, perhaps to change his appearance from the description given in the *Star* report. They then turned north across the river into Hammersmith. By 8:30 p.m., the men had reached the 'Palace of Varieties' at 82 King Street,

Hammersmith. Built in 1898, this thrived as a music hall, featuring stars like Dan Leno and Vesta Tilley. It closed in 1909, and has since been demolished.

Mazzola was asked by True to return after the second performance was over, so the chauffeur drove back to his garage in Knightsbridge – where he found Chief Inspector Brown and three other detectives waiting for him. Learning of True's present whereabouts, they ordered Mazzola to take them to the theatre at once. True and Armstrong had initially taken seats in the stalls, but switched to a box during the interval. The lights had again dimmed when, at 9:45 p.m., the detectives moved in swiftly through the rear to apprehend their man. Aware that True carried a gun, Detective Inspector Albert Burton grabbed his wrists. The cowardly killer made no attempt to resist. Outside the box, the pistol was taken from True's hip pocket. It was loaded with three cartridges, two of them filed down like dum-dum bullets. The officers also found over £17 in cash, a gold wedding ring and a pawn ticket for a gold watch and bracelet. More of Olive's jewellery was found in True's overcoat in Mazzola's car. When he asked where he was being taken to, the detectives curtly told him 'Wilton Street Police Station', where he would be questioned about the murder of Olive Young. 'It's no use me putting up a defence now,' True said, adding, 'but I will do at the proper time, otherwise I will only have to repeat myself.' He then changed his mind and blurted out a similar yarn to the one he'd told Mazzola earlier: that he had visited Young's flat where she and another man were arguing, which prompted him to leave shortly thereafter. All of which completely contradicted what the maid, Miss Steel, had told the police.

Ronald True was formally charged with Olive Young's murder the following morning, 7 March 1922.

A travesty of justice – in reverse

'The dispensing of injustice is always in the right hands.'

> Stanisław Jerzy Lec (aka Baron Stanisław Jerzy de Tusch-Letz), Polish poet and aphorist: *Unkempt Thoughts* (1962)

It is important to note that while remanded in HMP Brixton awaiting his trial, Ronald True was examined by the prison's senior medical officer, Dr William East. The latter came to the conclusion that the prisoner was insane – certainly not mentally able to instruct counsel, nor to understand the legal proceedings to which he was now subject. (True had told Dr East and his assistant Dr Young about his impersonator, the doppelgänger 'Ronald Trew'.) This being the case, and if the law was to be properly applied, the M'Naghten rule would have stood solid. True would have been found guilty of murder while mentally unbalanced, and packed off to spend the remainder of his days in an asylum for the criminally insane. There would have been no legal requirement for a full murder trial at all. But it didn't work out that way.

Despite the medical opinion that True was insane, he was tried. The upshot was that a meddlesome home secretary overruled the jury's guilty verdict and overruled two following upheld appeals, one of which was heard by none other than the lord chief justice of England. Had the strict letter of the law been followed, Ronald True would have been hanged. If ever there was a case of a 'reverse miscarriage of justice', this is it.

True relished his notoriety while on remand, but calmly continued to deny ever having murdered Olive Young, despite the overwhelming evidence against him. He remained quite unruffled, despite the prospect of being hanged. Indeed, one day in the prison hospital where he was being kept under observation, he met an inmate whom he knew was also accused of murder, and shouted out: 'Here's another for our "Murderers' Club" – we are only accepting members who kill them outright!' The inmate was eighteen-year-old Henry Julius Jacoby. On 14 March 1922, he had battered to death sixty-five-year-old Lady Alice White, a guest at the Spencer Hotel in Portman Street, London, where he worked as a pantry boy; her skull was crushed to fragments. He would be hanged at HMP Pentonville by executioner John Ellis on 5 June 1922. It may be of some interest to learn that the hangman felt some pity for the lad he was about to drop through the trap. '[Jacoby] seemed completely unconcerned about his impending fate as I measured him up as he played a makeshift cricket with one of the warders the afternoon before I would end his life,' Ellis reminisced. 'As I pinioned his wrists in the condemned cell, Jacoby made a point of thanking the governor and waiting prison officers for their kindness to him. As he went to the execution shed, he was the calmest person ever.'

Sir Richard Muir, KC, in charge of the prosecution, was well aware of the M'Naghten rule. He felt that this was a premeditated and calculated murder, the motive being robbery. As we have seen thus far, there can be no doubt about that. Muir pointed out that True's efforts to sell the victim's personal property and conceal clues were hardly the actions of a madman. Amazingly, however, the prosecutor could not find a single forensic psychiatrist throughout the whole of Great Britain, to agree with him. Not one shrink whom he approached thought that True was sane. Even odder was the fact that neither Brixton's senior medical officer nor his assistant were called to give their opinion that True was insane.

The Old Bailey

True's trial opened at the Old Bailey on Monday, 1 May 1922, with the controversial Mr Justice Sir Henry Wilfred McCardie presiding, a judge noted for opinions that often differed from those of the rest of the judiciary

True pleaded not guilty and went on to sit through the ensuing proceedings wearing his inane grin. He was calm and relaxed in the box, taking the occasional notes. His experienced counsel, Sir Henry Curtis-Bennett, KB, a rotund figure well known for his eloquence, had dissuaded his client from even opening his mouth.

In his opening speech for the Crown, Muir emphasised True's need for money and his efforts to evade suspicion after the killing. 'This murder was an exceedingly deliberate and brutal one, which was carried out with great thoroughness,' he told the jury. 'Nothing was left to chance.'

For the defence, Curtis-Bennett in his brief opening speech hinted that he would accept that True had killed Olive Young, but announced he would prove that the defendant had been abnormal since birth and was now plainly insane – 'a homicidal maniac' in fact! But, where did the strength of this mitigational defence spring from?

Aunt Grace Angus was the first defence witness to be called. She described her nephew as an only child, at odds with himself, who loved and yet tortured his pet rabbits and pony. 'He was remarkably untruthful,' she added.

Next into the witness box was True's wife, Frances. She described her tormented marriage to a morphine addict. She recounted how her husband had turned against both her and their son. 'He was very, *very* distressed and antagonistic to myself,' she said. 'He said he was going away... From that time, the middle of February, he completely disappeared. His mother and I were very anxious for his safety.'

Next came a troupe of witnesses, including several from True's brief flying career and the Southsea nursing home he stayed in. The defence were paving the way for the medical experts, the vital witnesses who might persuade the jury to spare True's life.

Examined by Curtis-Bennett, Dr East said that True had never fully developed a sense of right and wrong, and his condition had been worsened by his flying crashes and morphine addiction. When cross-examined, Dr East went on to say that the killer's actions had showed that he knew he had done a punishable act, but had also revealed his need for publicity, which, we can agree, would not give Ronald True the chance of a successful M'Naghten rule defence.

Muir was now placed in the most unfavourable of positions. With not a forensic psychiatrist in the land willing to support him, the lead counsel failed to undermine Dr East's certainty that True was insane, but he harped constantly on about True's guile and ruthlessness.

'You think [True] thought he had the right to commit murder, although murder, he knew, was punishable by law?' he asked.

Somewhat remarkably, Dr East agreed: 'Yes, that is what it comes to.'

'Does that mean that [True believed] he had a moral right to murder anyone that he chooses?'

'Yes,' Dr East replied, bluntly. The three other medical witnesses generally supported his views, emphasising that True no longer had the power to control his actions.

In his closing speech on 5 May, the fifth and final day of the trial, Curtis-Bennett disputed the idea that True had killed for greed, arguing that he could have obtained money from his mother whenever he wanted. This was a totally false submission, because True always squandered what allowance his mother gave him on the high life, supplementing it by thieving and conning day after day. No doctor, the barrister said, had spoken for the Crown's case and True's actions before and after the murder had plainly lacked reason or self-control.

For the prosecution, Muir was still determined to show the jurors that however unbalanced True might have appeared, the crime was a down-to-earth matter of common greed, a plan cunningly prepared with malice aforethought by its perpetrator.

Summing up, Mr Justice McCardie dealt sympathetically with the medical evidence but towards the end of his speech seemed to lean towards the prosecution's view. 'It was a case in which murder was followed by theft, and by a thief who selected the more valuable things,' he told the jury. He reminded them that True could be reprieved from a death sentence, even if convicted, a signal that he wanted the jury to adhere to the strict law on legal responsibility.

The jury retired at 6:05 p.m., and returned less than ninety minutes later. 'Guilty of wilful murder,' the foreman declared without hesitation. It was noticeable that the jury attached no rider asking for mercy. Even as lay people, they could see True for what he truly was: a murderous conman, a mendacious, conniving knave, a man who probably didn't even know the meaning of truth even when it stared right back at him.

True was asked if he had anything to say before sentence was passed. 'I am innocent, my Lord. That is all,' he replied, with a smirk on his face. The judge donned the black cap and sentenced True to be taken away to be hanged in due course. As His Honour rose from his bench, he picked up the pen he'd used to sign the order and snapped it in two – a practice well recognised by 'hanging judges' throughout decades.

Nonetheless, the prevailing medical and legal opinion was that True was clearly insane. After his appeal against conviction was dismissed, bringing him a few steps closer to the execution shed, on 25 May a panel of 'specialists' was appointed to assess his state of mind – routine procedure for condemned persons. All three agreed that True was a lunatic.

While awaiting execution, Ronald True penned this last letter to a former chauffeur named Frank Sims, whom he got to know in the Southsea nursing home: 'It's unfortunate that I shall probably cash my chips in just prior to my birthday…

but [I] am considering petitioning the King to extend the period.' He thanked Sims for testifying at the trial about his mental condition and gave him a list of horses worth betting on. 'It may interest you to know that the winner of the Derby is included in this little lot,' True noted. He ended with the words: 'Cheerio, old nut, and if you come to the same place as I am going to, I'll have a drink of nice, cold water ready for you to drink on your arrival.'

We can never know what Sims's thoughts were upon receiving this letter. Perhaps something along the lines of: 'Screw the cold glass of water, you ass wipe, what about all the money for freebee taxicab fares you owe me and Luigi Mazzola?'

On 8 June, the home secretary, Edward Shortt, duly announced that True was reprieved on the grounds of insanity. There was an immediate outcry, for only three days earlier, the poor eighteen-year-old pantry boy whom we met earlier was executed. On that occasion, the home secretary had rejected the jury's appeal for mercy. Newspapers were inundated with angry letters, arguing that there was one law for the rich, another for the poor – a valid argument that still remains so to this very day. True was followed by newspaper reporters as he was taken on his final road trip from HMP Pentonville, London, to the Broadmoor Asylum for the Criminally Insane in the peaceful fields of Berkshire. Once the huge gates had closed behind him, freed from the pressures of the outside world, it is said that he settled down to the happiest days of his life. At the time, he was one of the most popular and longest-staying patients the asylum had ever had.

'I had to respite [True]'

The home secretary, Edward Shortt, said these words when he overruled judge and jury twice running and granted True a reprieve, having refused one to murderer Henry Jacoby despite pleas for clemency from the jury. Jacoby's victim, Lady Alice White, was the 'establishment'; Ronald True was at least semi-establishment and his victim was portrayed as a woman of loose morals.

One of the psychiatrists called by the defence was Harley Street's Sir Maurice Craig, KBE, FRCP who specialised in the legal aspects of psychiatry (in the context of determining sanity or capacity to stand trial).

Craig was a pioneer in the treatment of mental illness. However, does his opinion, and that is *only* what it was – a personal view – stack up against what the twelve wide-awake jurors determined using streetwise common sense, i.e. that Ronald True was sane? Indeed, while True was on remand in Brixton prison the chief medical officer *and* Craig – the latter in his capacity as a psychiatrist – deemed True mentally unfit to stand his trial. So, make of that legal inconsistency what you will.

It has been said that the greatest tragedy of True's case is that so many people who realised how mentally ill he was did nothing to help him. Had they done something, they might have helped save the life of Olive Young.

Conclusions

As we draw this book to its close after our trip through the minds of the so-called criminally insane – some of whom might genuinely be as mad as hatters and thus are rightly deserving of our compassion, because they truly know not what they do – let me make the following observation. If forensic psychiatrists, from either side of a legal debate, continue to abuse the long-established M'Naghten rule to serve their own ends, we should remind ourselves of Sir Ludovic Kennedy's remark that appeared at the outset of this book:

Christopher, let's not fool ourselves that a murder trial is a search for the truth. It's anything but. It's a legal stage set with actors; a bewigged judge all wrapped up in ermine, the lawyers in gowns and horsehair wigs; psychiatrists who most often disagree with colleagues let alone their own thinking, with the better side winning, even at the cost of true justice.

I ask my readers to consider all that we have covered in this book, and then apply the following 'common sense' rulings from *Kahler v. Kansas* (Certiorari to the Supreme Court of Kansas, No. 18-6135. Argued: 7 October 2019. Decided: 23 March 2020). I will try to spare you too much legal jargon, but it seems to me that Kansas has lucidly, well and truly hit the nail on the head. So please bear with me.

> In a previous ruling – *Clark v. Arizona*, 548 U.S. 735, this Court catalogued the diverse strains of the insanity defense that States have adopted to absolve mentally ill defendants of criminal culpability. Two – the cognitive and moral capacity tests – appear as alternative pathways to acquittal in the landmark English ruling *M'Naghten's Case*, 10 Cl. & Fin. 200, 8 Eng. Rep.178.
>
> The morality incapacity tests asks whether a defendant's illness left him unable to distinguish between right and wrong with respect to his/her criminal conduct. Respondent Kansas has adopted the cognitive incapacity test, which examines whether a defendant was able to understand what he or she was doing when committing a crime. Specifically, under Kansas law [and this law accords most generally with the M'Naghten rule], a defendant may raise mental illness to show that he 'lacked the culpable mental state required as an element of the offense charged.' Kansas does not require any additional way that mental illness

can produce an acquittal, although a defendant may use evidence of mental illness to argue for a lessened punishment at sentencing. In particular, Kansas does not recognize a moral–incapacity defense.

In *Kahler v. Kansas*, James Kahler was charged with capital murder after he shot and killed four family members. The facts of the matter are as follows. In early 2009, Karen Kahler filed for divorce from her husband James and moved out of their home with their two teenage daughters and nine–year–old son. Over the following months, James Kahler became more and more distraught. On Thanksgiving weekend, he drove to the home of Karen's grandmother, where he knew his family was staying. He entered through the back door and saw Karen and his son. He shot Karen twice, while allowing his boy to flee the property. He then moved through the residence, shooting the grandmother and each of her daughters in turn. All four of his victims died. Kahler surrendered to police the next day and was charged with capital murder.

Prior to trial, his defence argued that Kansas's insanity defence violated due process because it permits the State to convict a defendant whose mental illness prevented him from distinguishing between right from wrong. Does this not echo the defence put forth in the Ronald True case? I think that it does. Of course True knew the difference between right from wrong; the jury sensed as much, and both of his appeals were turned down, the second one by the then lord chief justice of England. Yet a meddlesome home secretary – a pen-pushing public servant no more, no less – decided that he would take the law into his own hands and overrule justice with a stroke of his pen. In Kahler's case the trial court disagreed and the jury returned a conviction, as certainly *was* the case in True's trial at the Old Bailey.

During the penalty phase, Kahler was free to raise any argument he wished that mental illness should mitigate his sentence, but the jury still imposed the death sentence, exactly as did the jury in True's case. The Kansas Supreme Court rejected Kahler's due process argument on appeal. Can the reader now see the parallels here between Kahler and True, in the context of the M'Naghten rule? They should be as plain as day.

The first strain of any mental insanity defence revolves around a defendant's 'cognitive capacity' – whether a mental illness left him 'unable to understand what he was doing' when he committed a crime. The second examines his 'moral capacity' – whether his illness rendered him 'unable to understand that his action was wrong'. Thus, if a defendant lacks either cognitive or moral capacity, he is not criminally responsible for his behaviour. This, of course, is basic M'Naghten rule stuff. However, a third 'building block' of sanity tests, which gained popularity from the mid-nineteenth century on, focuses on 'volitional incapacity' – whether a defendant's mental illness made him subject to irresistible impulses, or unable to otherwise control his actions. And bringing up the rear is the 'product-of-mental-illness' test, which broadly considers whether the defendant's criminal act stemmed from a mental disease.

Your author roundly apologises to the reader for labouring the issues here. But having looked into the minds of those apparently possessed by homicidal madness during this metaphorical road trip, can we say in all certainty that the M'Naghten rule has not been abused in order to allow the 'better side' to win?

So let's ask ourselves:

1. Did any of the perpetrators of criminal acts featured in this book *truly* lack cognitive capacity, rendering him or her incapable of understanding that their actions were wrong?
2. Did any of those cold-blooded killers *really* lack all moral capacity, rendering them unable to understand that their actions were wrong, against the law and contrary to basic human decency?
3. Did these murderers not have any volitional capacity? Were they subject to irresistible impulses and unable to control their actions?
4. How many of them really did suffer from a genuine disease of the mind?

We can apply the same questions, and expect the same answers, for many of the stone-cold killers who are given comfy beds in secure mental hospitals today. That's a subject for the sequel of this book, but it's an undeniable fact that many killers are released from secure institutions on the say-so of inept psychiatrists only to kill again and again. Consider the example of the UK's Graham Young. Known as the 'Teacup Poisoner', as a youth he was committed to Broadmoor Hospital, only to be freed on the recommendation of a resident psychiatrist who believed that he was now 'cured of his psychopathy'. Young went on to kill several more times. Was the hospital held to account? Damn right it wasn't.

In the US, after serving a mere fifteen years for murdering two children, paedophile Arthur John Shawcross, aka the 'Monster of the Rivers' – whom I interviewed twice at the Sullivan Correctional Facility in New York – was released on the advice of several of the prison's psychiatrists, although several of their rather more sensible peers disagreed with the decision. Shawcross went on to murder at least ten more women before he was caught. Did these psychiatrists receive even a rap over the knuckles? No they did not.

More recently in the UK, emerging serial killer and homicidal psychopath Colin Pitchfork was freed on life licence. Again, this was on the recommendation of a prison psychiatrist who argued that Pitchfork's psychopathic tendencies had been cured, despite many warnings – some from within the prison system and some from figures outside it, including me – that he would strike again. Within days of his release he was rearrested for breaching his licence conditions and appearing to approach some young girls, and returned to prison, for eighteen months. By the time you get to read this book, he will be back on the streets again and he could be living next door to you and watching your daughter at play. Did 'Mr Shrink-in-Charge' lose his job? Did he even forfeit a day's pay? Damn right he did not. And why not, you may ask.

Like all of the other shrinks who hold 'opinions', it is not their own children who are being raped, butchered and killed, that's why. Those who flagrantly abuse the M'Naghten rule to line their own pockets by appearing in court as a so-called expert are the lowest of the low.

Nonetheless, as I always try to do when exiting a book, I feel a change of tone is necessary so that we may end on a lighter note. So where was I when I started out on this road trip into the minds of the (allegedly) criminally insane? Ah, yes, I remember now: in Cebu, Philippines, where no one ever wears a hat, not even of the Mad Hatter's variety. So who said that this isn't a mad, mad world? Not I.

Happy days and no nightmares, please.

christopherberrydee.com